Edexcel GCSE

Citizenship Studies

Short Course

Student Book

Anthony Batchelor, Gareth Davies, Pauline Standen

Published by Pearson Education Limited, a company incorporated in England and Wales, having its registered office at Edinburgh Gate, Harlow, Essex, CM20 2JE. Registered company number: 872828

Edexcel is a registered trade mark of Edexcel Limited

Text © Pearson Education Limited 2009

First published 2009

12 11 10 09
10 9 8 7 6 5 4 3 2 1

British Library Cataloguing in Publication Data
A catalogue record for this book is available from the British Library

ISBN 978 1 846905 35 3

Typeset by Pantek Arts Ltd
Illustrated by Darren Prentice and David Eaton
Picture research by Louise Edgeworth
Printed in the UK by Scotprint

Acknowledgements

The author and publisher would like to thank the following individuals and organisations for permission to reproduce photographs:

Alamy Images: Jon Arnold Images Ltd 7c, 7l, 22l, 22r; Digital Vision 56; Eye-Stock 27 (background); Tim Graham 94; Jane Hallin 106; Tim Keatley 92; Peter Marshall 74, 81; Jeff Morgan recycling & waste management 139; Andrea Murphy 10b; PCL 107 (background); Photofusion Picture Library 7r, 23; Powered by Light/Alan Spencer 20; David Stares 6r, 19; Mark Sykes 130t; Peter Titmuss 36r; tompiodesign.com 114 (background); Jim West 29; Janine Wiedel Photolibrary 83; Calyx Multimedia : 105; Corbis: Rick D'Elia 138; Howard Davies 112r; Fancy/Veer 66; Fat Chance Productions 64l; Najlah Feanny 32; Tom Grill 16-17; Olivier Hoslet/epa 110; Simon Marcus 11; Ahmad Masood/Reuters 108, 118; Gideon Mendel 58; Durand Patrick/Corbis Sygma 116t; SW Productions/Brand X 140; DK Images: 13; Nigel Hicks 54; Getty Images: 59, 73bl; B2M Productions/Digital Vision 67; ColorBlind Images/Iconica 130b; De Agostini 30 (background); Newcastle United 63; iStockphoto: Bart Coenders 126-127; Joe Gough 6l, 18l; Elena Korenbaum 36l; Diane White Rosier 10c; Alyn Stafford 10t; Jupiter Unlimited: AbleStock.com 142; Stockxpert 39; PA Photos: 76r; AP Photo/Ron Edmonds 86; Barry Batchelor/PA Archive 37r; SANDRO CAMPARDO/AP 31; Chris Clark/PA Archive 40; EMPICS Entertainment 41; Danny Lawson/Pool/PA Wire 73t; Dominic Lipinski/PA Wire 38; PA Wire 79; Karel Prinsloo/AP 112l; Stefan Rousseau/PA Wire 76l; John Stillwell 15t; John Stillwell/PA Archive 43; John Stillwell/PA Wire 52; Lewis Whyld/PA Archive 37l; Photofusion Picture Library: Brian Mitchell 6c, 18r; Mary Reid: 24; Reuters: Ian Hodgson 57; Marc Serota 121; Rex Features: 15b, 33; Scott Aiken 64r; Fotex 62; Ken McKay 68; Sipa Press 116b; TopFoto: PA Photos 77, 78, 104; UPPA 73br

Every effort has been made to contact copyright holders of material reproduced in this book. Any omissions will be rectified in subsequent printings if notice is given to the publishers.

Disclaimer
This Edexcel publication offers high-quality support for the delivery of Edexcel qualifications.

Edexcel endorsement does not mean that this material is essential to achieve any Edexcel qualification, nor does it mean that this is the only suitable material available to support any Edexcel qualification. No endorsed material will be used verbatim in setting any Edexcel examination/assessment and any resource lists produced by Edexcel shall include this and other appropriate texts.

Copies of official specifications for all Edexcel qualifications may be found on the Edexcel website – www.edexcel.org.uk

Acknowledgements

We are grateful to the following for permission to reproduce copyright material:

ABC News for the Table 'Average sales of selected UK daily newspapers August/Sept 2008' copyright © ABC News; Age Concern and Help and Aged for company logo's, reproduced with permission; The Central Intelligence Agency for data from The World Factbook "Country Comparisons – Life expectancy at birth"; and the table "Estimated life expectancy for a child born on 18 December 2008 in selected countries" Green highlights G7 countries, source: Central Intelligence Agency www.cia.gov; Department of Economic and Social Affairs for an extract from Millennium Development Goals Report 2008 copyright © United Nations, 2009. www.un.org. Reproduced with permission; eBayTM for permission to use the eBay logo. eBay is a trademark of eBay Inc; Financial Times for an extract adapted from "Council tax rises to exceed inflation" by Jim Pickard, Financial Times 1 January 2009 copyright © Financial Times 2009; Fubra Limited for an extract adapted from The Guides Network (2008) Recycling Guide www.Recycling-Guide. org.uk, reproduced with permission; The Home Office for 3 graphs showing international migration to and from the UK, immigrants in the working-age population and top occupations for non-UK workers, source: The Home Office, as published in The Guardian 10 September 2008 © Crown copyright 2008; The Independent for the front page of The Independent 21 July 2006 copyright © Independent News and Media Limited 2006; National Farmer's Union (NFU) for their company logo, reproduced with permission; The National Youth Agency for the BUZZ OFF logo & company name brand. BUZZ OFF campaign is a partnership between 11 MILLION, led by the Children's Commissioner for England, young people from Groundwork's Corby Young People Friendly Neighbourhoods project, The National Youth Agency and Liberty, reproduced with permission; NI Syndication for the front page of The Sun 25 January 2007 copyright © NI Syndication Limited 2007; Office for National Statistics for the tables "Membership of selected environmental organisations in the UK" published in Social Trends 33; "Crimes recorded by the police: 2007/8" adapted from Home Office, published in Social Trends 39; "Recorded crimes detected (criminals caught) by the police in England and Wales in 2005/2006 (%)" published in Social Trends 37; "Contrasts between urban and rural areas"; and the graphs "Voting turnout in the 2005 General Election" British Election Study, published in Social Trends 37, Figure 13.17; "Union Membership" source: Labour Force Survey (autumn quarters); and 'Union Membership, Union density down slightly in 2006' source: Labour Force Survey www.statistics.gov.uk © Crown copyright 2006, 2007, 2008; Ordnance Survey for Map of Kirklees www.kirkleespartnership.org/images/locality-map-blue.jpg, reproduced by permission of Ordnance Survey on behalf of HMSO, © Crown Copyright 2009. All rights reserved. Ordnance Survey Licence number 100030901; Social Exclusion Unit for statistics from Reducing re-offending by ex-prisoners Report by the Social Exclusion Unit, July 2002 © Crown copyright 2002; Solo Syndication for an extract adapted from "Keep fit or risk loosing NHS care" by James Chapman published in The Daily Mail 1 January 2008 copyright © Solo Syndication 2008; Taylor & Francis Books (UK) for data from The Almanac of British Politics by Robert Waller and Byron Criddle, 2007, copyright © Taylor & Francis Books (UK) 2007; UK Independence Party for an extract from the blog of Nigel Farage, 22 October 2008 http://www. ukip.org/content/nigel-farages-blog/818-crisis-management-brusselsstyle, reproduced with permission; UK Parliament for a quotation by Robin Cook, May 1997 and Gordon Brown, December 2008, Crown © copyright 2008; and The World Bank for the graph "Highly-indebted poor countries" as published on http://news.bbc.co.uk/1/low/business/4084574.stm copyright © World Bank.

In some instances we have been unable to trace the owners of copyright material and we would appreciate any information that would enable us to do so

Contents: delivering the EDEXCEL GCSE Citizenship Studies (Short Course) Specification

Welcome to Edexcel GCSE Citizenship Studies!

What do I need to know, or be able to do, before taking this course?

Citizenship Studies is an exciting course to take for GCSE. It's not just about sitting in classrooms but gets you out and about. You will be involved in community activity which you plan and organise. You will plan a campaign for an issue that you choose and really care about. The course builds on citizenship lessons from Years, 7, 8 and 9 and all sorts of things you have done before in English, Geography and History.

Why should I study this course?

If you are interested in the world and people around you, this is the subject for you. It helps you to make decisions for yourself on all sorts of issues. We are bombarded with information about things like the environment, fair trade and people's rights across the world, but most of us find it hard to work out what's right and wrong. Citizenship helps you to develop the skills you need to decide for yourself. You will investigate issues that really matter and work out what can be done about them. You will also learn skills in taking action and presenting cases.

What will I learn?

If you are going to investigate current issues, you need to know how the world works. The course will help you to understand how an individual can change things, so it explores how we make laws, our place within the economy, what pressure groups do, and how we all relate to the rest of the world. The media are also important because they influence how we think – so we need to work out what their messages really mean. There is also a focus on communities, how we all live together, and our similarities and differences. The aim is to help you to understand and play a part in the world locally, nationally and internationally.

How will I be assessed?

There is a Short Course and a Full Course GCSE in Citizenship Studies. If you choose the Short Course there is one exam and a community activity for coursework, called controlled assessment. If you choose the Full Course GCSE there are two of each. The first exam will test your knowledge and understanding of the material, and the second asks you to think about it from different points of view. They are based on real examples of things that are going on in the UK and further afield. The coursework for the Full Course also involves running a campaign. This might be for something local or a much bigger issue like protesting about child labour or encouraging people to be more environmentally friendly. Whichever course you choose, the exam is worth 40 per cent and the controlled assessment counts for 60 per cent.

What can I do after I've completed the course?

You will learn lots of skills that will be useful in later life. Being able to see the world from other people's points of view will always help you to understand what's going on around you. The range of activities you will be involved in will help you to work with others and see the benefits of being part of a team – and even leading a team. You will learn to put a message together to persuade people of your point of view.

There are lots of opportunities to put these skills to work when you reach 16. Whatever you do next – A Levels, a Diploma or an apprenticeship – you will find that citizenship is an integral part of the course.

How to use this book

Welcome to Edexcel GCSE Citizenship Studies! This book has been written to help you to increase your interest in Citizenship, and also to help you do your very best in the Short course exam.

The authors of this book are examiners for Edexcel GCSE Citizenship studies. They really want you to succeed in the exam, so have included everything you need to know and think about here. Even better, they have taught and examined many, many students just like you, so know exactly the sort of mistakes some students make, so they have included tips and examples throughout the book, to help you to do your very best in the assessment.

Let's see what you should look out for in the book.

At the start of the book you will find an introduction to the three key concepts in your Citizenship Studies course, called **All About You**.

If you take a look at the specification, you will see that this book is organised in exactly the same way, making it clear what you will cover and how.

The book is divided into **units**. At the beginning of each unit is a section which tells you what the unit is about and why it is important in the exam.

The units are then divided into **chapters**. Each chapter is covered in distinct two page sections, so you can see everything on a subject at a glance.

Objectives appear at the beginning of every chapter. These tell you what you need to learn.

What's the issue? introduces the topic through a source or discussion on a subject which you may already know about.

Key terms are certain terms that you should understand, and also say what they mean. You will find them listed in the glossary at the back of the book

---

Chapter 1: A changing and diverse society
Rights and responsibilities for all

You will learn about:
- obligations and responsibilities linked to rights
- human, legal, moral, political, social and civil rights and responsibilities.

18

What's the issue? Rights without responsibilities?

Everyone has a **right** to marry, sign up for a **civil partnership**, or to qualify and enter a profession such as medicine or teaching, but such actions carry **obligations** and **responsibilities**.

Do marriages or civil partnership ceremonies involve legal or moral obligations, or both?

Once teachers have qualified, they have the right to teach. Is this a human right, a legal right or a moral right?

The teacher is responsible to: the children, their parents, other teachers at the school and the school governors. The teacher has legal and moral responsibilities. What do you think they are?

In what ways are the responsibilities of doctors the same as those of teachers?

If you see someone in trouble it is morally wrong to ignore them, though getting involved might be dangerous. How can you protect yourself and help others?

Different kinds of rights
Human rights are stated in documents such as the **Universal Declaration of Human Rights**. They include the **right to life**, the right to an education and the right to work. They are supposed to apply to every **citizen** on the planet. However, they are not usually applied in a particular country until they are written into its laws and then become legal rights.

Legal or social rights are human, moral, political or civil rights once they have been built into the laws of a state. If an individual is denied such rights they can go to court or another official body to get the treatment they are entitled to receive; this may differ from country to country. People in countries where the human right 'not to be subjected to inhuman or **degrading treatment**' is not part of the **law**, have much less protection than those in countries where there are these laws.

Moral rights are rights based on **values** or **conscience** – your sense of right and wrong. In the UK they relate strongly to treating others with **respect** and not letting down other people – particularly friends, relatives or colleagues. It's not always illegal to tell lies about someone but it's certainly morally wrong.

Political or civil rights are rights such as freedom of movement and association, freedom to **vote**, **discrimination**. In the southern USA it was the courage of people such as Rosa Parkes and meant black people could sit on a bus even if a and that black children could attend 'white' scho

What obligations and responsi these rights?
Once you have a driving licence you have the rig responsibilities go with that? You need to be fit treat other road-users with respect. Many traffic of the drivers involved is ignoring these obligatio

Respons based on all the pl the right team me obligatio up on tim not to le

Each player has his obligations to the team and his fellow players.

Activity

In pairs, think about the rights of buyers and auction site. Draw up a table with two colum 'Responsibilities'. Add three rights and respo has and three rights and responsibilities that you think is most important: the rights or the

Review and research

The checklist
- Rights cannot be separated from respon
- Human rights might not be applied until i built into a country's laws.
- Legal rights can be enforced in the court carry obligations as well.
- Conscience and values are at the heart of and responsibilities.
- Political and civil rights include freedom right to vote and the guarantee of equali

Chapter 1: A changing and diverse society

Diverse UK

You will learn about:

- key features of diversity and why 'multiple identities' help provide an understanding of life in the UK today
- how migration over many years has changed UK society.

What's the issue? East End – one world or two?

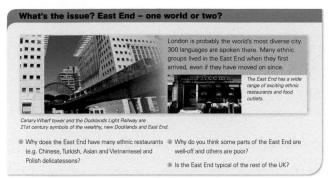

London is probably the world's most diverse city. 300 languages are spoken there. Many ethnic groups lived in the East End when they first arrived, even if they have moved on since.

The East End has a wide range of exciting ethnic restaurants and food outlets.

Canary Wharf tower and the Docklands Light Railway are 21st century symbols of the wealthy, new Docklands and East End.

- Why does the East End have many ethnic restaurants (e.g. Chinese, Turkish, Asian and Vietnamese) and Polish delicatessens?
- Why do you think some parts of the East End are well-off and others are poor?
- Is the East End typical of the rest of the UK?

The many ethnic groups in the East End mean it is a ***multicultural*** *area in which* ***diversity*** *is celebrated. Think about some different forms of cultural diversity in the area where you live.*

Why are 'multiple identities' important?

The idea of '**multiple identities**' reminds us that we all play lots of different roles. We identify with our parents and brothers or sisters, our school, our favourite pop group or football team, the area where we live and the place where we work or go to school.

Someone from abroad who comes to live in Britain will have friends and family from their own **culture** but will make friends with people who already live here. Then they will start to identify with the place they now live.

Racist tensions arise when people are relatively isolated and therefore ignorant. This is less likely to occur when people from different ethnic groups know, like and trust each other and share the foods or festivals from each other's cultures.

Activity

Who do you think you are? Draw a mind map. Start a circle in the middle of the page and write 'me', or stick a photograph of

...ondon

...**m seekers** from Zimbabwe, Iran or Serbia, people ...ountries because of **persecution** or poverty – fear was ...hem from their own country.

Such groups included Jews who came to Britain to escape Nazi persecution in the 1930s. 'Push' factors also explain more recent arrivals from places such as Uganda and Vietnam.

A diverse London market scene

Pull factors

'Pull' factors explain the arrival of those attracted to the UK looking for a better life for themselves as **economic migrants**. When former communist countries in Europe joined the EU after 2004, 'pull' factors caused many people, such as Poles, to come to London. 'Pull' factors also explain why some former **Commonwealth** citizens come to London to study or to fill job vacancies, many getting jobs with the NHS or London Transport.

Employment

Historically, there were jobs in the docks and in manufacturing industries such as clothing, furniture and construction, all attracting people to a particular area. Once new settlers had established themselves, they or their children moved away to get better houses and jobs. However, parts of their culture – from **religion**, food and music to art, dress and language – continued to be celebrated by local **communities**. No wonder the East End is such an interesting place to live.

Theme 1: Rights and responsibilities

ResultsPlus
Exam Question Report

23

Many well-qualified young people from other EU countries often want to come and work in the UK. Briefly explain how such immigration may benefit the UK. (2)
May 2008 question 8di

Answer: When well-qualified young people from other EU countries come to work in the UK, we will benefit from having more professional people such as doctors. People who come to work from overseas in other jobs will help to overcome skills shortages, e.g. plumbers or bilingual workers. They may accept lower pay, and they will also pay taxes, so more money will be paid to the government.

How students answered

Some students answered the question poorly. Students offered disparaging comments about people from other countries – not appropriate on any exam paper; least of all a Citizenship paper!

Most students gave a reasonable answer to this question and recognised that an ageing population and low birth rate meant that we were short of workers.

Some students gained good marks. Students were aware that the government were now targeting particular areas of skill shortage.

Review and research

The checklist

- London is a multicultural city where people from many ethnic groups live harmoniously, typical of many cities in the UK.
- The East End is an area of contrasts with both poverty and wealth.
- Because of 'multiple identities', people with different backgrounds, skills and loyalties may all identify as 'East Enders'.

Further issues

- Why do racial tensions break out in some areas but not others?
- Which cultural forms best define the East End today?
- Is Britain right to restrict the numbers of economic migrants coming to the country?
- Should the numbers of asylum seekers be limited?

Taking it further

Find out more information on multiculturalism on websites such as the Multicultural London and Economic and Social Research Council (ESRC).

Theme 1: Rights and responsibilities

... freedom ...m from ... Movement and ...her King that ...n was standing

...go with

...a car. What ...drive and to ...occur when one

...not always ...ootball match, ...h teams have ...e field but, as ...y also have ...and get fit, to turn ...to the rules and ...-mates down.

...Internet ...ights' and ...t a seller ...Which do ...es?

ResultsPlus
Exam Question Report

19

Briefly explain the difference between a human right and a legal right. (2)
May 2008 question 4e

Answer: Human rights are rights everyone has, they relate to all age groups, e.g. freedom of speech. Legal rights are decided by law. They may relate to a particular age group, e.g. you need to be 18 to buy alcohol.

How students answered

Some students answered this question poorly. Students gave answers that were too vague and did not make the difference clear.

Most students gave a reasonable answer to this question. Simple definitions involving both terms are essential.

Some students gained good marks. In the best answers, the difference was also supported by an example.

Further issues

- Why might some countries ignore human rights in their laws?
- If someone is denied their legal rights, what could they do to get them?
- Why might moral obligations seem more important than legal responsibility?

Taking it further

Find out more about the background to rights and responsibilities using the Directgov website.

The **Review and research box** gives you a summary of what you have learnt in this chapter, in the **Checklist**, and also further ideas to follow up in research, and potentially as starting points for Unit 2, in **Further Issues** and **Taking it Further**.

Results Plus boxes The information in these boxes is based on how real students in the past have performed in the exam. See pages 8–9 for more information.

Activities Once you have learnt and understood something, the Activities help you to apply your knowledge to really make use of it, as you will need to in the exam.

Unit 2 includes important information about the controlled assessment where you will look into a particular issue and create an activity about that issue. You will need to think about the evidence you will collect and present. By working through this section of the book, you will be more prepared to plan and collect the right information and evidence to ensure you do your very best.

Good luck with your course – and have fun!

Examzone and Results Plus

At the end of each theme, there is a section called 'Examzone'. This will help you to check what you have learnt and to revise for the exam. It also includes longer practice questions and sample answers so you can find out the best way to tackle them.

We've broken down your revision into six stages to ensure that you are prepared every step of the way.

Zone in: How to get into the perfect 'zone' for your revision

Planning zone: Tips and advice on how to plan your revision effectively

Know zone: All the facts you need to know and exam-style practice at the end of every theme.

Don't panic zone: Last-minute tips for in the exam

Examzone: Help on how to answer different question types

Zone out: What do you do after your exam? This section contains information on how to get your results and answers to frequently asked questions on what to do next.

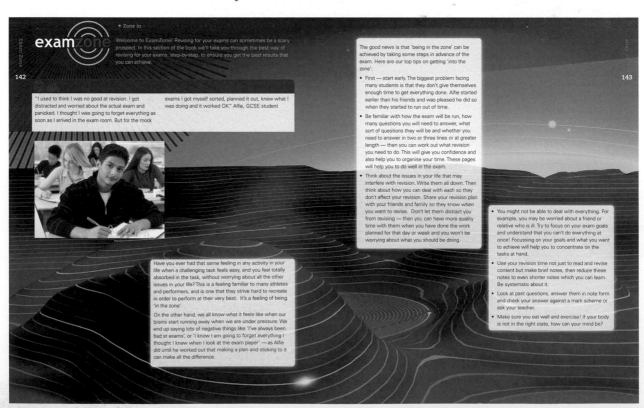

ResultsPlus

These features are based on the actual marks that students have achieved in past exams. They are combined with expert advice and guidance from examiners to show you how to achieve better results.

There are three different types of Results Plus features throughout this book:

Briefly explain the difference between a human right and a legal right. (2)
May 2008 question 4e
Answer: Human rights are rights everyone has, they relate to all age groups, e.g. freedom of speech. Legal rights are decided by law. They may relate to a particular age group, e.g. you need to be 18 to buy alcohol.

How students answered

Some students answered this question poorly. Students gave answers that were too vague and did not make the difference clear.

Most students gave a reasonable answer to this question. Simple definitions involving both terms are essential.

Some students gained good marks. In the best answers, the difference was also supported by an example.

Exam question reports

These show previous exam questions with details about how well students answered them.

- Red shows the number of students who scored low marks.
- Orange shows the number of students who did okay.
- Green shows the number of students who did well.

They explain how students could have achieved the top marks so that you can make sure that you answer these questions correctly in future.

ResultsPlus
Watch out!

State *two* of the rights which are guaranteed for UK citizens by the Human Rights Act, 1998. (2)
Adapted from May 2007, question 6e

Under half of the candidates were able to state accurately two human rights guaranteed to UK citizens. Freedom in itself is not a human right, since it must be linked to a freedom from or a freedom to something. A significant minority of candidates linked this question to legal rights, or more specifically to the consumer or employment rights.

Watch out!

The examiner knows where students tend to do things well and also where they can go wrong. So pay attention to these – they could really help you save or gain marks!

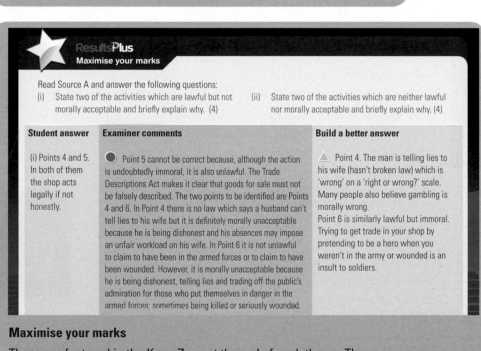

ResultsPlus
Maximise your marks

Read Source A and answer the following questions:
(i) State two of the activities which are lawful but not morally acceptable and briefly explain why. (4)
(ii) State two of the activities which are neither lawful nor morally acceptable and briefly explain why. (4)

Student answer	Examiner comments	Build a better answer
(i) Points 4 and 5. In both of them the shop acts legally if not honestly.	● Point 5 cannot be correct because, although the action is undoubtedly immoral, it is also unlawful. The Trade Descriptions Act makes it clear that goods for sale must not be falsely described. The two points to be identified are Points 4 and 6. In Point 4 there is no law which says a husband can't tell lies to his wife but it is definitely morally unacceptable because he is being dishonest and his absences may impose an unfair workload on his wife. In Point 6 it is not unlawful to claim to have been in the armed forces or to claim to have been wounded. However, it is morally unacceptable because he is being dishonest, telling lies and trading off the public's admiration for those who put themselves in danger in the armed forces; sometimes being killed or seriously wounded.	△ Point 4. The man is telling lies to his wife (hasn't broken law) which is 'wrong' on a 'right or wrong?' scale. Many people also believe gambling is morally wrong. Point 6 is similarly lawful but immoral. Trying to get trade in your shop by pretending to be a hero when you weren't in the army or wounded is an insult to soldiers.

Maximise your marks

These are featured in the KnowZone at the end of each theme. They include an exam-style question with a student answer, examiner comments and an improved answer so that you can see how to build a better response.

All about you

Learning about identities and diversity

There are three sets of key concepts in the GCSE Citizenship Studies course. They are:

- identities and diversity
- rights and responsibilities
- democracy and justice.

The next few pages introduce them, so you can handle them with confidence. You will also see how facts, opinions, bias and empathy are important terms which will help build a good understanding of Citizenship.

- Identity reflects how we see ourselves and what we do and think. There are many different lifestyles in the UK – different people work on farms, in offices, on off-shore drilling platforms, in television studios, in shops or on buses. Some people are very religious, while others aren't religious at all. People are so different – rich or poor, black or white, younger or older, married, single or cohabiting, gay or straight.

- This diversity does not prevent people from living happily together, though there can be problems and tensions. When people with different views and experiences do live alongside each other in the UK, they contribute to the UK's increasingly multicultural society.

- 'Diversity' may lead to discrimination where people are picked on because they have different identities, such as racist chants against black players in football matches or, more seriously, Hitler killing Jews in the 1940s.

Let's now meet **Adam, Yoko, Mary** and **Praful**, four young people who chat to each other most days on *Facebook*. They all study Citizenship and they want to help us introduce the subject to you.

Adam's 17, he finished his GCSEs (including Citizenship Studies) last year and he has a part time job at a local garage. He wants to join the army but his dad was killed fighting in Iraq and his mum isn't keen on the idea. He plays football whenever he gets a chance and goes running every day – he sees himself as a footballer, a runner, a mechanic, a scout, a Methodist and a supporter of Man United.

Yoko is 16 and she has three brothers and a sister. Her grandparents came to the UK from the West Indies and her mum and dad want Yoko to do well. She loves dancing and wants to train to be a fashion designer or a commercial artist. She identifies with her family's West Indian roots but feels she is British herself, feeling she belongs to several different communities at the same time.

Mary is 15 – she's a swimmer and wants to represent Great Britain in the Olympic Games. She's keen on ecology and conservation so in her free time she helps out at an animal welfare centre; later on she hopes to be a veterinary nurse. Mary's mum is Australian and her dad is Canadian so she doesn't know who to support when she watches sport.

 Praful is 17 and he fled from Myanmar (Burma) ten years ago with his parents. His parents are doctors; his dad is Buddhist and his mother Christian and Praful has decided to be Buddhist. He wants to go to the same university in the UK that his dad attended. Praful wants to be a journalist, has GCSEs, speaks four languages and is keen on martial arts.

Adam started off, asking Praful:

'Do you think your parents are really British now, even though they were born and brought up in Myanmar? Who would they cheer for if Myanmar played England or Scotland or Wales at football?'

Praful was quick to reply:

'When bad things happen to you and your family and friends, you feel so relieved when you are allowed to start a new life in a country like the UK. You probably still think about the world of friends or relations where you came from (if you can keep in touch) but that's the past. My dad supports Arsenal; for me and my parents being British is the future, a new start.'

Mary said:

'Praful and his parents may be more 'British' than me and my parents because they wanted to be British citizens while for us it just happened automatically. People have come to Britain from many countries either as refugees or conquerors, so 'being British' could mean that we have blood in our veins from Vikings or Normans – there is no such thing as 'British blood'.'

Praful then said:

'I love the idea of equality in the UK. When you go into a shop there is a multicultural feeling – the sales assistant could be from anywhere in the world and just be accepted as a fellow human being. You can't be 'more' or 'less' British than someone else. I have been here for ten years, have been educated here and don't feel any different from anyone else.'

Yoko then moved the conversation on to identities and diversity:

'When explorers reached other countries they often looked down on the local people who seemed different and spoke new languages. Now we know that because someone is different it doesn't mean they are inferior – something which you quickly realise as soon as you get to know someone. We all have lots of identities – how we see ourselves. I see myself as being British, black, female, I go to Evangelical church and I love fashion and dancing.'

Adam said:

'I would love to be a soldier just like my dad was. I agree with Yoko, there are many ways you can identify someone. I'm British, I'm white, I'm in the scouts, I'm a mechanic, I go to the Methodist church, I'm pretty good as a runner and in goal. I support Man United and am interested to see what happens to Man City.'

Do you agree with the views the group members expressed? Note that Adam makes two *kinds* of statements. He says: 'I'm white, I'm in the scouts, I go to the Methodist church' and all these statements are facts because they can be checked and proved. But when he says 'I'm pretty good in goal', that is an opinion because some people might not agree.

Learning about rights and responsibilities

Living in the UK, it is easy to take all your rights for granted. Many of the rights enjoyed by people in the UK are listed in the Human Rights Act 1998 which came into force in 2000. They include:

- Everyone has the right to life.

- No one can be tortured or punished in a degrading way.

- Slavery and forced labour are not allowed.

- Everyone has the right to liberty and security.

- Everyone has the right to a fair and public hearing in court if they are accused of committing a crime.

- No-one can be punished for an action which was not a crime when it was committed.

- Everyone has the right to privacy and family life.

- Everyone has the right to freedom of opinions, beliefs and religion.

- Everyone has the right to freedom of speech and expression.

- Everyone has the right to protest peacefully and to join (or not join) a trade union.

- Men and women have the right to marry and have children.

- Everyone has the right to own and enjoy their property.

- No-one is to be denied the right to an education.

- Free elections are to be held at regular intervals with secret voting so that people can choose the government they want.

- The death penalty has been abolished.

- No-one is to be discriminated against, on any grounds, in getting these rights.

Other rights, such as the right to work, are listed in the Universal Declaration of Human Rights.

But we have to recognise that this list of the human rights enjoyed by UK citizens is much longer than the very limited freedoms granted to people in some other countries.

The key idea you'll learn from this section is about the balance between 'rights' and 'responsibilities'. Although we have the right of free speech, our responsibility is to be fair and to speak truthfully. If we go around telling lies about people or unfairly damaging their reputation then we could be in trouble in the courts ourselves.

As you read the conversation between Yoko and her friends, try and work out which statements are facts and which are opinions. You will also begin to understand the idea of 'bias'.

Yoko's teacher had asked her to prepare a five minute talk about rights and responsibilities and she was asking the others what they thought she should say.

Adam started off:

> 'Begin with the distinction between *human* and *legal rights*. Some human rights, like the right to work and to have fair conditions at work, have been declared by the United Nations. They are a bit like general principles but they don't mean anything till they have been built into a country's laws – and many countries haven't done that.'

Yoko asked if someone could spell things out a bit more, so Mary said:

> 'We have the rights given by the Council of Europe because the UK passed the Human Rights Act 1998. The right to be safe at work in the UK is there because the UK passed the Health and Safety at Work Acts. This is good because it proves the UK takes human rights seriously and turns the general principles Adam talked about into detailed laws.'

With this Yoko wanted to be sure she had got the distinction between legal and human rights right:

> 'So legal rights probably contain more detail than human rights. They are shaped to be right for that country – when they write their employment laws, one country may have stricter health and safety rules than another or might put a maximum on the number of hours worked by a factory worker, while another might not.'

Adam came in:

> 'Well done! You've got it. But don't forget about 'responsibilities' as well as 'rights'. For example the Human Rights Act says everyone has a right to liberty but that obviously doesn't apply to the 80,000 people in prison because they haven't kept to their side of the bargain. Citizens are expected to obey the laws and if you don't meet your responsibilities you may lose your rights!'

Mary jumped in next:

> 'There's no death penalty in the UK and everyone has the right to life. Although it's rare, there are cases in the UK when individuals lose their life, as when there are deaths of people in prison or people are killed by speeding police cars. Then the question is whether the victim or others were to blame.'

Adam said he had read press stories about people getting killed:

> 'Sometimes opinions in papers are so varied you might think the different papers weren't talking about the same event. One paper might say someone who died in prison was aggressive and deserved everything he or she got, while another might emphasise that prison officers are supposed to uphold everyone's rights, include prisoners, which doesn't include letting someone die, even accidentally.

Note that the first two sentences in Yoko's statement are factual because they can be verified but where she says 'This is good…' is an opinion because whether or not something is good cannot be proved and it is an opinion because it will probably not be agreed by everyone.

People at work

Adam is making a good point about 'bias'. This is where the report of an event goes further than giving straight-forward details and tells the story in a way that supports their own particular view of the world, which may differ from someone else's view. Newspapers openly support different views and in elections they frequently back different political parties. *The Daily Mirror* is traditionally biased towards Labour while *The Daily Mail* is biased towards the Conservatives. Recognising 'bias' is an important skill.

Learning about democracy and justice

Democracy is the idea of majority rule – the person or party with more than 50% of the votes wins an election and makes the laws, but they must respect the rights of the minority. A different way of looking at democracy is to go beyond elections and look at other ways in which informed individuals can express their views – joining pressure groups, demonstrating, interacting with newspapers and television, blogging and signing up to e-petitions.

The idea of justice is also important: it says that once laws have been made, decisions about whether these laws have been broken will be made by judges and courts in a totally unbiased way.

● Problems arise when democracy and justice don't go together.

● A dictator who is not fairly or democratically elected by a majority of the people may make bad laws. If the laws are unfair it's difficult for honest judges and courts to achieve judgments.

● Even where elections are held, there are real problems if a president dismisses the judges because they don't take the decisions in the courts that he wants.

In addition to looking for examples of facts, opinions and bias, you will start to learn about the important Citizenship idea of 'empathy'.

Praful's points about councillors is a good example of empathy, where we imagine ourselves in the same position as someone else and so have a better chance of understanding their actions, feelings and point of view. If we heard that a woman has killed her husband, we would criticise her, but if we heard that the husband had brutally attacked the wife and their children, a sense of empathy would mean we understand better how and why she acted as she did.

We asked Mary to say what the key idea is in democracy. She said:

'Elections are most important – particularly general elections, which have to be held once every five years. The candidate with the most votes wins the constituency and the party representing most (usually a majority) of the constituencies forms a government.'

We asked Adam whether he thought democracy 'works' in the UK. He said:

'It works well if the parties offer really different policies so people can choose between them – as long as people pay attention and find out about the different policies.'

Praful said there were problems with the voting system:

'In 2005 the government had a big majority in the House of Commons but Labour won only about a third of the votes cast – that's not majority rule!'

Yoko could see general elections to elect a government were important but added:

'There are too many elections. Why can't we just have general elections?'

Praful was quick to reply:

'The UK has to elect MEPs to the European Parliament every five years. In Scotland and Wales the Scottish Parliament and Welsh Assembly really matter to people, and local councils also need to have councillors elected democratically, otherwise they would be completely out of touch with what local people want. People like to feel their representative knows and understands their needs and is 'on their side'.'

Adam said:

'Apart from elections, some issues should be decided by a 'people's vote' in a referendum instead of elections, like the one held in the UK in 1975 when the country voted to stay in the European Common Market (now European Union).'

Mary said:

'Many people prefer to join pressure groups like Greenpeace to push forward the things that are really important to them; campaigning by pressure groups is an important additional part of democracy.'

Praful agreed:

'If something really matters to them, people will want to get involved. Look at the big crowds which successfully protested in Herefordshire when schools there were threatened with closure in 2008.'

Adam added:

'Another good way of putting ideas forward is to keep an eye on the e-petitions on the 10 Downing St website and sign up to those you support.'

Then the discussion moved on to justice. Yoko asked:

'Can someone please tell me what is meant by saying 'Justice is blind'? It's something my teacher said recently.'

Adam said:

'The answer is that it shouldn't matter if someone is rich or poor, young or old, they are equally entitled to be protected by the rule of law, so the scales of justice must not be weighted in anyone's favour or loaded against them. Judges mustn't ever favour the rich or powerful.'

We asked Yoko whether she thought courts were fair and unbiased. She said:

'No, because poor people cannot afford the best lawyers and legal aid seems to be more about saving money on lawyers' fees than providing the best defence possible and true justice.'

Mary agreed:

'There's a danger of unfairness because someone might not have a good lawyer or even a lawyer at all. But it's good to have innocence or guilt decided by a jury of 12 unbiased men or women.'

Yoko disagreed:

'I'm not as much in favour of juries as Mary because often they get verdicts wrong. People can spend years in prison for things they haven't done like Barry George who was wrongly imprisoned for the murder of Jill Dando, and Sally Clark who was wrongly imprisoned for killing her two baby sons.'

Mary responded:

'Yes, that's bad but the police and the lawyers are the people who decide what a jury hears in court, so they should carry more of the blame than the jury.'

Justice is blind

In this discussion we have examined elections, referendums, people power and key points about the justice system involving lawyers, judges, juries and legal aid. We have also looked at the important idea of 'empathy'. How far do you agree with the students' points of view?

Citizenship Today

Your course

In Unit 1: Citizenship Today you will study three themes. You will learn about Rights and responsibilities, Power, politics and the media, and The global community. The themes focus on democracy and justice, rights and responsibilities, and identities and diversity. The box on page 17 shows what you will learn about.

Your exam

Your exam will last 1 hour and you will be marked out of 50. You will be tested on all themes in Unit 1 over two sections: Section A and Section B.

Section A

In Section A you will need to answer questions on all three themes. You will be provided with different sources, such as photos or newspaper articles, and will need to answer a set of questions for each theme based on these sources. The questions will be a range of short-answer and multiple-choice questions.

Section B

Section B consists of an essay question. You will have to choose one essay question from a choice of three. There is one essay question for each of the three themes for you to choose from.

What will I learn about?

Theme 1: Rights and responsibilities

In this theme you will explore and develop your understanding of what it means to be a citizen in the UK today. You will look at:

- diversity in the UK, and the impact of migration and integration on identities and communities

- political, legal and human rights

- how different kinds of rights have developed

- the rights and responsibilities of consumers, employers and employees.

Theme 2: Power, politics and the media

In this theme you will look at:

- how the media informs and influences the public, including how information from pressure and interest groups is used

Theme 3: The global community

In this theme you will also focus on ethical considerations in actions and policy making. You will cover:

- the role of the voluntary sector in supporting communities

- global warming and climate change

- the economy in relation to citizenship

- the UK's role in the world

- the challenges facing the global community.

- law and the justice system

- democracy in the UK.

Chapter 1: A changing and diverse society
Rights and responsibilities for all

You will learn about:
- obligations and responsibilities linked to rights
- human, legal, moral, political, social and civil rights and responsibilities.

What's the issue? Rights without responsibilities?

Everyone has a **right** to marry, sign up for a **civil partnership**, or to qualify and enter a profession such as medicine or teaching, but such actions carry **obligations** and **responsibilities**.

Do marriages or civil partnership ceremonies involve legal or moral obligations, or both?

Once teachers have qualified, they have the right to teach. Is this a human right, a legal right or a moral right?

The teacher is responsible to: the children, their parents, other teachers at the school and the school governors. The teacher has legal and moral responsibilities. What do you think they are?

In what ways are the responsibilities of doctors the same as those of teachers?

Different kinds of rights

Human rights are stated in documents such as the **Universal Declaration of Human Rights**. They include the **right to life**, the right to an education and the right to work. They are supposed to apply to every **citizen** on the planet. However, they are not usually applied in a particular country until they are written into its laws and then become legal rights.

Legal or social rights are human, moral, political or civil rights once they have been built into the laws of a state. If an individual is denied such rights they can go to court or another official body to get the treatment they are entitled to receive; this may differ from country to country. People in countries where the human right '*not to be subjected to inhuman or degrading treatment*' is not part of the **law**, have much less protection than those in countries where there are these laws.

If you see someone in trouble it is morally wrong to ignore them, though getting involved might be dangerous. How can you protect yourself and help others?

Moral rights are rights based on **values** or **conscience** – your sense of right and wrong. In the UK they relate strongly to treating others with **respect** and not letting down other people – particularly friends, relatives or colleagues. It's not always illegal to tell lies about someone but it's certainly morally wrong.

Political or civil rights are rights such as freedom of speech, freedom of movement and association, freedom to **vote** and freedom from **discrimination**. In the southern USA it was the Civil Rights Movement and the courage of people such as Rosa Parkes and Martin Luther King that meant black people could sit on a bus even if a white person was standing and that black children could attend 'white' schools.

What obligations and responsibilities go with these rights?

Once you have a driving licence you have the right to drive a car. What responsibilities go with that? You need to be fit and able to drive and to treat other road-users with respect. Many traffic accidents occur when one of the drivers involved is ignoring these obligations.

Responsibilities are not always based on law. In a football match, all the players in both teams have the right to be on the field but, as team members, they also have obligations to train and get fit, to turn up on time, to stick to the rules and not to let their team-mates down.

Each player has his obligations to the team and his fellow players.

Activity

In pairs, think about the rights of buyers and sellers on an Internet auction site. Draw up a table with two columns headed 'Rights' and 'Responsibilities'. Add three rights and responsibilities that a seller has and three rights and responsibilities that a buyer has. Which do you think is most important: the rights or the responsibilities?

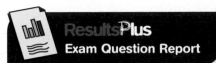

Exam Question Report 19

Briefly explain the difference between a human right and a legal right. (2)
May 2008 question 4e
Answer: Human rights are rights everyone has, they relate to all age groups, e.g. freedom of speech. Legal rights are decided by law. They may relate to a particular age group, e.g. you need to be 18 to buy alcohol.

How students answered

Some students answered this question poorly. Students gave answers that were too vague and did not make the difference clear.

Most students gave a reasonable answer to this question. Simple definitions involving both terms are essential.

Some students gained good marks. In the best answers, the difference was also supported by an example.

Review and research

The checklist

- Rights cannot be separated from responsibilities.
- Human rights might not be applied until they have been built into a country's laws.
- Legal rights can be enforced in the courts but they often carry obligations as well.
- Conscience and values are at the heart of moral rights and responsibilities.
- Political and civil rights include freedom of speech, the right to vote and the guarantee of equality.

Further issues

- Why might some countries ignore human rights in their laws?
- If someone is denied their legal rights, what could they do to get them?
- Why might moral obligations seem more important than legal responsibility?

Taking it further

Find out more about the background to rights and responsibilities using the Directgov website.

Freedom to... and freedom from...

You will learn about:
- how freedoms of speech, movement, opinion, privacy, association and the vote were obtained
- why these are important.

What's the issue? Voting at 16?

'Over 1.5 million 16- and 17-year-olds are denied the vote in the United Kingdom. For years there has been a consistent demand from young people for Votes at 16, and a clear case for change. That case is now overwhelming.

At 16, we can leave school, work full time and pay taxes, leave home, get married, join the armed forces, and make lots of decisions about our future.

At 16, people become adults and take control of their own futures – so why can't we have the basic right of all adult citizens of a say in how the country is run?

We're all interested in issues; from climate change to **racism**, from education to crime. Voting is the fundamental way that we have our say on issues, and we think that at 16, young people are mature enough to be properly listened to.'

Source: Votes at 16 Coalition, www.votesat16.org.uk

- Why is voting important?

- Have all 18-year-olds always been able to vote? Should the age when they can work and marry be raised to 18?

- If 16-year-olds are mature enough to work and marry, are they responsible enough to be able to vote?

The five 'giant evils'

People have freedoms to... do things, e.g. speak out, vote and live where they want. People also need freedom from... things like ignorance, disease, squalid housing, **poverty** and idleness – known as the five '**giant evils**'. To beat them, the **Welfare State** was set up to improve education, health (**NHS**), housing, social security and to aim for full employment.

Where do your freedoms come from?

Some freedoms – such as freedom of speech, expression and **opinion** – come from common law and have built up since the 13th century.

Other freedoms are incorporated into international statements of human rights such as the **United Nations** Universal Declaration of Human Rights, to which the UK has signed up.

Many freedoms have been won by groups of people who stood up for what they believed in – think of Martin Luther King in the USA.

Freedom and religious beliefs

In the past, some people were persecuted for their religious **beliefs**. Although freedom of worship is now guaranteed in the UK, some citizens are not always **tolerant** when they meet those who hold different religious views from themselves. However, in 2007 it became a criminal offence (**Racial and Religious Hatred Act 2006**) to use threatening words or behaviour to stir up hatred against any group of people because of their religious beliefs or their lack of religious beliefs.

Freedom from discrimination

In recent years, the UK has passed a number of anti-discrimination laws to stop discrimination on the grounds of gender, age, sexual orientation and disability. Anyone who feels they have been discriminated against when applying for a pay rise or a job, or in a shop or pub, can seek support from the **Commission for Equality and Human Rights**.

Freedom of movement

Freedom of movement between European countries exists because the UK belongs to the **European Union** (EU). Although you can travel to most places for holidays beyond Europe, the right to settle and work in these other countries is still restricted, as it is in the UK to non-EU citizens.

Other rights and freedoms

In the UK, other rights such as freedom of association (for example, the ability to join a **trade union**) were resisted until **parliament** passed laws to legalise them, mainly in the 1900s. Some trade union rights, such as the right to strike, are still restricted. The right to **vote** was achieved for all men and women over 21 in 1928. This makes **society** more democratic. In 1969 the voting age was reduced to 18.

Once it is agreed that everyone has rights that should be protected, ideas like **democracy**, **justice**, **tolerance** and **respect** can be used to support everyone. That is what an equal society is all about.

Many people from Commonwealth or other European countries have come to live and work in Britain. Why do people leave their home countries to travel and settle in the UK?

Activity

Study the following data.

England and Wales	Minimum ages
Criminal responsibility	10
Get a part-time job	13
Get a full-time job (if left school)	16
Marry (with parents' consent)	16
Buy a lottery ticket	16
Age of consent (sexual activity)	16
Drive a car	17
Buy an air gun	18
Vote	18
Be a candidate for Parliament	18
Buy cigarettes	18
Buy fireworks	18
Make a will	18
Own a house	18
Drive a heavy goods vehicle	21

The first of these is a **freedom from**; the rest are a **freedom to**. Consider arguments for and against changing each of the ages.

Review and research

The checklist

- If people do not have freedom from illness, poverty or ignorance they will find it difficult to enjoy freedom *to* do and achieve things.

- Young people aged 16 or 17 can get married or serve in the armed forces, so the Votes at 16 campaign says they should also have the right to vote.

- Minimum ages are set for various activities to keep individuals safe – and society too!

Further issues

- Are there any restrictions on freedom of speech that should be allowed?

- Why should we show tolerance to other people and their values or beliefs?

- How can individuals use democracy and justice to support themselves and their community?

Taking it further

Look at websites of groups such as Liberty and Justice to research more about equality and human rights.

Diverse UK

You will learn about:
- key features of diversity and why 'multiple identities' help provide an understanding of life in the UK today
- how migration over many years has changed UK society.

What's the issue? East End – one world or two?

London is probably the world's most diverse city. 300 languages are spoken there. Many ethnic groups lived in the East End when they first arrived, even if they have moved on since.

The East End has a wide range of exciting ethnic restaurants and food outlets.

Canary Wharf tower and the Docklands Light Railway are 21st century symbols of the wealthy, new Docklands and East End.

- Why does the East End have many ethnic restaurants (e.g. Chinese, Turkish, Asian and Vietnamese) and Polish delicatessens?
- Why do you think some parts of the East End are well-off and others are poor?
- Is the East End typical of the rest of the UK?

*The many ethnic groups in the East End mean it is a **multicultural** area in which **diversity** is celebrated. Think about some different forms of cultural diversity in the area where you live.*

Activity

Who do you think you are? Draw a mind map. Start a circle in the middle of the page and write 'me', or stick a photograph of yourself onto it. Now write words around the circle to describe the different roles and identities you may have.

Why are 'multiple identities' important?

The idea of '**multiple identities**' reminds us that we all play lots of different roles. We identify with our parents and brothers or sisters, our school, our favourite pop group or football team, the area where we live and the place where we work or go to school.

Someone from abroad who comes to live in Britain will have friends and family from their own **culture** but will make friends with people who already live here. Then they will start to identify with the place they now live.

Racist tensions arise when people are relatively isolated and therefore ignorant. This is less likely to occur when people from different ethnic groups know, like and trust each other and share the foods or festivals from each other's cultures.

Migration to London

Push factors

Like modern-day **asylum seekers** from Zimbabwe, Iran or Serbia, people have fled from other countries because of **persecution** or poverty – fear was a 'push' factor driving them from their own country.

Such groups included Jews who came to Britain to escape Nazi persecution in the 1930s. 'Push' factors also explain more recent arrivals from places such as Uganda and Vietnam.

A diverse London market scene

Pull factors

'Pull' factors explain the arrival of those attracted to the UK looking for a better life for themselves as **economic migrants**. When former communist countries in Europe joined the EU after 2004, 'pull' factors caused many people, such as Poles, to come to London. 'Pull' factors also explain why some former **Commonwealth** citizens come to London to study or to fill job vacancies, many getting jobs with the NHS or London Transport.

Employment

Historically, there were jobs in the docks and in manufacturing industries such as clothing, furniture and construction, all attracting people to a particular area. Once new settlers had established themselves, they or their children moved away to get better houses and jobs. However, parts of their culture – from **religion**, food and music to art, dress and language – continued to be celebrated by local **communities**. No wonder the East End is such an interesting place to live.

Review and research

The checklist

- London is a multicultural city where people from many ethnic groups live harmoniously, typical of many cities in the UK.
- The East End is an area of contrasts with both poverty and wealth.
- Because of 'multiple identities', people with different backgrounds, skills and loyalties may all identify as 'East Enders'.

Further issues

- Why do racial tensions break out in some areas but not others?
- Which cultural forms best define the East End today?
- Is Britain right to restrict the numbers of economic migrants coming to the country?
- Should the numbers of asylum seekers be limited?

Taking it further

Find out more information on multiculturalism on websites such as the Multicultural London and Economic and Social Research Council (ESRC).

A pick-and-mix society

You will learn about:
- different kinds of communities living in the UK.

What's the issue? Why so different?

Constituency	% professional workers in the population (2001)	Average weekly disposable income (2006)	Average property value (2006)	People who rent their house / flat (2001)	% non-white citizens (2001)
Hodge Hill	13.9%	£267	£116,000	35.2%	27.9%
Ladywood	18.0%	£266	£133,000	45.7%	64.9%
Leominster	28.0%	£376	£220,000	12.4%	0.7%
Ludlow	27.5%	£367	£218,000	11.9%	0.9%
Solihull	32.9%	£424	£231,000	8.4%	6.5%
Sparkbrook	19.3%	£273	£133,000	31.4%	64.8%
Sutton Coldfield	36.5%	£433	£226,000	9.4%	5.8%

This table shows seven West Midlands areas (constituencies), each represented by an MP. In 2005, three of these areas were Labour, three Conservative and one LibDem. Five are urban areas and two are rural areas.
Source: The Almanac of British Politics, Robert Waller and Byron Criddle, Routledge

- Which do you think are the rural **constituencies**?
- Which party do you think was elected in each constituency in 2005? Why do you think this was?
- What differences do work, income and housing make?

*About two thirds of people take part in democratic voting in UK **elections**. Why do you think they do that? Why do you think some people don't take part?*

*Why did the **government** decide in 2002 that new arrivals wanting to become British citizens must take a test?*

Becoming a UK citizen

If you were born in the UK with British parents, you probably take it for granted that you are British.

However, people from other countries can take a *Life in the UK* citizenship test to become British citizens. This means that they can prove they know about life in the UK and can speak English. In 2007, about 165,000 people decided to take the test, however 2,300 were turned down because they had insufficient knowledge of English or life in the UK.

A Citizenship ceremony in Kingston-upon-Thames in 2007 with the Mayor Councillor, Mary Reid and Ian Reid.

New UK citizens can also celebrate becoming British citizens in a citizenship ceremony. For this, they swear **allegiance** to **the Queen**, sing the national anthem and pledge to respect the UK's rights and freedoms.

In 2006 nearly 600,000 people arrived in the UK, but some 400,000 left. Over half of these were British citizens, of whom almost a third went to Australia and New Zealand, a quarter to Spain or France and about one in twelve to the USA.

Communities and lifestyles

Those coming to the UK legally often settle in areas where others from their former country live. They join groups and interact with local people. Later, they often move on to other areas.

Well-integrated communities see people from different ethnicities happily living alongside each other. Here, existing residents in the area do not feel their jobs, culture or housing needs are threatened by the arrival of newcomers. In less integrated areas, some people feel threatened by new arrivals.

Many UK citizens move home, often for work reasons, so in many communities some people are always moving in and others out. Often young people need to move to go to college or university, to get a job and be able to afford to buy a home.

Life expectancy is an average which reflects the number of years a particular group could expect to live. It varies between groups because of **lifestyle**, diet, poverty, occupation, pollution and quality of both housing and healthcare and it shows that the Welfare State has so far not achieved equality of lifespan within different communities. In 2009 a boy born in better-off Hampstead, London, would typically live about 11 years longer than a boy from poorer St. Pancras, five stops away on the London Underground.

Activity

Why do you think over 200,000 British citizens went to live in other countries? In groups, discuss whether you would like to go and live in another country and become a citizen of that country instead of the UK. Which country would you choose and why?

Watch out!

Give *two* reasons why peoples' life expectancy might be higher in some places than in others. (2) Adapted from May 2008, question 6d

Answers to this question were disappointing. The question asked for reasons why life expectancy might be higher, not lower, in some places than in others, so no marks could be awarded if the question were answered for lower rather than higher life expectancy. Too many candidates thought that life expectancy will be lower in areas with a high murder rate. There was a widespread lack of understanding about the links to life expectancy of such factors as levels of affluence, health (and access to health care), quality of environment and aspects of lifestyle.

Review and research

The checklist

- Communities in the UK differ greatly in terms of household income, jobs, housing and ethnicity.

- New and existing citizens often move between communities.

- Successful integration depends on local residents not feeling threatened by new arrivals in terms of jobs, culture or housing.

Further issues

- How is community integration and a sense of belonging best achieved?

- Why is life expectancy longer in some communities than others?

- Apart from voting, how can people demonstrate support for democracy?

Taking it further

Find out more about the *Life in the UK* test from the Border and Immigration Agency website.

Chapter 2: Consumption and employment
Shopping around

You will learn about:

⊚ the rights and responsibilities of sellers and consumers.

What's the issue? How consumers' interests are protected

Every **consumer** needs to be very clear about their rights.

Current laws	What they say	This means ...
Consumer Credit Acts 1974–2006	If you use a **credit card** to buy faulty **goods** or a **service** which provides less than it promises, it may be possible to claim from the credit card company.	... you will get **compensation** if the holiday or PC you buy doesn't work out.
Consumer Protection Act 1987	It is always illegal to sell unsafe goods. If you are injured through using faulty goods, you can claim damages from the manufacturer or, in the case of goods produced overseas, the importer.	... you can claim if electrical items prove dangerous or furniture turns out to be made of a material that could easily catch fire.
Food Safety Act 1990	It is illegal to sell food or drink that does not comply with food safety rules.	... a restaurant can be closed down if it serves unsafe meals.
Sale of Goods Act 1979	New or secondhand goods bought from a **trade** or mail order firm must: (1) be of satisfactory quality, (2) do what the seller or manufacturer says they will do, (3) be as described in an advert, on the packaging or by a sales assistant.	... if clothes bought by mail order turn out to be of poorer quality than you had been led to expect, the seller could be in trouble.
Supply of Goods and Services Act 1994	Goods sold must be fit for purpose, safe, durable, of acceptable appearance/finish and free from minor defects. People providing a service must do so with reasonable skill and care, in a reasonable time and at a reasonable price.	... the law covers not only goods but also services such as those provided by hairdressers or driving school instructors, electricians or gas fitters, estate agents, plumbers or mechanics.
Trade Descriptions Act 1968	It is a crime to make misleading claims about items for sale, e.g. falsely describing goods or services or claiming a £99 price has been halved if £198 was not charged for 28 consecutive days previously.	... false claims could refer to food that was said to be 'organic' (but wasn't) or to jeans with a Levi's label that had been made by some other firm.
Weights & Measures Act 1985	It is a crime to sell short measures or underweight goods.	... a pint of milk really has to contain a pint!

⊚ Why might it be safer to pay for a big purchase with a credit card?

⊚ What stops a shopkeeper claiming there is a sale on when no prices have really been reduced?

⊚ What rights do you have if you buy a tracksuit and the stitching comes undone the first time you wear it?

⊚ If a shopkeeper sells you an electric fire saying it was very safe, what is the position when it gives you an electric shock?

It is important to understand your rights as a consumer.

Buyer beware: save up or use credit?

People used to save up to buy things. Today more people pay for things by borrowing. This is convenient but can be expensive, as you may be charged interest if using a credit card. Credit cards allow you to buy goods on credit but you must make a monthly repayment that includes interest (which can be as much as 20% per year). A credit card is convenient and if you use it to buy an item such as a holiday, you can get your money back if things go wrong. Some credit cards start off with a **low interest** rate of 0–5% but after a few months this doubles, trebles or quadruples. So a £40 jacket can end up costing £100 or more unless you make a big payment every month.

Some shops will give you a store card to make purchases from them but the interest rates are generally higher than for credit cards. A personal loan or **hire purchase** may have a slightly lower interest rate than a credit card but you have to pay a fixed amount over a fixed number of months.

There are alternatives to credit cards. If you want to use a card rather than cash, you can get a pre-payment card – you pay into the card in advance, rather like a mobile phone top-up card. A **debit card** simply transfers money from your bank account without charging interest.

Buyers' rights

There are laws to ensure that what you buy is of good quality. It is illegal to sell unsafe goods or goods which are poor quality, which don't last a reasonable time, or which don't do what the seller or manufacturer say they will do.

Sellers' rights

If your purchase turns out to be faulty or unsuitable soon after you buy the goods, go back to the shop first to give them a chance to put things right – they may exchange the goods if they haven't been used.

However, if you bought a dress or a shirt which you knew was torn when you bought it, you will not get your money back if you try to return it later for that reason. Or, if a child's skateboard gets damaged through hard use, it would be unreasonable to take it back to the shop three months later complaining it was scratched. Sellers have rights too!

If you change your mind about a purchase or are given an unwanted present, you have no rights to a get the money to buy something different though some shops may let you change the goods for something you want.

Consumers who buy goods or services for their own use have many rights. Do sellers have as many rights?

Activity

On your own, work out how much you would have to pay for £100-worth of sports kit if you used a store card charging 22% interest per year and paid £5 per month. Which payment methods for purchases are cheapest and which, most expensive?

Activity

Look at the table in the *What's the Issue?* box. Discuss the examples of 'what this means' and come up with another example for each law. What can you do if something you buy fails to meet these standards?

*If you have a problem with something you have bought and the seller doesn't help, go to the **Citizens Advice Bureau**. They may suggest you approach the local **council's Trading Standards** Department who may prosecute the seller for misleading descriptions or safety issues. If you are concerned about unsafe food, ask the council's Environmental Health Department to investigate.*

Review and research

The checklist

- Buying an item such as a holiday with a credit card gives you potential rights to compensation. However, credit cards and other forms of borrowing can be expensive.
- Goods must always be fit for purpose, safe, durable, of acceptable appearance/finish and free from minor faults.
- Unsafe goods should never be sold and can lead to manufacturers being prosecuted.

Further issues

- How can consumers gain a better understanding of their rights?
- Do the disadvantages of credit cards outweigh the advantages?
- Are consumer rights unfairly loaded in favour of consumers against sellers?

Taking it further

Get more information about consumer matters from your council's Trading Standards website or the Office of Fair Trading's Consumer Direct service.

Working it out

You will learn about:
- the rights and responsibilities of employers, employees and trade unions
- the role of the individual in the economy and the right to representation in the workplace.

What's the issue? Who belongs to a trade union?

- How do the patterns of trade union membership for men and women differ?

- Why are some workers more likely to join a union than others?

- What are the arguments for or against going on strike to settle a dispute?

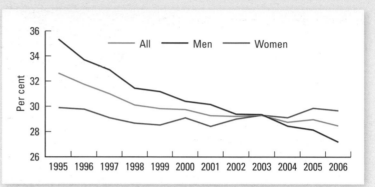

Declining trade union membership, 1995–2006
Source: Labour Force Survey, 2008, www.statistics.gov.uk, reproduced under the terms of the click-use licencese

On average, workers in the UK work more hours than workers in other EU countries. Is this good or bad?

Results Plus
Watch out!

Briefly explain *two different* reasons why an Asda employee might want to belong to a trade union. (4)
Adapted from May 2008, question 5c

Many candidates showed a disappointingly low level of knowledge and understanding of why employees might want to belong to a trade union and the benefits they could gain.

The changing world of work

In the 1940s and 50s, most people expected to have a job for life. By 1979 well over 50% of workers belonged to a trade union to improve working conditions, pay, hours and holidays and to try to get **employment laws** made fairer.

When **unemployment** rose in the 1980s, trade union membership fell sharply. New jobs were often offered on short contracts so **employees** saw little point in joining a union. **Strikes** were less popular than previously. Nowadays many workers don't expect to stay with one **employer** for a long time.

The Labour Force Survey shows that by 2006, the proportion of workers in unions had fallen to 28%. More full-timers (31%) were union members than part-timers (21%).The highest rate of union membership was in Northern Ireland (40%) and the lowest in England (27%). In the South East 21% were union members and in the North East, 39%.

Can individuals make a difference?

Amstrad's Alan Sugar, Virgin's Richard Branson and Easyjet's Stelios Haji-Ioannou prove that outstanding entrepreneurs can make a difference in business. Trade unions have also recruited influential leaders like Bill Morris and Tony Woodley. More people have set up their own businesses in recent years.

Individual workers can be key players in many firms. That's why firms match applicants against a **person specification** (listing skills, qualifications and experience needed) and a **job description** (what duties or responsibilities the job involves) before they appoint them.

28

What rights do workers have?

Workers are now protected by laws such as:

- **Sex Discrimination Act 1975**
- **Race Relations Act 1976**
- **Equal Pay Act 1970**
- **Disability Discrimination Act 1995**
- **Health and Safety at Work Act 1974**
- **Employment Rights Act 1996**
- **National Minimum Wage Act 1998.**

In 1997 Tony Blair's government signed up to the EU Social Chapter, giving more rights to workers.

A worker's **contract of employment** gives details such as entitlement to sick pay and holidays, place of work, rates of pay, dress code, working hours, disciplinary procedures and when the contract may be ended by either party.

Many employees are required to wear a uniform.

What rights do employers have?

Contracts of employment apply to both employer and employee. If an employee's conduct is unsuitable they will receive a **verbal warning**. If the poor conduct continues the employee may receive a **written warning**; further misconduct may lead to a third stage: **dismissal**. Sometimes an individual's behaviour may be so out of line (e.g. racial or sexual harassment, or dishonesty) that they can be dismissed immediately.

When a firm needs to cut its labour force, some workers are made redundant. They will be told to leave and won't be replaced. Statutory rates for **redundancy** compensation in 2008 were one week's pay for each full year of service, but 50% less for those under 22 years old and 50% more for workers aged 41 or over.

Is it fair that compensation for redundancy, linked to the number of weeks' pay per year of service, should vary for different age groups?

Review and research

The checklist
- Trade union membership has fallen sharply.
- Employees no longer seem to want a 'job for life' and expect to change jobs.
- Some individuals make a big difference.
- Many laws passed in the last 40 years have improved working conditions for employees.

Further issues
- Why are fewer workers now members of trade unions?
- Have employment laws improved the experience of working in the UK?
- Should the number of hours per week an employee works be restricted?

Taking it further
Find information on employment from the government websites. Find out about trade unions from websites of the Trades Union Congress (TUC) or unions such as Unite or Unison.

The United Nations

You will learn about:
- the UN Universal Declaration of Human Rights
- the work of the UN Council on Human Rights
- the importance of the UN Convention on the Rights of the Child.

What's the issue? Human rights for all?

The UN Universal Declaration of Human Rights was adopted in 1948 and describes rights in great detail. It is important that everyone knows the details so that people can't get away with ignoring these rights. Here are just two of the thirty provisions:

18 Everyone has the right to freedom of thought, conscience and religion; this right includes freedom to change his religion or belief, and freedom, either alone or in **community** with others and in public or private, to manifest his religion or belief in teaching, practice, worship and observance.

23 1. Everyone has the right to work, to free choice of employment, to just and favourable conditions of work and to protection against unemployment.

2. Everyone, without any discrimination, has the right to equal pay for equal work.

3. Everyone who works has the right to just and favourable remuneration ensuring for himself and his family an existence worthy of human dignity, and supplemented, if necessary, by other means of social protection.

4. Everyone has the right to form and to join trade unions for the protection of his interests.

The UN building

- Which countries have failed to apply these rights and make them part of their legal code?

- How well do these rights 'work' for UK citizens?

- What other rights do you think people are entitled to? When you have thought about this, see how many of your ideas are listed in the Declaration.

We saw in All about you and also in Chapter 1 that human rights need to become legal rights and be included in a country's laws, so why have many countries been slow to act?

The UN Council on Human Rights

To support the Universal Declaration:

- a Human Rights Council has been established to press for improvements where human rights are denied – but the Council is criticised because countries often seem to take regional loyalties (e.g. in Africa or Asia) more seriously than human rights.

- a **Commissioner** has been appointed to work with government leaders
- the Commissioner seeks publicity to help individuals worldwide put pressure on leaders who abuse human rights
- information about abuses is circulated to world leaders so they can be raised in face-to-face meetings or at international conferences.

The UN aims to eliminate:

- racial discrimination
- discrimination against women
- **genocide** and torture
- child mortality and execution of children for crimes committed when under 16
- extreme poverty and hunger
- exploitation of migrant workers.

The UN aims to support:

- universal primary education of children
- people with disabilities
- sufferers of HIV/Aids, malaria and other diseases.

In 2008 South African judge, Navanethem Pillay, was appointed to the position of Human Rights Commissioner.

The UN Convention on the Rights of the Child (CRC)

The convention was set up in 1990 and the UK joined in 1991. Some countries were criticised – including the UK – for their treatment of children. Criticisms of the UK included:

- levels of child poverty and inequality
- levels of injury sustained by children
- the numbers of young offenders placed in **custody**
- the low age of **criminal responsibility**
- the rights of UK parents to hit their children
- high exclusion rates in UK schools
- lack of a national strategy for the social inclusion of disabled children.

These criticisms are considered in the UK by the Department of Children, Schools and Families and four **Children's Commissioners** including Al Aynsley-Green in England in 2009.

Activity

In groups, examine the criticisms of the UK. Are some more serious than others? Identify the four you think are most important. What should be done about them?

Review and research

The checklist

- The UN Declaration of Human Rights defines human rights in detail.
- Human rights are not built into some countries' laws – so some people are not protected.
- The UN Commissioner puts pressure on countries to improve their record.
- The Convention on the Rights of the Child shows that even in the UK there are major problems.

Further issues

- Can countries rightly think it is no-one else's business whether their citizens have human rights?
- Should the UN intervene actively if countries fail to meet recognised standards of human rights?
- Is 'human rights' a Western idea which contradicts the traditional culture and values of other countries?

Taking it further

Investigate the key provisions of the Universal Declaration and the CRC. Look at the Human Rights Watch website to see the latest human rights issues and cases.

Europe

You will learn about:

- the European Convention on Human Rights
- the European Court of Human Rights
- the European Court of Justice.

What's the issue? Is punishment degrading?

Article 3: No-one shall be subjected to torture or to inhuman or degrading treatment or punishment. That's what the **European Convention on Human Rights (ECHR)**, written in 1950, says. That's the rule that the **European Court of Human Rights** in Strasbourg uses to decide cases about punishment. But what does 'degrading' mean? Would it include proposals to make petty criminals in the UK wear distinctive uniforms when carrying out **community sentences** – like offenders in Phoenix, Arizona (illustrated)? This was introduced in the UK in 2008 following a suggestion by government **minister** Hazel Blears. But the **pressure group** Liberty, asked: 'How do you create a culture of respect by degrading people?'

These offenders in Phoenix, Arizona had to wear distinctive uniforms to carry out community sentences.

In *Tyrer v UK 1978*, the European Court of Human Rights ruled that 15-year-old Anthony Tyrer was subjected to 'degrading punishment' when an Isle of Man court ordered him to be birched. Effectively this ended corporal **punishment** on the island and, ultimately, in the UK generally.

People sometimes claim the phrase 'degrading punishment' is too vague – saying the convention really guarantees nothing. **Judges** might forbid one punishment now but later, other judges could support such punishment and forbid another.

- Do you agree it is right to ban inhuman or degrading treatment?
- How would you feel if you could be subjected to such punishments?
- Should rights be expressed in more definite terms, so they are easier for judges to interpret consistently?

Activity

Consider the questions above and then look at the full European Convention on Human Rights. Are there other phrases that could be interpreted in different ways by different judges? What are the exceptions in the Convention?

European Convention on Human Rights (ECHR)

The aim of the convention is to give people who live in European states a list of rights.

The following basic rights and freedoms are set down in the Convention:

- the right to life
- the right to liberty and security
- the right to fair trial
- the right to no punishment without law
- the right to respect private and family life
- the right to marry
- the right to a remedy of human rights abuses
- freedom of thought, conscience and religion
- freedom of expression
- freedom of assembly and association

- prohibition of torture and of inhuman and degrading treatment
- prohibition of slavery and forced labour
- prohibition of discrimination
- prohibition of the abuse of rights.

The full Convention lists some exceptions to these rights. For example, a person has a right to life unless they are killed in self-defence.

European Court of Human Rights (ECtHR)

The European Court of Human Rights in Strasbourg is part of the **Council of Europe** (not European Union). In 2005 the Court received 45,500 applications from the 41 member countries. Since 2000 UK courts have taken the UK cases because the **1998 Human Rights Act** meant that the ECHR provisions became part of UK law. UK citizens can still take a case to ECtHR if they don't win in UK courts and ECtHR rulings are binding on the UK government – but it can take four or more years to get a ruling.

The 'McLibel Two'

McDonald's sued the '**McLibel Two**' (David Morris and Helen Steel) for **libel** because of leaflets they distributed, entitled *What's Wrong with McDonald's*. Morris and Steel represented themselves against McDonald's expensive **lawyers**, but lost to McDonald's in 1997.

Morris and Steel felt they did not receive a fair trial, so took their case to the ECtHR. In 2005 ECtHR ruled they should have been given **legal aid**, that their trial had violated Article 6 (right to a fair trial) and Article 10 (right to freedom of expression). It awarded Morris and Steel £57,000.

The European Court of Justice (ECJ)

The **European Court of Justice** sits in Luxembourg to rule on European Union law. It can overrule UK law. Most ECJ cases are brought by member states or other EU organisations, or involve legal questions raised by national courts.

In a rare case brought by an individual citizen in 1995, Mr Richardson complained that women over 60 were entitled to free prescriptions, but he had to pay until the age of 65. The ECJ ruled that the UK's prescription charges exemption scheme was in breach of the Directive by setting different rules for men and women. UK men over 60 have paid no prescription charges since 1995 because of the **judgement**.

In the future could people think it's degrading to send people to prison and lock them in small rooms (sometimes with other prisoners and no privacy) for over 22 hours a day?

33

What would be the advantages of taking a case to a UK court rather than the European Court of Human Rights?

David Morris and Helen Steel

Why do you think the two European courts have been established instead of one?

Review and research

The checklist
- Both ECJ and ECtHR decisions overrule national courts.
- ECtHR deals with more 'individual' cases than ECJ but ECJ decisions do affect the lives and rights of many people.
- Provisions expressed in general terms allow judges to interpret cases to keep decisions up to date.

Further issues
- What does 'degrading' mean in the European Convention?
- In what ways do both European courts assist UK citizens?
- Does Europe need both ECtHR and ECJ?

Taking it further
Investigate the key provisions of the European Convention on Human Rights and the cases which the ECJ considers.

1998 Human Rights Act

You will learn about:

- how UK citizens can claim their rights
- how rights are safeguarded at a local, national or global level.

What's the issue? How the 'system' worked for EM

EM's son was born in 1996 in Lebanon, and her husband immediately tried (but failed) to abduct him to Saudi Arabia. After this he subjected her to extreme violence. She obtained a **divorce** from the Islamic court and was awarded custody of her son until his seventh birthday. Islamic law in Lebanon means that after that date her husband would have custody of their son.

Because she objected to this law, she left Lebanon without permission, taking her son with her. They arrived in the UK from Lebanon in 2004. She says she is now sought by Lebanon for the offence of kidnapping and that she is accordingly at risk of ill-treatment in prison and, she fears, death. She says she would be the subject of discrimination in a custody battle. She also claims that any separation from her son, even if in accordance with Islamic law in Lebanon, is contrary to her human rights.

She claimed asylum in the UK, was turned down and in 2005 a deportation order was made. After a series of unsuccessful **appeals**, the case went to the **House of Lords** in 2008. The House of Lords upheld EM's appeal, allowing her to remain in the UK with her son. The court decided that if she were sent back to Lebanon, this would be a breach of the Human Rights Act, which guarantees that everyone has the right to respect in private and family life, and home life.

- Do you think this was the right decision? Is it fair on the father? Discuss in groups.

Activity

Discuss why the ECHR was incorporated into UK law in the Human Rights Act. Are newspapers and others justified in criticising the Act?

The Human Rights Act (HRA)

On page 30, you learned about the European Convention on Human Rights (ECHR). For many years, using the Convention meant taking the case to the ECtHR in Strasbourg, which took time and money, because it was not actually part of UK law. However, from 2000, the Human Rights Act (HRA) has made the rights from the ECHR enforceable in our own courts, making it quicker and simpler to use.

If existing UK law conflicts with ECHR, senior judges have to consider making a 'declaration of incompatibility'. The Government then decides whether it should amend UK law.

Whilst it is always wrong to do wrong, human rights law recognises the question of how wrong it is, which depends on why a person acted as they did in the first place. Now UK courts take HRA into account (a big change).

Criticism of the Act

Some people and **newspapers** have criticised the Human Rights Act because it gives rights to everyone (even criminals in some cases) because of the danger they would otherwise face.

Are newspapers and others justified in criticising the Act?

Judges overrule court

Call to kill Act

Human Rights Act triumph

Loony Act – They Can't be Serious

Opinions over HRA are divided. What do you think?

Getting your rights – locally, nationally and globally

The incorporation of ECHR into UK law as HRA has changed the justice system – locally, nationally and globally. Many rights (**pension**, health, benefits, etc.) can be easily claimed and the best source of information is your local Citizens Advice Bureau.

All UK citizens also have the right to approach the Commission for Equality and Human Rights (CEHR), if they believe they are being denied their human rights. In 2007 CEHR took over responsibility from three previous bodies – Commission for Racial Equality (CRE), Disability Rights Commission (DRC) and the Equal Opportunities Commission (EOC).

At a global level, the UN has in the past established separate tribunals to hear cases such as genocide in Rwanda and the former Yugoslavia. In 2002 it established a permanent **International Criminal Court (ICC)** to deal with genocide, crimes against humanity and other crimes such as aggression, drug trafficking and terrorism. As a permanent body it exists to deter war crimes. A weakness is that by 2008, countries such as the USA, Russia, China and India had not joined.

Review and research

The checklist

- Incorporating ECHR into UK law as HRA has been a big change, but it should save time and cost for UK citizens.

- Decisions are not always popular but there is now a better chance that people receive the rights which they are entitled to.

Further issues

- Can good reasons ever justify bad actions?

- How is access to more rights likely to affect a person's identity?

- What service does the Citizens Advice Bureau provide in your area?

- Why have some countries failed to join the ICC?

Taking it further

Find some more cases involving human rights, perhaps on the CEHR website or those of pressure groups such as Justice or Liberty.

Chapter 4: Can our rights be overruled?

If we don't live up to our responsibilities ...

You will learn about:
- how rights are linked to responsibilities
- how rights and responsibilities are challenged.

What's the issue? Should the NHS deny treatment?

Smokers, drinkers and the obese beware: keep fit or risk losing NHS care.

Patients' rights are to be spelled out in a new NHS constitution, which is likely to cover core treatments to which they are entitled and the right to be treated in clean hospitals. But with the rights will come the responsibility to lead a healthy lifestyle. Smokers and people who drink or eat too much could be refused treatments. Already around one in ten hospitals refuse to carry out joint replacements for obese patients or orthopaedic surgery on smokers.

Doctors say the risks of operating on obese patients are higher and the treatment may be less effective. Smokers also have a higher risk of complications after surgery. Health trusts in North Staffordshire have the toughest restrictions. Patients must have a body mass index below 30 and have not smoked for three months to qualify for any routine operation.

Source: adapted from Daily Mail www.dailymail.co.uk, 1 January 2008

- Should we deny the *right* to medical treatment to people who don't behave *responsibly* (e.g. put themselves at risk by excessive drinking or eating too much or smoking)?

- What attitude should the NHS take to people who deliberately put themselves in danger, such as racing drivers or boxers?

Activity

We all have the right to listen to our music but not if we play it too loudly and annoy others – some people have even been evicted from their house for this kind of nuisance. In a group make a list of other occasions when a right needs to be balanced by responsibility.

One person's right versus another person's responsibility

One example involves the case of Natallie Evans and her former partner, Howard Johnston.

Natallie is now infertile following treatment for ovarian cancer. Before this medical intervention she had successful IVF treatment with Howard in 2001 and six embryos were created, which were fertilised with his sperm. However, he withdrew his consent for the embryos to be used when they separated in 2002 and Ms Evans spent years fighting the case through the courts.

Natallie Evans and her former partner Howard Johnston

After exhausting the UK legal system, Ms Evans turned to the European Court of Human Rights. In 2008 the judges said they 'did not consider that the applicant's right to become a parent should be accorded greater weight than (Mr. Johnston's) right not to have a child with her'.

After the hearing, Ms Evans said: 'All I was fighting for was my right to become a mother' but Howard Johnston did not want to be the father of a child who would grow up not knowing him.

The judges balanced Natallie's right to private and family life with the responsibility which would have been imposed on Howard as the genetic father; a role he did not wish to have now the relationship had broken up. Did they make the right decision in either law or ethics?

Review and research

The checklist

- Rights and responsibilities are like a two-sided coin – you can't have one without the other.

- One person exercising a right might impose a responsibility on another person and both need to agree to this.

- Rights are never absolute or unlimited.

Further issues

- If you contribute to your own illness, should you expect the NHS to help you get better?

- If you play loud music, is it fair on those who are sitting near you on a bus or who live near you?

- How much should we consider others? For example, should owners of cars that pollute the environment pay more tax than those who don't?

Taking it further

Look at websites dealing with health, education and the environment and find news stories about rules and relationships. Consider whether the balance between rights and responsibilities is appropriate.

A justification for identity-checking, surveillance or detention

You will learn about:
- how fears of terrorism may lead to the restriction of rights and freedoms
- arguments for and against restricting rights and freedoms.

What's the issue? Identify cards – good or bad?

New ID card revealed by Home Secretary

The new UK **Identity Card**, initially to be issued to foreign nationals, was revealed in 2008. The credit-card sized document will show the holder's photograph, name, date of birth, nationality and **immigration** status with an electronic chip holding details including fingerprints, and a digital facial image.

Home Secretary Jacqui Smith said: 'ID cards will help protect against **identity** fraud and illegal working, reduce the use of multiple identities in organised crime and terrorism, and make it easier for people to prove they are who they say they are.'

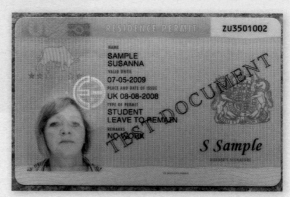

Sample UK Identity Card

But many people think that ID cards are a bad idea. Their reasons include:

- The government might lose the data, which would put people in real danger. They have lost the names and addresses of millions of child benefit recipients and recruits to the armed services.

- The Spanish ID card did not stop the Madrid train bombers and a British ID card wouldn't have stopped the 2005 bombings in London.

- Home-grown terrorists or suicide bombers might want their names to be recognised once they have carried out their attacks so ID cards are unlikely to deter them!

- ID cards are, in fact, likely to increase the problem of ID theft, because the card will be something really worth forging.

A person can already prove their identity with a passport or driving licence.

- What is the aim for ID cards?

- Will ID cards compromise people's privacy but fail to deter terrorists or criminals?

- Why do we need ID cards – isn't it enough to produce a driving licence or passport to prove who we are?

Freedoms in danger?

Richard Thomas, Information Commissioner, says British people are the most spied-on in the world. In the UK people suspected of terrorist-related activities can be held in detention without being charged for 28 days. The government wanted to increase this to 42 days but many **MPs** and members of the House of Lords were deeply uneasy about this. But even at 28 days, the UK is massively out of line with other countries. The figures for other countries are:

Maximum number of days in detention without being charged

Country	Days
Canada	1
USA	2
Russia	5
France	6
Ireland	7
Turkey	7.5
Australia	12
UK	28

Young people often complain that they are stopped and searched too often by police. Would official ID cards overcome this problem?

Are we citizens in a surveillance society?

Activity

Discuss as a group: does all this information-gathering make us any safer?

Many now believe we are citizens in a '**surveillance society**'. Technology allows speed and closed circuit television cameras to monitor our movements. Store, bank and credit cards mean every transaction we make can be recorded. In addition, the government is setting up a database to monitor every telephone call, text and e-mail at an estimated cost of £12 billion to keep us safe.

How much privacy would a citizen truly have if all these sources of information were collected together?

Review and research

The checklist

- UK identity cards are meant to combat the threat of terrorism and crime.

- People can be held in detention without charge in the UK for much longer periods than in any other country.

- Fears that Britain is being turned into a 'surveillance society' are said to be unjustified because such monitoring helps to keep us safe.

Further issues

- How justified are our hopes and fears over the introduction of ID cards?

- Is the UK in danger of sacrificing too many rights in an attempt to resist terrorism?

- Can intensive surveillance ever be justified or is it an affront to our right of privacy?

Taking it further

See developments reported on the Information Commissioner's Office (ICO) website including the monitoring of the Freedom of Information Act.

Does religion divide or unite society?

You will learn about:
- how different faiths have different beliefs and traditions
- how far believers are entitled to go to defend or promote their faith.

What's the issue? Different religions in society

UK citizens have rights to religious freedom and in many parts of the UK leaders of different faiths work together and have much in common. Faith groups undertake much good work but sometimes only certain faiths get involved. In multicultural areas such as Leicester, Luton or Bradford, Christians, Jews, Muslims, Hindus, Buddhists, Sikhs and others are also involved in good works.

The Church of England and the Methodists have male and female clergy, allow priests to marry and reluctantly accept divorce, while the Roman Catholic Church expects its priests to be male, single and celibate and the church won't tolerate divorce. Christian groups can have different beliefs, celebrate different festivals and often their followers are denied particular foods or have to behave in particular ways.

Glasgow football teams, Celtic and Rangers

Some believers from different churches and religions can sometimes behave like 'rival tribes'. Think of the tensions in Northern Ireland after the 1960s and all the deaths and injuries that occurred. Think of the continued conflict between Muslims and Jews in Israel and Palestine. Nowhere are the loyalties to particular traditions more obvious than when the Glasgow football teams, Celtic and Rangers, play each other. About three quarters of Celtic supporters see themselves as Catholic while two-thirds of Rangers fans say they are Protestant.

- Why are some religions not included in faith groups in some areas?

- How similar or different are the beliefs and practices of different religions?

- Are different religious groups sufficiently tolerant in their responses to people they disagree with?

Protest, tolerance and law

Different religious groups have been involved in loud protests in recent years. For example, Muslims protested over Salman Rushdie's writings and the cartoons they considered blasphemous. In 2004, Sikhs broke windows in a Birmingham theatre when they successfully demanded that a play, *Behzti*, which they objected to, should not be performed. Christians have been involved in protests against the ordination of women priests.

Human rights groups also campaign against female circumcision, which is part of the culture and tradition of some religions but contrary to UK law. This results from the Female Genital Mutilation Act 2003, which applies whether the procedure is carried out in the UK or if a girl is taken outside the UK for the operation.

Tolerance is the avoidance of discrimination between groups on grounds of faith or belief. Some question whether UK citizens are sufficiently tolerant in thoughts and actions. It is hoped that protests by or against religious groups can be limited to normal debate. In this way, a group can find peaceful ways for its followers to inform MPs and the government of their views.

The UK passed a law in 2006 which creates an offence of 'stirring up' hatred against a person on the grounds of their religion. Although UK laws allow citizens the right to practise their religion, they also have a responsibility to obey UK law. A serious breach of UK law was the 'honour killing' in 2005 of 20-year-old Banaz Mahmod whose boyfriend was considered unacceptable by her family.

How do different ethnic groups acquire UK values and learn about UK laws? Which cultural traditions from their former country might be unacceptable in the UK? Which UK values might be different to their former country's values?

Activity

In a group, think about how different religions can put forward their views if they are uneasy about an issue. Will religions appreciate a future king becoming 'Defender of Faith'? Which groups might oppose this?

Does multicultural Britain need a multicultural monarch?

The Queen is Head of the Church of England and Defender of the (Anglican) Faith. Prince Charles has suggested that when he becomes king, he may wish to be 'Defender of Faith' so aiming to protect all religious observance and perhaps stop the UK's move towards secularism (belief in non-religious society).

Prince Charles: future 'Defender of Faith'?

Review and research

The checklist
- Religions do unite on some projects in the UK but often not all religions are included.
- Religion can cause deep divisions in society.
- Tolerance is the avoidance of discrimination between groups on the grounds of faith or belief.
- UK law makes it illegal to 'stir up' hatred against a person on the grounds of their religion.
- Some followers of some religions in the UK sometimes seem reluctant to recognise that the right to live and practise a religion in the UK requires acceptance and tolerance of UK laws and values.

Further issues
- Are there adequate channels in the UK for religious minorities to present their views to authorities?
- Should the UK demand that everyone living here always obeys UK law even if it challenges some of their cultural traditions?
- Should UK law do more to accommodate the cultural values of UK citizens?

Taking it further
Find out about religious activities where you live and whether all faiths are included.

What happens if different 'rights' conflict?

You will learn about:
- how freedom of speech can conflict with the right to privacy
- how the right to freedom of movement could clash with a right to work
- how other 'rights' can conflict.

What's the issue? Freedom of expression vs. privacy

Many public figures have accepted the right of freedom of expression enjoyed by the media but challenged the idea that newspapers, radio or television can deny them or their families their personal privacy. Their complaints included:

- Tony Blair – the media photographed his young children

- Prince Charles – there was publicity about Prince Harry's sports injury when he was young

- Michael Douglas and Catherine Zeta Jones – *Hello!* Magazine printed wedding pictures after the couple had sold the rights to *OK!* Magazine

- Naomi Campbell – the media highlighted a visit to a drug **rehabilitation** clinic.

- Is it right to limit publicity given to children while still at school?

- Do the general public have a right to know about famous people's private lives?

Conflicting rights

There is sometimes a conflict between different rights.

Freedom of expression vs. privacy

All the public figures in the examples above have pointed out the conflict between Articles 8 (privacy) and 10 (freedom of expression) of the Human Rights Act 1998.

Right of movement and right to work

The UK is a member of the EU, so our citizens have a right to live or work in any of the other member countries – just as citizens of those countries can come to the UK. At the same time UK citizens also have the legal right to work. Some groups suggest that the arrival of workers from other countries undermines our own labour market, causing UK citizens to lose their jobs.

In 2006 it was claimed that the reason UK unemployment figures had reached 1.68 million was because there had been a 'flood' of workers from eastern Europe – yet in 2007, after many more European workers had arrived, unemployment actually declined. Perhaps they took jobs that UK workers wouldn't do. Also, many UK citizens moved abroad to work. This suggests that the right to free movement does not clash with the right to work to the extent that some people initially feared.

What jobs do you think people from overseas might be willing to do in the UK, which UK citizens seem unwilling to do?

The case of Ali and Mohammed Safi and seven others

Hijackers acted out of fear for their lives.

In February 2000 nine Afghans hijacked a Boeing 727 on an internal flight from Kabul and forced the crew to fly to Stansted.

The nine were convicted in 2001 of hijacking, false imprisonment, possessing firearms with intent to cause fear of violence and possessing explosives, but the convictions were overturned in 2003 by an appeal court which found they acted out of fear for their lives. They felt that hijacking the plane was their only way of escaping Afghanistan.

Although an immigration adjudication panel ruled they could not be returned to Afghanistan, the Government thought that allowing them to stay in the UK would send the wrong signal. The Government left the nine subject to immigration control, unable to work but having to depend on state hand-outs, reporting regularly to the immigration authorities.

In their appeal, the **judge** ruled the hijackers should remain in the UK, subject to six-monthly review. Removing them would deny their Article 3 rights not to be subjected to inhuman or degrading treatment or torture in Afghanistan.

Activity

Discuss as a group whether this was the right decision. What are the arguments for and against?

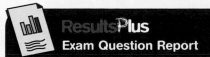

ResultsPlus
Exam Question Report

43

Which *two* of the following activities can be lawfully undertaken by a 16-year-old in England and Wales?
A Make a will
B Buy a lottery ticket
C Own a house
D Buy fireworks
E Give consent to sexual activity   (2)
May 2006, question 6e
Answer: B, E

How students answered

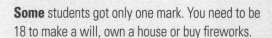

A few students scored no marks. Although you can guess multiple-choice questions, this is risky, so it is best to simply learn these facts.

Some students got only one mark. You need to be 18 to make a will, own a house or buy fireworks.

Most students answered this correctly and got two marks.

Review and research

The checklist

◉ The right to free expression in the UK must be understood alongside the right to privacy.

◉ The right of movement means that people can come from overseas to work but they often do jobs that UK citizens don't want to do.

◉ UK citizens have every right to fear terrorist activity which can threaten public safety but that does not allow us to deny rights to others or place them in a position of danger.

Taking it further
Find cases in which the Human Rights Act was used, on either government or pressure group websites.

Further issues

◉ Does it matter that different 'rights' conflict?

◉ Is any limitation on freedom of speech and expression ever justifiable?

◉ Should UK law 'protect' terrorists and hijackers?

44

Source A: Back from work experience...

When Mark, Keela and Suzi returned to school after work experience, they had to speak to their class about the activities of the shops where they worked. Did they break the law or make poor moral judgments? Each student mentioned ways in which they had been concerned.

Mark's examples:

1. Shop never returns the money of customers who return faulty goods – will only give a credit note.

2. Shop tears off 'sell by' dates on food items and leaves them on the shelves until sold.

Keela's examples:

3. Shop will not take back a returned item when the person has received the same item as a present.

4. Shopkeeper tells his wife he is going to a trade warehouse most days but in fact he goes to a betting shop.

Suzi's examples

5. Shop describes non-organic vegetables as 'organic' so higher prices can be charged.

6. Shopkeeper tries to win the sympathy and custom of shoppers by telling them he was wounded while in the armed forces, which is not true.

(a) A moral judgement involves: (1)

A acting to your own financial advantage

B an action in which the law is broken

C choosing between right and wrong

D doing something which is popular with others

(b) Which one of these laws was broken by at least one of the shops? (1)

A Consumer Credit Act

B Weights and Measures Act

C Consumer Protection Act

D Trade Descriptions Act

ResultsPlus
Maximise your marks

Read Source A and answer the following questions:

(i) State two of the activities which are lawful but not morally acceptable and briefly explain why. (4)

(ii) State two of the activities which are neither lawful nor morally acceptable and briefly explain why. (4)

Student answer	Examiner comments	Build a better answer
(i) Points 4 and 5. In both of them the shop acts legally if not honestly.	● Point 5 cannot be correct because, although the action is undoubtedly immoral, it is also unlawful. The Trade Descriptions Act makes it clear that goods for sale must not be falsely described. The two points to be identified are Points 4 and 6. In Point 4 there is no law which says a husband can't tell lies to his wife but it is definitely morally unacceptable because he is being dishonest and his absences may impose an unfair workload on his wife. In Point 6 it is not unlawful to claim to have been in the armed forces or to claim to have been wounded. However, it is morally unacceptable because he is being dishonest, telling lies and trading off the public's admiration for those who put themselves in danger in the armed forces; sometimes being killed or seriously wounded.	△ Point 4. The man is telling lies to his wife (hasn't broken law) which is 'wrong' on a 'right or wrong?' scale. Many people also believe gambling is morally wrong. Point 6 is similarly lawful but immoral. Trying to get trade in your shop by pretending to be a hero when you weren't in the army or wounded is an insult to soldiers.
(ii) Points 4 and 6 aren't legal or moral. The real point is that if activities are not moral they can't be legal.	■ Point 6 cannot be correct for the reason stated in (i) above. Point 4 also cannot be correct for the reasons stated above. 'Moral' and 'legal' do not overlap as exactly as the candidate's answer suggests. Two of Points 1, 2 and 5 need to be identified and briefly explained. Point 1 is wrong both legally and morally – if an item proves not to be 'fit for purpose', money must be refunded and the shopkeeper is treating the customer unfairly. Point 2 is unlawful because it breaches the Food Safety Act and immoral because it could make people ill. Point 5 breaches the Trade Description Act so it is unlawful and also immoral because a dishonest claim is made.	△ Point 1 is illegal because the shop mustn't sell faulty goods and a customer may be willing to have an alternative item or a credit note but they should not be denied their money back if that is what they want. Wrongly withholding a customer's money is undoubtedly immoral. Point 2 is also illegal (Food Safety Act) and to sell people goods that could make them ill just to make a profit is morally very bad.

ResultsPlus

Watch out!

- Pay attention to the command words.
- If you are asked to 'state' something you do not need to 'unpack' the material or explain it.

- If asked to 'briefly explain' you must do so and address all key words in the question.

Practice Exam Question

'The best way to promote multiculturalism is to get people interested in the foods of different cultures.'

Do you agree with this view? Give reasons for your opinion, showing you have considered another point of view. (12)

To answer the question above, you could consider the following points and other information of your own.

- How can and do people from different cultures get to know each other in the UK?
- In what ways, excluding food, do people differ from culture to culture?
- How and why do people become interested in popular foods from other cultures and countries?
- Why is 'foreign food' and multicultural living often more fashionable than 'traditional food' in the UK?

Getting started

- Think about the material in Chapter 1 and the work you did in class on this topic.
- Never lose sight of the main question – refer to it in your introduction, in the body of the answer and in the conclusion so the examiner can see how and why the points you are making are relevant.
- The four 'mini-questions' are there to help you get thinking. If you answer these 'mini-questions' in your answer make sure the 'mini-answers' clearly help to answer the main question.
- In these long answers you must always offer at least one other point of view – so 'for' and 'against' points are required.
- For your conclusion you need to explain definitely whether you agree with the original statement or not – and you must clearly say why.

Introduction

This is where you indicate the main points you are going to make – a sort of 'essay plan in words'. You may also want to include any definitions of key terms in the introduction.

Student answer

A 'multicultural society' is a society that includes both cultural and ethnic diversity within the population and 'multiculturalism' aims for a society that gives equal status to distinct cultural and religious groups with no one culture being dominant. Learning about and enjoying foods from other cultures is a good way to get to know people from other countries and their values but it isn't the only way and it may not be the best.

Examiner comment

The definition is good and helps to give structure to the answer. It also immediately confirms to the reader that the student knows what she or he is talking about. The second part of the introduction directly engages with the question and without getting into a great deal of detail at this stage indicates that the final conclusion may not completely agree with the proposition in the question.

Main body

Here your answer needs to establish a number of particular points – these should include arguments backed up with evidence – you could use the 'mini-questions' (called 'scaffolding') to help you to develop these but don't forget the main question. When you offer contrasting points, you will need to show by the time you get to the conclusion why you consider one to be stronger than the other.

Student answer

Lots of people travel globally for holidays or work and when they do they find different foods. Most people like an opportunity to try new foods and it often makes people feel adventurous. Back in this country we can go to ethnic restaurants (e.g. Greek, Italian, Indian, Chinese, Vietnamese) at first because we like the food but then we get to know members of the local community who live and work locally.

Once people in the UK liked to only eat their usual foods, but now many more people are willing to eat different foods – maybe because of the many 'ethnic food' programmes on TV – and we meet people from ethnic minority communities when we go to food shops to buy.

But we do not learn about cultures just from ethnic foods. Sometimes we meet people from different cultures at work, when shopping, at school or college or they may share interests or just live near each other.

Examiner comment

- The 'mini-questions' are used well.
- We start by considering how people from different cultures can get to know each other through overseas travel (this is good – a new point which is not in the mini-questions). This idea is then focused onto the UK in the third paragraph.
- How and why people become interested in popular foods from other cultures and countries is explained in the first and second paragraphs (good reference to another new point about television).
- A wider range of cultural differences is part of the discussion in the third paragraph.

Later on the answer points out that some people feel multicultural living is fashionable and argues that religion, language and dress values may be more important elements than 'food'.

Conclusion

Before you start writing your conclusion, always look again at the main question. The examiner will expect you to refer to it in your conclusion. Don't introduce new information. Just explain the points you have already made to show which argument is the stronger in your view and why.

Student answer

We can find out about lots of cultures from food so the question is partly right but I'm not sure if it's always the best way to promote or advance multiculturalism. For some UK people food will be the best way to get to know others, but there are now many people from other cultures who have other things in common with some of us – like a shared religion, or a shared interest in a sport such as swimming or running, or other pastimes such as chess or poetry. So the answer is 'sometimes but not always'.

Examiner comment

This conclusion rounds the essay off well. It is consistent with the argument suggested in the introduction and it doesn't introduce any new points. Because another point of view has been addressed a good mark will be awarded. If only one view had been given, the student would have received no more than about half marks.

Over to you

'Human rights are more likely to be implemented at the national rather than at the global level.'

Do you agree with this view? Give reasons for your opinion, showing you have considered another point of view. (12)

To answer the question above, you could consider the following points and other information of your own.

- How have the United Nations and European bodies promoted human rights?
- What happens at national level if a citizen is denied human rights?
- How important is it for human rights to be turned into legal rights at national level?
- How successfully can international bodies overrule national courts or governments?

Chapter 5: Media – representation and reality
Media representations

You will learn about:

- identifying facts, opinion and bias in different media sources
- similarities and differences between broadcast and print media and ICT
- empathy as a source of opinion.

What's the issue? Popular or quality?

The Sun **newspaper** front page followed an announcement of serious overcrowding in the prisons for which John Reid **MP** was allegedly responsible.

Popular newspapers, such as *The Sun*, *The Daily Express* and **The Daily Mirror,** sometimes like to have fun with their headlines, and often seem **biased**.

Quality newspapers, such as **The Times, The Guardian** and *The Independent*, usually have more sober, less humorous headlines, but they still have biased views. Their owners and **editors** usually dictate the 'policy line' they adopt.

'Popular' newspapers often have fun with their headlines.
Source: The Sun 25 January 2007

'Quality' newspapers often have more sober headlines.
Source: The Independent Fri 21 July 2006

- Is *The Sun's* headline a fact? What is the headline trying to do?

- Compare the front pages. What are the differences and similarities?

- Why are newspapers and Internet **blogs** more biased than radio or television?

Popular and quality newspapers

Newspapers are bought every day. Often, to persuade people to buy them, they will include interesting, sometimes outrageous, front-page headlines and pictures.

Popular papers sometimes print humorous front pages that poke fun at famous people or celebrities. They include large headlines and photographs, look at personal aspects of the news and often use a chatty style. The newspapers may also print unattractive photographs or rude cartoons of people they disagree with.

Quality papers are more likely than the popular press to include factual accounts. They deal with home and overseas news in detail and also cover sports and cultural events, mostly in a formal style. The leading article is often stated in a logical, reasoned way.

Putting forward a biased view

Quality newspapers tend to give a more factual account of the news. However, both popular and quality newspapers may give more emphasis to the side of the argument they favour and miss out aspects that don't fit in easily with their point of view. Not giving a completely balanced, fair account is called a bias, and involves people's **opinions**. For example, *The Daily Telegraph* regularly supports the **Conservative Party** and the *Guardian* backs the **Labour Party** or the **Liberal Democrats**, so they will tend to write in a way that supports the party they favour.

Bias is obvious in Internet blogs where individuals state openly, or campaign for, their own point of view.

Why is broadcasting less biased?

The **BBC Charter** and the Independent Broadcasting Authority Acts require **terrestrial** broadcasters such as the BBC and the independent television channels (for example, **ITV** and Channel 4) to be **impartial**. This means being fair and unbiased. This is why opinion news programmes offer different points of view and programmes such as BBC's *Question Time* include several panel members with different views. Any complaints about bias are investigated by the **Office of Communications (Ofcom)**, which regulates the broadcasters, making sure that they stick to the Broadcasting Code and, if necessary, imposes fines.

Empathy and soap operas

Empathy means putting yourself in the position of someone else to help you understand what they think or why they behave as they do. This can help you to forgive someone if they have behaved badly or oddly. It can have a big impact on your views. For example, when a character you identify with in a soap opera such as *Eastenders* or *Coronation Street* has a problem (perhaps deciding whether to have an abortion or experiencing gender or racial discrimination), empathy will make you feel you understand. If someone you know has a problem you can also use empathy to imagine what they are going through, and to change your own opinion. These issues can help form your opinions.

Activity

Look at a selection of newspapers, both quality and popular, for the same day and look for the different ways stories are written. Notice the ways in which each newspaper puts across its own opinion.

Activity

What does the Office of Communications do? How effective is it? Look at the Ofcom website and download a broadcast bulletin. How powerful do you think Ofcom is?

Review and research

The checklist

● Popular and quality newspapers, and Internet blogs, may include bias as they reflect the views of their owners, editors and authors.

● Terrestrial broadcasters are expected to be unbiased, balanced and impartial; they are regulated by Ofcom to ensure they stick to the Broadcasting Code.

● Our attitudes towards another person, what they say and how they act, are often influenced by empathy.

Further issues

● Do we buy newspapers for news or for entertainment?

● How has the wider use of the Internet affected newspapers and broadcasters?

● How can soaps affect people's opinions on key moral issues such as discrimination and abortion?

Taking it further

Carry out some research on one topical issue to see how differently it is presented by various media sources.

Issues and news agendas

You will learn about:
- the extent to which the media reflect, distort or create opinion
- how different forms of media are regulated.

What's the issue? Mosquito campaign goes into reverse

Biting back at the Mosquito

The Mosquito device has been used by some local shops to stop gangs hanging out nearby and causing damage. The sound emitted by the device causes discomfort to young people's ears, although over-25s cannot hear it. At first this was thought to be a success, with about 3,500 being installed in the three years up to 2009.

But now, after much blogging, **Youth Parliament** members from all over the UK have won the backing of **Children's Commissioner** Sir Al Aynsley Green, who launched the Buzz Off campaign, saying the Mosquito created a divide between young and old.

Using the Mosquito is still backed by the 30,000-member Association of Convenience Stores who claim it helps tackle anti-social behaviour. But Shami Chakrabarti, Director of the pressure group, Liberty, asks:

'What type of **society** uses a low-level sonic weapon on its children? Imagine the outcry if a device was introduced that caused total discomfort to people of one race or gender, rather than to our kids. The Mosquito has no place in a country that values its children and seeks to give them dignity and **respect**.'

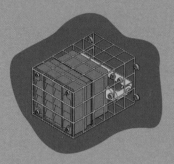
Mosquito device

Following the launch of a campaign by 11 MILLION, The National Youth Agency, Groundwork and Corby Young People Friendly Neighbourhoods, Kent County Council has prohibited the gadget on its buildings and called for a nationwide ban – a step enthusiastically reported by newspapers such as *The Daily Mail*.

- How have public views about the issue changed?
- How important are **pressure groups** for changing opinions and decisions?
- Why does Kent County Council now want the Mosquito banned?

The Buzz Off campaign logo

Why have views changed about using the Mosquito to move young people on from parks or shopping areas? How important do you think newspapers, the Internet or broadcasts were in causing the change?

Do the media create, lead, distort or follow public opinion?

Newspapers, particularly tabloids, and Internet bloggers often campaign for certain issues or promote a viewpoint:

- *The Sun* or *The Daily Mail* often criticise **immigrants** arriving in the UK.
- *The Guardian* and *The Independent* often oppose discrimination and promote social reform proposals.
- *The Times* and *The Daily Telegraph* generally highlight flaws in UK relations with Europe.

Sometimes the media exaggerate the dangers presented by particular groups, such as immigrants or 'hoodies' – most of whom are law-abiding **citizens**. If only a few people in a particular group cause problems, or commit crimes, the media may exaggerate this, causing the public to panic and believe that everyone in that group is a danger.

The media will not stick to an opinion that their audience doesn't like; they must keep the readers on their side. If pressure groups get involved, the media might decide to change the way they report a story.

Regulating the media

All parts of the media may be subjected to **censorship** – not allowed to publish certain information on grounds of public safety (e.g. **DA notices**) or decency. A DA notice is an official request to news editors not to publish or broadcast items on specific sensitive subjects. Additionally, all the media must obey the **law** of **defamation**. This is when a person's reputation is wrongly damaged by someone talking about them (**slander**) or writing about them (**libel**). Publications such as *Private Eye* have been charged with libel by several people in the past. In some of these cases, the court has decided that they were guilty of libel and *Private Eye* has had to pay money to these people to compensate them.

In addition, the media must respect people's right to **privacy** and not interfere in their private life.

All published media such as magazines and newspapers obey the Code of Practice adopted by the **Press Complaints Commission (PCC)** in August 2007. The PCC investigates complaints. If it finds the Code of Practice has been broken, the publication has to prominently publish the Commission's ruling in full on its pages.

In 2008 the Ofcom Broadcasting Code was finalised. It includes guidance on matters such as protecting under-18s, **religion**, due impartiality (fair and balanced views) and accuracy, undue prominence of views and opinions, **elections** and **referendums**, and fairness and privacy.

If someone believes their rights have been disregarded, Ofcom will examine any complaints.

Activity

Look for examples in the media of particular groups being demonised. Are any claims made based on prejudice or hate rather than hard evidence?

Activity

Look at the PCC website and note the main elements of the Code of Practice. Discuss recent cases on which rulings have been made.

Review and research

The checklist

- If the public view of an issue changes, the media will reflect this. Media outlets do not usually pursue opinions that their audience dislikes.
- Some sensationalised stories create 'folk devils' and 'moral panics'.
- The media must not break the law or breach codes of practice.

Further issues

- Are the media more interested in telling the truth or making profits?
- Can the media influence opinion in elections?
- Do codes of practice and laws relating to the media give individuals strong enough rights to complain?

Taking it further

Look at the provisions of the PCC Code of Practice and the Ofcom Broadcasting Code and some of the resulting cases and issues. Think about whether or not the regulations do enough to protect people. Can the media still misuse their power and damage individuals?

Chapter 6: Information is power
Public debate and policy formation

You will learn about :
- how politicians use the media to communicate with the public
- the extent of bias in the media.

What's the issue? When public opinion and public policy clash...

If you lived in a house beside a field, you would probably hate it if someone built an ugly over-sized house next door. If you didn't know about the new house in advance, you couldn't take steps to stop it.

To overcome the housing shortage, in 2008 the **government** proposed building ten new **eco-towns**. The announcement appeared in the media so that people living near the suggested sites knew in advance and were able to organise **petitions**, posters, protests and publicity.

If they had not been informed, the **contracts** for building the houses, offices, roads and new railway connections, could all have been signed and then it would have been too late to protest.

Where has the field gone?

Protesting against new development

- How can it be claimed that 'information is power'?

- What are the arguments for and against secrecy?

- How can the media help those who support or oppose particular proposals?

How widely do people have access to the media? Are there some people who are left out? Does this matter?

Activity

Go onto the 10 Downing St website to see what issues are being discussed. Go to the e-petitions part of the website and see what proposals citizens have put forward.

How the government uses the media to communicate with the public

When new laws are passed, the government can't assume that everyone will immediately understand the law change or that they will agree with it.

- Governments need to persuade people that a law should be obeyed. Before the smoking ban in public places was introduced in July 2007, the government used the media to highlight the health dangers of smoking.

- Proposed laws are now discussed on websites, on radio and television programmes as well as in newspapers and magazines. This is so people can offer feedback and make suggestions to improve the proposals. An example was the Crime & Disorder Act 1998 which established anti-social behaviour orders (ASBOs). It was first proposed in 1997, but the reaction of the Press, and pressure groups such as Liberty and **Justice**, meant the Act was changed from the original proposals.

- Government now holds frequent **consultations**. Consultations are where the government asks people to give their opinions on new ideas. This can be done in meetings, through letters, websites, emails or the media.
- Once a law is passed, the government also uses the media to tell people that the new law is now in force.

Politicians and the media

Politicians want the media to say good things about them. If the public likes them, this helps them get elected or re-elected. But sometimes the media criticise MPs for bad decisions over policy or their private behaviour. When the media reported that Derek Conway MP had employed his son, and that his wages were paid with public money, he was forced to leave the Conservative Party.

The media and elections

During elections, terrestrial TV programmes are balanced and unbiased because the law says they have to be. However, newspapers are very different. In the 2005 **general election**, popular papers such as *The Daily Mail* backed the Conservatives and the *The Daily Mirror* supported the Labour Party. Quality papers offered more balanced coverage but were still biased, with the *The Daily Telegraph* supporting the Conservatives and both *The Guardian* and *The Independent* backing Labour and the Liberal Democrats.

UK political party spending during the 2005 general election

If a **political party** has fewer wealthy supporters, lack of funding might limit the way it gets its message across to the general public. So giving political parties state funding has been considered (e.g. money from taxes).

Money spent on:	Making party political broadcasts	Establishing media teams	Advertising in media & poster boards
Labour	£470,218	£375,410	£5,286,997
Conservative	£293,446	£448,276	£8,175,165
Lib Dem	£124,671	£105,793	£1,583,058

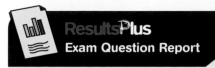

*Why do you think there is such a big difference in the amounts spent by different political parties? Is there a case for political parties to get their funding from the state? Visit websites, such as that of the **Electoral Commission**, to find more information.*

Review and research

The checklist
- Without information, people cannot act effectively.
- Consultation helps make new laws more acceptable.
- Because some political parties are less well funded than others, their messages are less likely to reach the public.

Taking it further
Talk to your teacher about submitting a petition proposal to the 10 Downing St website.

Further issues
- Should governments do what they think is right or should they try to take into account the pressure from media sources and groups?
- Is it a good thing that there are such big differences in political party spending during elections and can this be controlled?

Influencing public opinion

You will learn about:
- ways in which the media are used to influence public opinion and those in power
- the role and importance of opinion polls.

What's the issue? Where does public opinion come from?

Average sales of selected UK daily newspapers August/September 2008	
The Sun	2,914,643
Daily Mail	2,049,881
Daily Mirror	1,312,458
Daily Telegraph	798,159
Daily Express	689,890
The Times	600,437
Daily Star	599,356
The Guardian	303,402
The Independent	167,092
Financial Times	138,783

Source: ABC

Where does public opinion come from?

- Which newspapers have most impact on public opinion: the popular papers that most people read or the quality papers that fewer people read, which go into things in greater detail?

- As newspaper sales fall, which media source has the biggest influence on how we think and what we do?

- Why are popular papers much cheaper than quality ones?

Who influences us and how?

We are all influenced by experiences at home, school and work, or when we spend free time with friends. But companies and organisations can also influence us.

Advertisements try to influence you to buy jeans, personal computers or sports kit. Often they get well-known sports people or celebrities to recommend their product. If you like the celebrity involved, you may be persuaded to choose the brands they are advertising. In this case a celebrity is acting as an **opinion leader**.

Pressure groups, like **Greenpeace**, promote their causes through all forms of media. They gather information from public authorities (using the **Freedom of Information Act 2000**), university researchers, and answers to questions in **Parliament**. They influence people through appearing on radio and television programmes and also through helping MPs and government departments develop new **policies**.

Public opinion might be influenced most by large-circulation popular daily papers, but many people buy these papers for the sport, pictures, horoscopes, puzzles or celebrity gossip. They rely instead on radio and television to keep them up to date with recent news.

Fewer quality papers are sold but their readers include MPs and members of the **House of Lords**, senior **civil servants**, senior business people, **trade union** leaders, religious leaders and professionals such as **lawyers**, doctors, bankers and school, college and university teachers; the people who are often either decision makers, opinion leaders or both.

Radio and television programmes are supposed to be less biased than newspapers because they don't just put forward one point of view. Does it help you make up your mind if you hear more than one point of view expressed?

Do opinion polls reflect opinions or influence them?

To find out what the public think about an issue, a sample of different people are asked questions. Their answers are used to represent those of the public in general. This is known as an **opinion poll**. Accuracy of an opinion poll depends on the numbers of people asked, and who they are. The more people who respond, the more accurate a poll will be. If lots of polls produce similar responses, it is even more likely that they are accurate, though of course opinions do change.

A countryside Alliance percentage poster

During the debates on whether hunting should be allowed to continue, the Countryside Alliance's posters said '59% say keep hunting' based on an opinion poll. They were using the results of the poll to try to influence others, including MPs. But 59% doesn't show how many people were asked – it could have been 100, 1000 or any number.

Government and political parties use opinion polls to help them assess the popularity of people or policies. If an opinion poll shows that support for a political party is falling, the party leader may resign, as Conservative, Iain Duncan Smith did in 2004 and Liberal Democrat, Sir Menzies Campbell, in 2007.

Review and research

The checklist
- Opinion leaders advertise products or seek support for particular policies, parties or people.
- Pressure group concerns are publicised through all types of media.
- Opinion poll findings may be used to try to change the views of others.

Further issues
- Should newspapers and the Internet be made to avoid bias, as broadcasters are?
- Which types of newspapers have the biggest impact on public opinion?
- How do opinion polls assist policy making and democracy?

Taking it further
Choose a topic or issue. Look at newspaper and television stories over a two- or three-year period to assess how much public opinion on the issue has changed over time.

Chapter 7: Law and society
Crime: rising or falling?

You will learn about:
- levels of crime in the UK, who commits crime and its impact on society
- crime, conscience, law and morality.

What's the issue? Crime rates are falling – or are they?

Police records show 5.52 million offences were recorded in England and Wales in 2005/2006 and this fell to 5.42 million in 2006/2007. Although there were more crimes in some categories and fewer in others, the levels of crime seem to be falling.

Are crime rates now falling?

Crimes recorded by the police in England and Wales in 2007/08	(%)
Theft and handling stolen goods	36
Theft from vehicles	9
Theft of vehicles	3
Criminal damage	21
Violence against the person	19
Burglary	12
Fraud and forgery	5
Drugs offences	3
Robbery	2
Sexual offences	1
Other offences	1
All notifiable offences (=100%) (thousands)	4,951

Source: adapted from Home Office, reported in Social Trends 39
Reproduced under the terms of the click-use license

However, the **British Crime Survey (BCS)** estimated in 2008 that there were 10.1 million crimes committed against people living in private **households** in England and Wales; roughly double the number reported to the police. The survey reports that the elderly fear crime most, yet young people are most often the victims of crime.

- Why do people commit crime?

- Why are young people most often victims of crime?

- Can crime ever be justified?

Do you think that fewer crimes would be committed if the punishments were more severe? Is the real problem that too many people have not learned that committing crime (breaking the law) is wrong and can never be right, whatever excuses are offered?

Who commits crime? Who are the victims?

In 2006, 80% of offenders were male and 7% were aged under 18. 2.1% of all 15-year-old girls and 6.1% of all 17-year-old men were guilty of, or **cautioned** (given a warning) for one or more offence. Young people are often victims of:

- theft from rented flats
- thefts of cars (or from cars), or
- violence in the street.

Why might crime not be reported?

There could be several reasons why a crime is not reported. For example:

- not all crimes are noticeable (e.g. not paying for parking)
- people might think the crime is not important enough (e.g. stealing something of low value)
- the victim might be too embarrassed (e.g. if they have been sexually abused)
- the victim might know the offender (a friend or relative) and want to protect them
- the victim might not believe the police could find the person responsible.

There has recently been a lot of concern about knife crime. Is this is a real problem, or have the media exaggerated it?

Young people are often victims of violence in the street.

Crime, conscience, law and morality

Sometimes there is a difference between what you feel to be wrong and what is actually illegal. For example, Conservative MP Nadine Dorries believes it is morally wrong that there are so many abortions in the UK at present. However, these abortions are legal. Other MPs, such as Lib Dem Dr Evan Harris, disagree and believe that every woman has the right to choose for herself.

When rugby player, 23-year-old Daniel James went to Switzerland for an assisted suicide in September 2008, there was concern that his parents could be prosecuted (taken to court). This is because they went with him and it is against the law to help someone to commit suicide. In the end, the **Crown Prosecution Service (CPS)** decided not to prosecute. Similar issues arose when MS sufferer, Debbie Purdy from Bradford, went to court in October 2008 to ask for a guarantee that her husband would not be prosecuted if he helped her to die at some point in the future. She lost her case but said she would fight on.

There was a different outcome when long-term leukaemia sufferer, 13-year-old Hannah Jones, said she did not want to receive any more treatment, even though it might mean she would die. The health authorities went to court to try to make her have a heart operation but, in the end, they decided to respect Hannah's wishes and dropped their legal case. Some people, who believe that life should be saved at all costs, were worried about this decision.

*Is there a case for making **euthanasia** (helping to kill someone who has an incurable illness or injury, with that person's consent) legal in the UK? Or is human life so sacred that everything possible should always be done to preserve life?*

Review and research

The checklist

- Police records show that the crime reported to them is falling. But the British Crime Survey says that half the crimes committed are never reported.
- The young are more often victims than the old and most crimes are committed by men.
- Sometimes the law doesn't seem to match up with the choices people want to make in these modern times.

Further issues

- Which measure of crime should you believe – police statistics or the British Crime Survey?
- Do the media exaggerate fear of crime?
- Do today's laws match up with the moral values we hold in a modern society?

Taking it further

Look up crime figures in your area and compare them with the trends shown in the national data on page 56.

Reducing crime

You will learn about:

- crime detection – the work and effectiveness of the police
- the work of youth offending teams
- how the National Probation Service supports offenders, victims and society.

What's the issue? 73% of offenders are never caught so de we need more police?

This means that if 14% of burglars are caught (detected), then 86% aren't!

Would more police on the streets mean more offenders were caught?

- Why are detection rates much higher for some crimes than for others?
- Does society do enough to teach everyone that crime is wrong?
- How could detection rates be increased?

Recorded crimes detected (criminals caught) by the police in England and Wales in 2005/2006	(%)
Drug offences	95
Violence against the person	54
Theft and handling stolen goods	18
Theft of vehicles	15
Theft from vehicles	9
Sexual offences	35
Rape (including attempted)	28
Fraud and forgery	29
Robbery	18
Criminal damage	15
Burglary	14
Other crimes	71
All recorded crime detected	**27**

Source: Social Trends 37, reproduced under the terms of the click-use license

Activity

Find out the levels of crime reported to your local police force and compare their detection rates with the national ones for England and Wales, above.

If parents acted as responsible people, keeping their children in order and punishing them if they did bad things, would we need Youth Offending Teams?

Crime detection

Citizenship teaches us to behave as law-abiding people because it's the right thing to do – and not just because we don't want to be caught and punished! However, if fewer than one in three crimes are solved, it isn't surprising that some offenders think the law will never find them. From the table above, only 27% of crimes are detected and, if only half of all crimes are reported, that figure may well be much lower.

The role of the police

There are 160,000 police officers in the UK and 100,000 staff who support them. The police: (i) investigate serious crime and keep in contact with **communities**, (ii) are responsible for traffic management and help at serious accidents, (iii) help at sporting events and political **demonstrations**, (iv) deal with, and prevent, many serious incidents which are the result of **terrorism** (a growing problem).

However, the police are often criticised for a number of reasons:

- Crime detection rates are low (so perhaps we need more police officers).
- People say they want more police patrolling the streets on foot but the police say it's better to use cars to reach trouble-spots quickly.

- Sometimes the police are criticised for acting without having all the facts. For example, when they shot dead the innocent Jean Charles de Menezes in 2005 because they mistook him for a terrorist.
- The 1999 **MacPherson report** said London's Metropolitan Police force was 'institutionally racist' (suggesting that the entire police force were racist).
- Young people sometimes claim they are stopped and searched too often, without good reason.

What do Youth Offending Teams do?

With more parents working full time today, **Youth Offending Teams (YOTs)** try to prevent offending behaviour by children and young people aged 10 to 17. They are made up of representatives from the police, **probation** service, social, health and education services, drugs and alcohol misuse and housing officers. YOTs assess the needs of young offenders and identify the problems that make them offend, as well as measuring the risk they pose to others. They ensure offenders are dealt with quickly and encourage them to face up to the consequences of their actions. They promote reparation to victims by young offenders and reinforce parental responsibility.

The National Probation Service (NPS) – what does it do for local communities, prisoners and victims?

The **National Probation Service (NPS)** supervises drug **rehabilitation** schemes (helping people to try to come off illegal drugs) and offenders who are carrying out community service. This is compulsory unpaid work and is an alternative punishment given to people who have broken the law (instead of sending them to prison).

In 2007, six million hours of community service were carried out by offenders in England and Wales. This is the same as spending £33 million to help make local communities across the country better places to live. The work includes bringing run-down areas and buildings back into use, clearing churchyards, mending park benches, removing graffiti and supporting charities.

The NPS also works on sentence-planning with prisoners, supports victims of violent crime and supervises offenders in the community when they have completed their sentence.

Results Plus
Watch out!

'There would be less crime if punishments were more severe.' Do you agree with this view? Give reasons for your opinion, showing you have considered *another point of view*. You should support your arguments with *examples* wherever possible. (9)
Adapted from May 2006, question 9

80% of the candidates chose this question, but the overwhelming majority failed to consider an alternative view, thus limiting themselves to 4 marks out of a possible 9.
Most agreed with the view but failed to consider another point of view e.g. that most ex-prisoners re-offend or that countries with capital punishment might also suffer high crime rates. Too many candidates gave emotional answers with unsupported opinion rather than factual reasons.

People who complete community service are 14% less likely to re-offend than those who go to prison.

Review and research

The checklist
- 73% of offenders were not caught in 2006.
- There are 250,000 police and support staff but perhaps more are needed.
- Community punishments are generally more successful than sending offenders to prison.

Further issues
- Are criticisms of the police justified?
- Do you think community punishments are better than sending offenders to prison?
- Should parents be more responsible for the behaviour of their teenage children?

Taking it further
Make a list of the aims of Youth Offending Teams and the National Probation Service, and what activities they carry out in your area.

Courts at work

You will learn about:
- the different courts in England and Wales and who presides over them
- the differences between barristers and solicitors and the role of juries.

What's the issue? What's fair?

Martin was driving at about 60mph in a 40mph area when he injured an elderly woman on the pavement as he swerved to miss a lorry. He is charged with dangerous driving and could go to prison and receive a driving ban. Martin was driving to the airport with his daughter's passport, which she had left at home when setting out for New Zealand. To get the passport to his daughter in time, Martin planned to drive 40 miles on urban roads in 40 minutes. The case is now being heard in the Crown Court.

- Is Martin guilty or not guilty?
- If guilty, do you think Martin should be sent to prison and banned from driving?
- If Martin is found guilty, what reasons for a lenient sentence could his lawyers offer before he is sentenced?

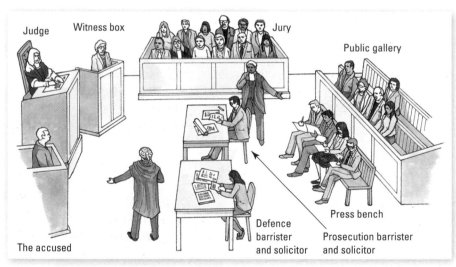

A courtroom trial

Activity

In a group, imagine if you were in each of these roles in turn — judge, victim, jury member, prosecution or defence barrister, the accused, press reporter, or an observer in the public gallery. Discuss your feelings.

Roles in the courtroom

The **judge** decides points of law (he knows what the law can and cannot do), keeps order (if people in the courtroom behave badly, e.g. start shouting) and decides sentences (whether someone will go to prison or, perhaps as an alternative, carry out community service – see page 59).

The **jury** decides if someone is innocent or guilty.

The *defence team* put forward reasons why the jury should find Martin not guilty or, if he is guilty, why he should not be punished too severely.

The *prosecution team* put forward reasons why the jury should decide Martin is guilty and should be punished.

A jury is told to be impartial (unbiased) as they listen to the case but they may find someone 'not guilty' if they think a 'guilty' verdict would lead to someone being very heavily punished. Also, what influences a juror? A 62-year-old woman might have a lot of sympathy with the victim while a dad with a 20-year-old daughter might be sympathetic to Martin.

Criminal courts in England and Wales

In increasing order of seniority the courts are:

- *Magistrates' courts* with up to three trained, but not qualified, lay **magistrates** (also known as Justices of the Peace, JPs) or one legally qualified *district judge*. They deal with 98% of criminal cases, and also act as youth courts if the accused is aged between 10 and 17.

- *Crown Courts* deals with more serious cases and decides sentences when a magistrates' court is not able to give a strong enough sentence (magistrates can only pass limited sentences).
- *High Court* (Queen's Bench, Family and Chancery Divisions) deals with some criminal but mainly civil cases (disputes decided by court).

People found guilty have a right to *appeal* against their conviction. The *Court of Appeal* hears appeals from the Crown Court. The *House of Lords* (to be replaced by the *Supreme Court* in 2009) deals with appeals from the Court of Appeal or High Court.

Magistrates and judges

In England and Wales there are 29,000 magistrates. They are now appointed from a wider cross-section of society than before, including women and people from ethnic minorities.

525 out of 3,000 judges in senior courts are women but, in April 2008, only 156 judges were from ethnic minorities. In September 2008 Sir Terence Etherton was the first openly gay judge to be sworn in as one of the 38 Lord Justices of Appeal in the Appeal Court.

Barristers and solicitors

In the UK we have *barristers* and *solicitors*. Solicitors do general law work. This includes writing wills or arranging for a house sale or purchase. They often represent clients in court themselves, particularly in magistrates' courts. Barristers are specialist lawyers. They often represent a solicitor's client in court if the case is more serious, for example, murder or rape. Barristers generally specialise in one area of law, e.g. criminal or family or contract law, and they can go on to become judges.

Juries and justice

In Crown Courts a group of 12 men and women aged between 18 and 70 become the jury and decide if an accused is innocent or guilty. Attempts have recently been made to get rid of juries or reduce their powers. Those who are opposed to juries say they are not able to understand long or complicated trials dealing with fraud or terrorism. Most people see them as an important part of a citizen's rights. Sometimes juries do not want to convict people if they were accused of a crime for which they could receive a heavy sentence.

Anyone over the age of 18 can be a juror. How would you feel if you were asked to be on a jury?

Results Plus
Watch out!

What is a jury? (1)
What is an ethnic minority? (1)
June 2005, question 6c, e

Make sure that you know key terms and what they mean. These should be easy answers. In the exam, most candidates understood that a jury is a group of people deciding innocence or guilt in a criminal court or liability in a civil court. However, it was disappointing that relatively few candidates could 'unpack' the term 'ethnic minority' as a group different from the main population of a country or locality in terms of their racial origin or cultural background. These could be easy marks to gain.

Review and research

The checklist
- A court hearing will be a very different experience for a victim, an accused or a juror.
- Judges and magistrates are increasingly chosen from all different areas of society.
- Juries usually decide if someone is innocent or guilty but sometimes they look for the 'greater justice'.

Taking it further
See if your teacher can arrange for you to visit a magistrates' or crown court or perhaps talk to local magistrates or the clerk of the court. Find out about the 'Kingsnorth Six'.

Further issues
- Should magistrates and judges be from a wider cross-section of society?
- Do we need to divide the legal profession between solicitors and barristers?
- Should juries continue in UK courts?

Crime and punishment

You will learn about:
- the role of prisons
- how the justice system deals with crime and antisocial behaviour.

62

What's the issue? Why do criminals commit crime?

Differences between UK prisoners and the general population	General population	UK prisoners
Ran away from home as a child	11%	48%
Taken into care as a child	2%	27%
Has a family member convicted of a criminal offence	16%	43%
Regularly truanted from school	3%	30%
Left school at 16	32%	88%
Attended a special school	1%	21%
Has no qualifications	15%	55%
Numeracy at or below level expected of an 11-year-old	23%	65%
Reading ability at or below level expected of an 11-year-old	23%	48%
Suffer from two or more mental disorders	4%	71%
Drug use in previous year	11%	62%
Hazardous drinking	28%	58%
Unemployed	5%	67%

How do prisoners differ from the rest of the population?

- How do prisoners differ from the rest of the population?
- How can you explain these differences?
- Do the differences suggest there are more effective ways of treating offenders?

Could alternative ways of dealing with offenders reduce the size of the prison population?

An alternative approach: Grendon Prison, Oxfordshire

In 2008 *The Independent's* Longford Award went to Grendon Prison near Oxford. They said it had achieved 'stunning results' in reducing the number of crimes committed by dangerous and disturbed criminals. The number of prisoners from this prison who commit a crime again after they are released is lower than elsewhere in the prison system, and levels of violence and self-harm are among the lowest in the country.

It is the only British prison operating as a 'therapeutic community': it requires its inmates to face up to their offending behaviour. Prisoners – who are mostly serving a life sentence, including murderers, rapists and sex offenders – have small group meetings with staff and psychotherapists. In these meetings they try to understand the reasons why they commit crimes. Just 8% of Grendon's lifers re-offend within four years of release, compared with 24% generally. For other crimes and sentences served in other prisons, the **recidivism** rate (the rate of re-offending and being

Activity

In a group, using websites and media reports, investigate ways in which Grendon Prison is different from other prisons. Think about why fewer of its inmates offend when released than those released from other prisons.

sent back to prison) is over 50%; higher for younger prisoners on shorter sentences, lower for older prisoners with longer sentences.

Grendon costs £42,000 per prisoner per year compared to £37,500 for other prisons. However, the extra money can be justified by the fact that former prisoners will cost less money in the future as they are less likely to commit another crime.

Do prisons work?

'Nothing sobers you up like going to prison', said professional footballer, Joey Barton after serving 74 days in prison for assault. However, the fact remains that over 50% of ex-prisoners are sent back to prison within a couple of months.

Although all prisons protect society from dangerous people, some people feel that they do not do enough to stop people committing crimes (so perhaps the high rates of people re-offending and being sent back to prison are not surprising). Perhaps the threat of prison doesn't work. If the basic education, health and employment needs of low-risk offenders were dealt with in the community, we would not need to build more prisons.

Joey Barton wants to turn his life around so he can be a 'shining beacon' for troubled youngsters.

What's the alternative?

- An **Anti-Social Behaviour Order (ASBO)** is a court order that tells an individual over ten years old how they must *not* behave, particularly if they have a record of bad behaviour. Although some ASBO holders do go on to behave properly, others continue to cause trouble and, sooner or later, they are sent to prison or a youth offender institution (YOI).
- Community punishments are cheaper and more effective than sending offenders to prison or a YOI and re-offending is considerably lower. Community service, in which offenders do unpaid work to improve their community, is less disruptive to an offender's life. Of those sent to prison, two thirds lose their job, one third lose their home and four in ten lose contact with their families.
- **Restorative justice** is also effective. Here, the offender and the victim meet and the offender explains their actions and apologises to the victim. This helps offenders understand the effect of what they have done to their victims; most victims agree that an apology represents genuine remorse.
- The Howard League for Penal Reform, which campaigns for improvements to prisons, argues that if more community sentences were given to low-risk offenders, the prison service would be able to carry out more work with those higher-risk offenders who do need to be in prison in order to protect the public.

Review and research

The checklist
- Many offenders might avoid crime if they were helped to gain skills and qualifications or to get a job.
- If more prisons followed the 'Grendon principles', fewer prisoners might re-offend.
- Although ASBOs have had mixed success, community punishments and restorative justice approaches have been more successful.

Further issues
- How can offending behaviour be explained?
- Are deterrents successful or unsuccessful?
- What are the best ways to tackle offending behaviour?
- What are the advantages and disadvantages of replacing many prison sentences with community punishments?

Taking it further
What have you learned in Citizenship studies that might help to prevent crime before it even occurs?

Getting a decision: the purpose of civil law

You will learn about:
- how civil law differs from criminal law
- civil law and the wide range of civil cases
- the courts that deal with civil cases.

What's the issue? Criminal law and civil law: what's the difference?

Criminal law: how is this different to civil law?

Criminal law: Has someone…
smoked on a train or a bus?
stolen something?
driven dangerously?
attacked, injured or murdered someone?
…then a punishment is given

Civil law: Is there a dispute over…
whether a fence between two houses is in the right place?
whether a deceased person's will is valid (should their wishes be carried out)?
who should be awarded custody of a child?
someone being wrongly dismissed from their job?
the terms of a contract (e.g. to build or sell a building), and if they've been fully met?
defamation: speaking (slander) or writing (libel) to unfairly attack someone's reputation?
…then the case will either be resolved in court or through more informal measures, such as counselling, mediation or arbitration

- Why do most criminal cases result in the accused going to court?
- Are courts the best way to deal with civil cases?
- What other methods could be used to decide cases?

Criminal and civil law in action

Criminal law deals with someone committing a crime and a punishment being given. Crimes include smoking on a train or bus, driving dangerously, stealing or attacking, injuring or murdering someone.

In a criminal case, if someone admits a minor offence they may be cautioned (given a warning) or told to pay a fixed penalty fine (e.g. parking or speeding offences). In serious criminal cases such as driving dangerously, stealing or murder, a person will probably receive **legal aid** to pay for legal advice and representation; if found guilty, a person may be imprisoned to keep society safe and to be rehabilitated (taught to behave better) so they do not commit crime in future.

Civil law involves a dispute (an argument) between two parties, which is resolved in court or by other means.

In civil cases, a **claimant** may seek a specific order to be made, for example, to move a fence, distribute a dead person's possessions in a particular way or to give someone their job back. Often, someone is asked to pay **compensation**, e.g. if building work is completed late.

Civil courts in England and Wales

1 *Tribunals* hear appeals on matters such as immigration, social security, child support, **pensions** and tax.

2 *Magistrates' courts* deal with some family and domestic matters.

3 **County courts** and **small claims courts**, are where most civil cases (about 90,000 a year) are dealt with.

4 *High Court*:
   (i) Queen's Bench Division, e.g. cases where an individual seeks damages (compensation) for negligence.
   (ii) Family Division, e.g. cases such as **divorce**, adoption and custody and appeals on such matters from magistrates' courts.
   (iii) Chancery Division, e.g. cases such as charities, trusts, contested wills, tax disputes, bankruptcy and patents.

5 *Court of Appeal* (Civil Division) hears appeals from the High Court, tribunals and certain cases from County Courts.

6 *House of Lords* – Supreme Court from October 2009 – deals with appeals from the Court of Appeal or, occasionally, the High Court.

How does a fine in a criminal court differ from compensation ordered in a civil court?

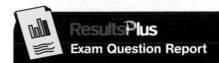
ResultsPlus
Exam Question Report

A journalist is found guilty of libel by a court. What might be the likely outcome for the journalist and/or the newspaper? (1)

May 2008 question 7f

Answer:

Someone who is found guilty of libel by a court usually has to pay compensation to the person who they wrote about. The journalist could be fined or lose his job.

How students answered

A few students gave vague answers, lacking sufficient explicit detail.

Most students made brief reference to damages paid and costs.

Review and research

The checklist
- Criminal law involves punishment for crime while civil law aims to settle disputes.
- Orders from civil cases often involve compensation (damages) being paid.
- Some civil matters involve specific judgements, e.g. if a will is valid, child custody or whether an immigrant should be allowed to stay in the country.

Further issues
- Could more cases be dealt with informally rather than going to court?
- Do legal aid rules mean some people are denied access to justice?
- Why are court hearings so expensive: could costs be reduced?

Taking it further
Find the nearest county court to your school or college and the types of cases they deal with.

Settling disputes

You will learn about:
- civil law relating to employment and consumer rights and the family.

What's the issue? What is a contract?

How do contracts work?

Often the contract will include conditions and it may break down if these are not met. For example, a **contract of employment** will list details such as the jobs to be undertaken, the hours an **employee** must work, how much holiday to take, what uniform to wear, the notice period for leaving; an employee who doesn't obey these conditions may be dismissed (sacked). Employees also have legal rights such as the National Minimum Wage.

- What legal rights do **consumers** and employees have?

- Why is it always important to read all the 'small print' in a contract before signing it?

- If you have a dispute, how could the **Citizens Advice Bureau** help you sort it out?

Contract: an offer made by one person and accepted by another, with a payment in cash or kind being made by one party to the other. Often involves signing a document but is also valid if a spoken agreement.

What is a contract?

How do employees know if they are working safely and have been trained properly?

Employment rights

Look again at the **employment laws** listed on page 29.

All workers are entitled to paid holidays. Part-timers must be treated in the same way as full-time employees. Employers must not treat you unfairly because you belong to a union, or because you refuse to join or decide to leave one – the choice is yours. It is against the law to discriminate on the grounds of age, race, gender, sexual orientation or disability.

Employees must tell the truth about themselves when they apply for a job, otherwise they could be dismissed later. **Dismissals** must be based on clear rules laid down in the firm's disciplinary procedures (rules about dealing with bad behavior at work), usually involving **verbal**, **written** and **final warnings** before being dismissed. Otherwise a tribunal may rule an employee has been unfairly dismissed. Only in cases of **gross misconduct** can sacking someone instantly be justified, and the worker can still appeal to an **employment tribunal**. Gross misconduct is when an employee has done something very serious, for example, stealing, or assaulting another member of staff. Workers cannot be dismissed on the grounds of pregnancy or for taking a reasonable amount of time off to care for a sick child or close relative.

Activity

Make a list of differences between dismissal and redundancy. How and why are they treated differently?

Consumer rights and wrongs

In Chapter 2, you studied the laws which say **goods** or **services** (such as hairdressing) must be fit for purpose and do what they claim to be able to do. When you buy goods, you effectively have a contract with the seller.

If you take faulty goods back within the agreed timescale and the shop tells you to contact the manufacturer, they are wrong – they sold you the goods and the contract is with them. It is their responsibility to sort out the problem.

If a shop offers you a replacement for faulty goods instead of your money back, you can still insist on having your money back if you wish. The same applies if they offer you a credit note.

Goods or services (such as hairdressing) must be fit for purpose and do what they claim to be able to do.

Civil law and the family

Divorce

Marriage is also a contract. Many married couples get divorced because the marriage has 'irretrievably broken down'. Reasons could include evidence that a husband or wife has committed adultery (i.e. has been unfaithful) and that their partner would find it impossible to live with him or her.

Divorcing or separating parents usually agree how their children will be cared for and the financial arrangements for them. If parents cannot agree, the court may issue some or all of the following orders:

- a residence order – who the children should live with
- a contact order – who the children are allowed to see, or receive letters or telephone calls from
- a prohibited steps order, which prevents named persons from taking certain steps, such as taking a child abroad without first getting the court's permission
- a specific issues order, which says how a matter about the children should be handled – e.g. their schooling.

Courts can also make care orders or emergency protection orders if the children are being abused or at risk of harm.

Wills

The best way for someone to ensure their possessions are given out as they wish after their death is to write a will. Sometimes a person writes a will and forgets all about it. In the meantime, circumstances change and someone who has become important in their life isn't mentioned in the will.

If this happens an application may be made for a Deed of Variation to change the will.

Someone who dies without making a will is said to have died 'intestate'. There are rules to decide who will inherit their possessions.

Review and research

The checklist

- Every employee has rights and obligations set out in a contract of employment.
- Every time you buy something, you enter into a contract with the seller.
- Court orders can be made to give rulings to divorcing parents on how to look after their children.
- We can protect our family by making a will and keeping it up to date.

Further issues

- How can people ensure they are aware of their rights?
- Why do many workers not join trade unions? Why do some employers not want their employees to join trade unions?
- Does the law protect children enough?

Taking it further

Use the Internet to discover what happens to the possessions of someone who dies intestate (who has not made a will).

The people speak

You will learn about:
- the main elements of a parliamentary democracy and patterns of voting in elections and referendums
- alternative forms of participation.

What's the issue? Voting and democracy

In a **democracy**, the person or party that gains a majority (i.e. more votes than anyone else) wins the election. Democracy is based on the idea of a majority **vote** so, ideally, a winner should receive over 50% of the vote representing a real majority. In 2006 Leona Lewis was the happy winner of X Factor. Over 8 million votes were cast by the public – that's about the same number of people who voted Conservative in the 2005 general election and almost as many as the 9.5 million who voted Labour. But there are differences between X Factor voting and UK general elections.

Leona has the X factor!

In the X Factor there is no limit to how many times someone can vote, people vote for an individual performer whose singing they like, voting is not secret and voting by phone means you have to pay to vote.

- What difference would it make if people could vote as many times as they liked in UK general elections?
- What problems could arise if people just voted based on the personality of political candidates rather than policies or their previous record in office?
- Why is it important for people to be able to keep their vote secret if they want to?

Why might Labour MPs sometimes not support a Labour government or why might Conservative or Liberal Democrat MPs go against the official views of their party?

Results Plus
Watch out!

Briefly explain what you understand by the following terms:
(i) referendums (1)   (ii) by-elections (1)
Adapted from May 2006, question 2a

Hardly anybody knew that a referendum was a national vote on a specific issue or that a by-election took place following the death or resignation of an MP in a consituency. It is important to learn these key terms.

Parliamentary democracy versus presidential rule

In a general election, you can vote only once. Your vote is secret. Most people vote for a candidate because they support the party and its policies, but some people may choose to vote on 'personality' grounds. All votes are counted and if serious mistakes are made, a new election may be held. In the UK we elect MPs to the **House of Commons** and the party with the most MPs elected forms a government. This as known as a parliamentary democracy.

The USA has **presidential rule** instead, so the government depends on the President. Barack Obama's win meant that a Democratic party government (or administration) took office in January 2009, replacing the Republican party administration led by President George W Bush from 2001.

Patterns of voting in UK elections

- In the 1950s and 1960s, most people who were rich, university-educated or who considered themselves to be **middle class** voted Conservative. Most people who were not so well off, belonged to a trade union, or felt they were **working class** voted for the Labour Party.

- Today, class is not considered to be so important, and other political parties – such as the Liberal Democrats, the **Green Party**, UK Independence Party (UKIP), and the Scottish and Welsh Nationalists – have gained support.
- Twenty or thirty years ago many more people than today identified strongly with one party or another and didn't change who they voted for.
- In the 2005 general election, one of the biggest differences was in the ages of those who voted – over 80% of older people cast their vote, but less than 50% of younger people did so. Politicians knew they must please older voters (who mostly voted Conservative) more than younger ones, who often did not vote.
- However, in some university areas many young voters did vote. Many of them liked the policies of the Liberal Democrat party which included opposition to the Iraq war and top-up fees, and the party's support for more spending on education. This resulted in Liberal Democrats electing seven or eight more MPs in university towns, showing that young voters can have a political influence when they vote.

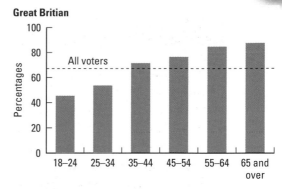

Voting turnout in the 2005 General Election
Source: British Election Study, reported in Social Trends 37, reproduced under the terms of the click-use license

What are referendums? How are they different?

A referendum ('direct democracy') is a vote in which the public says 'yes' or 'no' to a proposal. In 1975 a vote was held to decide whether the UK should stay in the EEC (now the **European Union**). Referendums are also held when a change is proposed to the government system, for example, in 1998 a referendum decided that London should have a **mayor**.

Other forms of participation

In a democracy, people are free to choose not to vote in elections or referendums, although good citizens should not leave voting to others. There are other forms of participation than voting. For example campaigning to defeat bullying, discrimination or **homophobia** (fear or hatred of homosexuals), doing **voluntary work** for a charity such as Oxfam or Christian Aid to help people in the UK or overseas, writing a regular blog or to the letters column of a newspaper or joining a pressure group such as Greenpeace or Friends of the Earth and supporting their campaigns.

Activity

Find out from your local newspaper, council offices, public library, the BBC or Electoral Commission website, the voting figures and percentage turnout for recent elections in your area.

What are the advantages and disadvantages of giving a bigger say to the general public in referendums?

Review and research

The checklist

- The government is appointed from the party that wins a majority of MPs in a general election.
- In voting, the close link between parties and class seems to have weakened in the past 25 years or so.
- Referendums give people a direct chance to say 'yes' or 'no' to particular proposals.

Further issues

- How could voting be made easier and more popular?
- Are young voters given enough information to decide how to vote?
- How can other forms of participation change things?

Taking it further

Go onto the website of your local council to find out about elections locally and which areas are represented by different parties. Which party do the councillors who represent where you live belong to?

Elections

You will learn about:

- elections in the UK
- the 'first-past-the-post' electoral system and other voting systems used in the UK and possible reasons for people not voting.

What's the issue? Time to end the 'winner's bonus'

In the 2005 general election, nearly two thirds (65%) of the population did not vote for the present Government (Labour). Labour won 55.2% of the seats but only 35.3% of the votes – a **winner's bonus**.

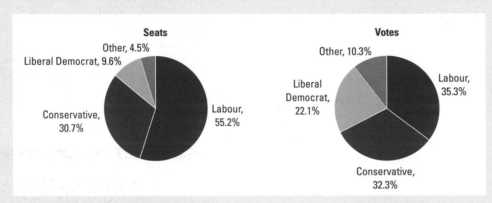

Seats
- Other, 4.5%
- Liberal Democrat, 9.6%
- Conservative, 30.7%
- Labour, 55.2%

Votes
- Other, 10.3%
- Liberal Democrat, 22.1%
- Labour, 35.3%
- Conservative, 32.3%

Seats and votes in the General Election 2005
Source: Electoral commission website

- Why are the shares of seats in Parliament so different from the shares of votes? Does it matter?

- If the **first-past-the-post** system gives winners a big bonus of seats, why would they want to change it?

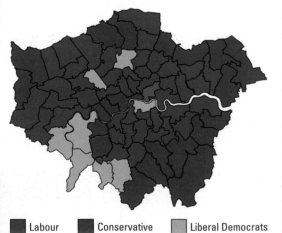

■ Labour ■ Conservative ■ Liberal Democrats

How London constituencies voted in 2005

About elections in the UK

General elections are held at least every five years although not all Parliaments run for the whole five-year period. The average time between elections is four years. However, **European Parliament** elections are held on fixed dates every five years.

Is it fair?

This system of voting is known as 'first-past-the-post'. To become an MP, a candidate has to gain more votes than any candidate in that **constituency**. He or she does not need to win the majority of the votes cast. For example, if, within a constituency, 40% voted Labour, 30% Conservative and 30% Liberal Democrat, the Labour candidate would win, despite the fact that 60% people had voted against him/her. The party with the most MPs forms the Government, even though most people's votes may have been for other parties. Local councils are also elected using first-past-the-post, and councillors usually belong to political parties who may control the council.

Proportional representation

Proportional representation (PR) aims to match the number of seats a party wins to the number of votes cast for it. This means that the number of MPs in the parliament is more likely to reflect the total number of votes per party.

This would mean that there might be a mixture of parties sharing power in a **coalition** government or a **minority government** where one party does not a have the majority of seats.

There are three PR systems already in use in the UK. All aim to equalise the share of votes and seats, though in slightly different ways:

- **Regional Lists** are used for European Parliament elections.
- The **Additional Member System** is used for the Scottish Parliament and **Welsh assembly**.
- The **Single Transferable Vote System** is used for the **Northern Ireland Assembly** and council elections in Scotland.

Parties with widely scattered support such as the Green Party or UKIP have won seats to the European Parliament where PR is used but have not been able to win first-past-the-post elections to the House of Commons.

Should we keep the first-past-the-post electoral system?

Some people say yes because it guarantees a stable government for most of the time, so one party is clearly in charge and can make decisions more easily, and everyone can easily identify their MP, who will take up any problems they have.

Other people say no because it is not fair that a party with a minority of votes should form a government and more people will vote if they think that their vote will count, and democracy demands that we have 'one vote one value' as well as 'one vote one person'.

Non-participation

In the 1950s over 80% of those entitled to vote did so (the **turnout**) yet in 2005 it was only 61%. Nowadays the parties seek support through the media, leaflets, the Internet, texting and telephoning. But without direct face-to-face contact, many people see no reason to vote, perhaps because the differences between the parties don't seem great enough to matter. More than 60 seats changed hands in the 2005 election. This included some which had seemed 'safe', having previously been won by the same party by a good margin for many years. So perhaps voters have more power than they think. In Blaenau Gwent, a Labour seat with a majority of over 19,000 (60%) was won by an Independent in 2005.

ResultsPlus
Watch out!

Give and briefly explain *two* reasons why it might be a good idea to replace the existing 'first-past-the-post' voting system used in the UK general elections with a system of proportional representation. (4)
Adapted from May 2006, question 4d

Most students scored no marks in this question. The benefits of proportional representation over the present method of 'first-past-the-post' were simply not known. To gain full marks, an answer could outline how seats in the House of Commons were allocated in proportion to votes achieved by different parties and that, in a proportional system, smaller parties such as the Green Party might gain some representation in parliament.

Activity

In a group, discuss more arguments for and against keeping the first-past-the-post system for UK general elections.

Would you be more likely to go and vote if someone came to see you and spoke to you rather than sending leaflets, texting or telephoning?

Review and research

The checklist
- The first-past-the-post system gives us a stable government.
- Others say we would be better off with proportional representation (PR) even if that meant the UK had coalition or minority governments.
- The forms of PR in the UK at present include the regional list system.
- Participation in elections has gone down – this could be dangerous for democracy.

Further issues
- Are the benefits of changing the system greater than the disadvantages?
- Would a ruling party that benefits from the present system ever be likely to change it?
- How can more people be encouraged to participate?

Taking it further
Find out about different types of proportional representation used in the UK.

Political parties

You will learn about:
- political parties in and out of Parliament
- the differences in success and policies of the main political parties
- how political parties try to win support.

What's the issue? Which parties matter most?

Around 320 UK parties are registered with the Electoral Commission. They can put forward candidates for UK general or local elections and have their party logo printed alongside their candidate's name on a ballot paper. In the 2005 general election 11 parties won representation in the House of Commons. Some were stronger, some weaker than in 1992:

	1992 seats	2005 seats	Change 1992–2005
Labour	271	356	+85
Conservative	336	198	−138
Liberal Democrat	20	62	+42
Democratic Unionist Party (DUP)	3	9	+6
Scottish National Party (SNP)	3	6	+3
Sinn Fein (SF)	0	5	+5
Plaid Cymru (PC)	4	3	−1
Social Democratic & Labour Party (SDLP)	4	3	−1
Independent Kidderminster Hospital & Health Concern	0	1	+1
Respect	0	1	+1
Ulster Unionist Party (UUP)	9	1	−8
There is one Independent (Peter Law MP) and two more parties – the Green Party and UKIP – have seats in the European Parliament.			

Party representation in the House of Commons in the 1992 and 2005 general elections

- Why do you think people shift their support from one party to another?

- When or why might people vote for a mainly local party?

- Why might someone decide to support a 'fun' party, for example, the Fancy Dress Party?

All the MPs in Cornwall are Liberal Democrats, in Surrey they are Conservatives and in Tyne and Wear they are Labour. Why are some national parties more successful in some areas than others?

Different parties, different goals

Labour, Conservative and Liberal Democrats want to win power and form a government. In 2008 the SNP and the Green Party formed a minority Scottish government, Wales has a Labour-PC coalition and the Northern Ireland **power-sharing executive** is made up of DUP, SF, SDLP and UUP **ministers**.

Apart from the parties which aim to win power nationally or regionally, there are local political parties such as the Doncaster First Party or Mebyon Kernow – the party for Cornwall. These parties have more limited ambitions. Each party's supporters share agreed policy goals which members vote for at party meetings. There are also parties which are more about fun than serious politics such as the Church of the Militant Elvis Party, the Fancy Dress Party, or the Official Monster Raving Loony Party.

How important are party leaders?

All parties want a popular figurehead as their leader. Unpopular leaders generally fail to meet supporters' expectations and quickly resign, as Conservative Iain Duncan Smith did in 2003.

Gordon Brown

The Labour party was out of power from 1979 to 1997 but their image changed when Tony Blair became leader and, for the first time ever, the party won three successive Labour victories. Gordon Brown took over from Tony Blair as **Prime Minister** in 2007.

As Conservative leader, Margaret Thatcher was admired by millions of supporters and she led the Conservative Party to three of its greatest victories, resigning in 1990. In 2005, David Cameron became the Conservative leader.

David Cameron

Nick Clegg

The Liberal Democrat party was formed by the merger of Liberals and Social Democrats in 1988. Their most successful leader was Charles Kennedy. In 2008 Nick Clegg became the Liberal Democrat leader.

Different party, different policy

Elections are battles between different parties with different policies and the result decides which policies will actually come into force. Sometimes there don't seem to be many differences as parties use opinion polls and focus groups to find ways of making policies sound good and get the most support. The best way to recognise the differences between the parties is to study their history and basic philosophy:

- The Conservatives became prominent in the late 19th century and the party was formed to keep those people in Parliament who believed in individualism, preserving the United Kingdom and private enterprise. More recently, the party has favoured selling off nationalised industries because it believes that anything the state can do, the **private sector** can do better.
- Labour was formed in the early 20th century by **socialist** societies and trade unions who wanted to get working people into Parliament at a time when MPs were not paid a wage. They wanted the state to improve people's living conditions and not leave everything to private enterprise, even if this meant increasing taxes. Reducing **social exclusion** (where some individuals or groups feel they are outside society) is currently an important goal.
- Liberal governments of the early 20th century started the **Welfare State.** This include providing **state pensions** and **unemployment benefits**. Since the party merged with the Social Democratic Party in 1988 (a breakaway from Labour), it has developed strong **beliefs** in social justice (where all are treated fairly), Europe, sustainability (using natural resources carefully) and opposition to the Iraq war.

Review and research

The checklist
- We need to distinguish between parties competing for power nationally, regionally or locally and 'fun' parties.
- Many people identify with a party because they like and trust its leader.
- Understanding a party's history and philosophy is a good way to understand its roots and its policies.

Further issues
- Why has the number of political parties increased in recent years but party memberships fallen?
- Are UK parties democratic enough?
- Why is the idea of state funding for political parties gaining support?

Taking it further
Look at the websites of the main parties to find their current policies on a topic of your choice.

Representation

You will learn about:
- the relationship between constituents and MPs
- the duties of an MP and whether the MP is a 'delegate' for the party.

74

What's the issue? Representatives – who needs them?

If 40 people live in a community, they could easily vote from time to time on issues that affected them. This would be an example of direct democracy. But in practice the UK is now home to 40 million adults so the practical way to make decisions is to elect representatives – **councillors** at local level and MPs at national level – this is an example of representative democracy.

Jeremy Corbyn MP

Constituencies are areas represented by an MP. They typically have about 70,000 electors, although the smallest has barely 20,000 voters, and the largest over 107,000. Around 8,000 votes would probably be enough to win in the smallest constituency but an MP might need 30,000 or 40,000 to be sure of winning in the larger one. We may have 'one person one vote' but not 'one vote one value'.

Between 2001 and 2005, the Labour MP who rebelled most against Labour's voting instructions (148 times, to be exact) was Islington North MP, Jeremy Corbyn. 19 other Labour MPs rebelled on more than 33 occasions because they disagreed with the party on key issues.

- Is 100,000 people too many for one MP to represent?
- As they are elected as a member of a particular party, should MPs always vote as their party says?
- When might it be justifiable for an MP not to follow the party line?

Are MPs sufficiently representative?

More women have been elected to Parliament in the last 15 years and, partly as a result, more attention has been given to child and family issues. However, only 19% of MPs are female: 125 out of 646. Also, ethnic minorities are under-represented (15 MPs in 2009) compared with the UK's total ethnic minority population. Could this be because, in some areas where large numbers of people from ethnic minorities live, taking part in politics has not been a part of their lives?

What do MPs do for their constituents?

Once elected, MPs deal with the problems raised by their **constituents** (the people who live in their constituency). This is regardless of whether or not the constituents voted for them. Most MPs conduct a weekly or fortnightly 'surgery' where local people can go to discuss issues. MPs also receive many letters and e-mails. They run websites which keep people informed and these give constituents an opportunity to offer comments or make contact.

Activity

Look at the websites of several MPs in or near the area where you live. Decide which you think offers the best service to constituents – and why.

MPs have the following roles:

◉ MPs write to or meet ministers or other responsible organisations about issues raised by constituents. Few people ignore a letter from an MP!

◉ An MP can ask a question in Parliament, so that both the minister and the civil servants in the department have to study and consider the issue raised.

◉ An MP may arrange an **adjournment debate**. This gives backbench MPs the opportunity to debate issues they are concerned about in their constituency. Alternatively, they may propose a **private member's bill** – a way for individual MPs to introduce their own new laws. Although they are rarely successful, it is an important way for MPs to get an issue they care about put onto the political agenda.

What else do MPs do?

MPs have five important functions:

1 Represent the people, including speaking on issues of public concern.
2 Debate, amend and vote on legislation (new laws).
3 Examine and check up on the work of the government at **Question Time** in Parliament and on **select committees** or by referring possible cases of maladministration to the **Ombudsman** (who independently investigates complaints).
4 Sometimes work as ministers.
5 Authorise and review **taxation** and government expenditure (how the government is spending public money).

Should MPs use their own judgement or do as they are told?

Edmund Burke said that when MPs arrived at Parliament they should use their own judgement and not do as they are told. In the 21st century all parties want their MPs to follow the 'party line' but this doesn't always happen. In reality MPs do use their judgement and when they all support their party it is either because they agree or because they have been persuaded!

Results Plus
Exam Question Report

What is a parliamentary constituency?
A The actual place in the House of Commons where an MP sits.
B The geographical area represented by an MP.
C A set of rules for organising the work of Parliament.
D The location of an MP's office.   (1)

May 2006, question 7d
Answer: B

How students answered

Many students incorrectly chose A, C or D.

33% of students knew that the geographical area represented by an MP is called a constituency.

Review and research

The checklist

◉ MPs are the key figures in a representative democracy but are not wholly representative of the UK population.

◉ Representation is one of the five key functions of MPs.

◉ MPs are expected to act on their judgement, not to act as obedient delegates who simply carry out party instructions.

Further issues

◉ Should MPs be more representative of UK society in social and economic terms? How could this be achieved?

◉ How effective are MPs?

◉ Should MPs be more independent of their parties?

Taking it further

Look at Hansard, or BBC Parliament or the Parliament website. Talk to your MP if you get a chance to do so, or e-mail her or him. Then consider which of the MP's functions you consider to be the most important – and why.

Government

You will learn about:
- key features of the UK government, the role and importance of the Cabinet
- the nature and activities of the opposition parties.

What's the issue? Government and Parliament: what's the difference?

Parliament, often described as 'the **legislature**' because it passes laws, is made up of 646 MPs (650 in the election after March 2009) and approximately 730 members of the House of Lords. They can belong to any of the political parties or none of them and vote to decide issues and **bills** being considered.

Government is the **executive** putting laws into effect.

Secretaries of state and ministers (heads of government departments) are all members of the House of Commons or House of Lords.

When the Prime Minister asked Peter Mandelson (who was not an MP at the time) to become Businesss Secretary, he was made a **peer** (Lord Mandelson of Foy and Hartlepool). This means that Parliament can hold him (or any other minister) **accountable** by asking them to come to Parliament to answer questions or to speak in a debate on relevant issues.

Peter Mandelson is the Secretary of State for Business, Enterprise & Regulatory Reform, (BERR) in 2009.

Every government department also has a professional civil servant called a **Permanent Secretary** to manage staff, allocate responsibilities and ensure the department carries out the wishes of the **secretary of state** or minister. Altogether there were 480,000 civil servants of various grades in 2008, of which 53% were women.

Sir Brian Bender is the Permanent Secretary at the BERR Department in 2009.

A lot of the work that used to be carried out by government departments themselves is now done by decentralised agencies. These are given money (funded) by government to do a particular job, e.g. the Food Standards Agency, the Drivers and Vehicle Licencing Agency (DVLA) or the Environment Agency.

- Who belongs to Parliament but is not in the Government?
- Who works in the Government but is not in Parliament?
- How is Government different from Parliament?

Why is the Cabinet important and what does it do?

The Prime Minister appoints about 20 of the most senior ministers to meet together weekly as the **Cabinet**. The Cabinet reviews developments, looks at proposals from sub-committees and decides policy. Among those present are ministers such as the Foreign Secretary, **Home Secretary**, Justice Secretary, Chancellor of the Exchequer and Defence Secretary. They decide the most important issues to be presented to Parliament. If they believe new laws are needed, they decide what the main points of these new laws should be. Once a decision is made, a Cabinet member is expected to support it. A Cabinet member who cannot support a particular decision is expected to stay quiet or to resign from the Cabinet.

Do civil servants influence ministers too much?

The Cabinet reviews developments, looks at proposals from sub-committees and decides policy.

The role of the opposition parties

The **Shadow Cabinet** consists of MPs (shadow ministers) from the main **opposition** party in the House of Commons (the Conservatives in spring 2009). Other opposition parties, such as the Liberal Democrats, will also appoint a team of shadow ministers as spokespeople. Each member of a Shadow Cabinet will closely follow the work of a particular government department (e.g. Health, Education or Environment) and speak for his or her party on the policy area in question, asking questions and making criticisms, which the government minister will have to answer.

Much of the work of the House of Commons takes place in committees. Each departmental select committee checks and reports on the work of a particular government department to make sure it is working effectively. Select committees usually include about a dozen MPs from parties, in proportion to their strength in the House of Commons. After an investigation they will publish a report which is debated by the House of Commons; the government will defend itself against any criticisms made and sometimes decides to change its policy or priorities as a result of the committee's recommendations.

Review and research

The checklist

◉ 'Parliament' refers to all members of the Houses of Commons and Lords while 'Government' refers to the ministers appointed by the Prime Minister who run various departments.

◉ Every department is led by a minister who is supported by a senior civil servant known as a Permanent Secretary and a team of less senior civil servants.

◉ The role of opposition parties is to challenge the government, expose poor performance and put forward their own policies.

Further issues

◉ Are key decisions made by the Prime Minister or by the whole Cabinet collectively?

◉ Are decisions within ministries taken by ministers or civil servants?

◉ How could individuals persuade government to change their policies?

Taking it further

Research a recent Question Time for a particular department either by watching BBC Parliament or by consulting the Parliament website.

Legislation

You will learn about:

- proposed bills and where they come from
- the factors most likely to decide a bill's success
- the main stages of a bill becoming an Act of Parliament.

What's the issue? Where do new laws come from?

When someone wants to introduce a new law, they either propose a bill or a **statutory instrument**.

Government bills	Private members' bills	Private bills	**Delegated legislation** (or statutory instruments)
– Proposed by the government and then become Acts of Parliament.	– Put forward by a backbench MP (not a minister or shadow minister), then become Acts of Parliament. – Usually about things that people are unlikely to be against. – Only about 5/6 a year passed between 1997 and 2007.	– Come from large corporations or local authorities and sometimes need special laws which just apply to them (e.g. to regulate a university or harbour or railway line). – When passed, they become Acts of Parliament.	– Allows the government to make changes to a law without having to start again with a new bill. The original law has a clause which allows this. – The change is usually drafted by or for a minister.

- Why do backbench MPs sponsor legislation and why aren't they more successful?

- Thousands of statutory instruments are passed every year. Why do you think that is?

- Are Private Acts of Parliament really needed?

Mr Speaker presides over the House of Commons.

Delegated legislation (or statutory instruments)

Thousands of these orders are passed every year compared to just a few dozen Acts of Parliament. About two-thirds of statutory instruments are not actively debated by Parliament and simply become law on a specified date. There is a committee which checks that the Minister proposing the change is not using his powers wrongly.

Which bills become law?

If the government has enough of a majority and all its MPs support the bill, the bill will pass. However, if the bill contains some points which could upset some of their MPs, the government may have to change some of the proposals. If the government includes things in a bill which are unpopular, it will not pass because it will be rejected by the government's own MPs or because the House of Lords opposes it. In 2008 there was a proposal to detain people suspected of terrorism for 42 days without charge; this was strongly opposed and the government withdrew the proposal.

A bill can start in either the House of Commons or the House of Lords and then goes to the other House. Generally it does not become law until it has been passed by both Houses and received the **Royal Assent**. The only two exceptions are that (1) the House of Lords cannot delay a **money bill** which deals with taxation and spending and (2) a bill which the Lords refuse to pass in one year can become law without their support a year later.

Backbenchers' bills are generally debated on Fridays when many MPs travel back to their constituencies, so some supporters may not attend if their constituency is a long way from London. These bills are sometimes actively backed by certain pressure groups and their campaigning may provoke other groups to organise opposition. For example, when the RSPCA attempted to ban hunting, the Countryside Alliance group put together powerful support in favour of it.

The stages a bill must go through in both houses are:

Debates in the main chamber of the House of Commons are often poorly attended and not many MPs show up. What other work might MPs at Westminster be doing if they are not sitting in the chamber listening to a debate?

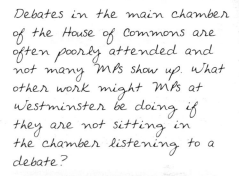

Both the House of Commons (above) and the House of Lords are arranged so government and opposition members face each other.

First House

- **First reading:** the bill is introduced but not debated.
- **Second reading:** general debate.
- Committee stage: a group of about 20 MPs will work through the bill in detail and make any changes necessary.
- **Report stage:** opportunity for further amendments.
- Third reading: final chance for debate. If the House votes in favour it is passed by that House.

Second House

The bill has to go through the same stages in the second house (usually the House of Lords). Both Houses must agree on all the words in the bill.

Act of Parliament

The proposals of the bill have now become law.

Royal Assent

A bill cannot become law without the formal permission of the **monarch (the Queen)** or those acting on her behalf.

Review and research

The checklist
- Government and private members' bills are both public bills.
- Private bills apply to particular areas or organisations.
- A government with a united majority can pass all the legislation it wants as long as it has enough time.

Further issues
- Should backbench MPs be allowed more time to get their own legislation passed?
- Are there enough safeguards when delegated legislation is passed?
- Could the process of making laws be simpler?

Taking it further
Examine the part the House of Lords plays in the legislative process: do they improve or simply delay law-making?

Chapter 9: Active participation
Influencing decisions

You will learn about:
- pressure groups and the importance of consultation, including the role of the voluntary sector
- how actions contribute to policy proposals, public debates and outcomes
- the force of public opinion locally or nationally.

What's the issue? Why are some groups more influential than others?

A pressure group is a group of people with a shared view of issues and events who try to persuade councils or government to do what they want or not to do what they don't want. Many established bodies such as charities, businesses, sports clubs, theatres and media companies act as pressure groups at one time or another.

The government is helped by 'insider' groups such as Age Concern and Help the Aged, the National Society for the Prevention of Cruelty to Children (NSPCC), and the National Farmers' Union (NFU). The government welcomes their suggestions and advice and, when it is considering a new policy, it often consults 'insider' groups privately first.

This is very different from the treatment given to 'outsider' groups who oppose government policy, such as Fathers4Justice, Plane Stupid or the Stop the War Coalition. The only way such groups can hope to achieve the policies they want is to demonstrate, engage in stunts and hope their publicity will swing public opinion behind them so government has to take their views seriously.

- When might a charity, religious group or sports club act as a pressure group, trying to change govenment policy?

- Can you think of other 'insider' groups?
- Can you think of other 'outsider' groups?

How much does the attention given to a group and whether it is seen as an 'insider' or 'outsider' depend on the government itself rather than the group?

Why consult? Is the majority always right?

Modern governments know that people are more likely to obey laws they understand and support, so they often hold a period of consultation and public debate before they finalise new policies. In recent years, consultations have taken place on matters such as:

- *Should there be a badger cull (this is when a certain number of badgers are killed) to reduce the risk of bovine TB?*
  In 2008, against the advice of the NFU, the government decided that there would not be a badger cull in England. Members of the Badger Trust argued very strongly there was no 'scientific, economic or practical case' for a cull.

- *Should wind farms be built in particular areas?*
  The UK might face possible shortages of electricity and so it has been suggested that more wind farms should be built to generate extra electricity. However, some people who live in the areas where the wind farms could be built have campaigned against them. They say that the wind farms would not generate that much electricity and they would also spoil the view, reduce the price of houses and be dangerous for birds. Alternatively, their opposition could be put down to '**NIMBY**' thinking – this means '**Not In My Back Yard**'.

- *Should eco-towns be built to provide more houses with low carbon emissions?*
  Many people objected strongly in 2008 when the government proposed to build twelve eco-towns. People were especially angry in Warwickshire. Here, it was proposed that a town called Middle Quinton could be built.

Local protests against an eco-town – is this Nimbyism in action?

Councillors in Stratford-upon-Avon said that it would not be sustainable and that it would ruin the countryside. The government plans to carry out more consultations in 2009.

Does the fact that people feel strongly opposed to a proposal always mean it should be abandoned? In the past, many people were very unhappy about new towns being built, such as Milton Keynes. However, such towns were quickly accepted and they were often praised once they had been built. The fact that people are protesting may mean that if the project goes ahead it will be carefully planned so that it takes account of people's worries.

- *Should a new East-West railway line (Crossrail) be built through London?*
  If **public transport** across London is improved, there will be fewer carbon emissions (less pollution) and less congestion (when heavy traffic builds up and clogs the roads). People will be able to get to where they want to go more quickly. After consultation, the government approved the Crossrail project. However, it may cause a lot of disruption while it is being built and this is what opponents are very worried about.

Is the majority always right even if they are behaving selfishly or have not fully taken the 'big picture' into account?

Review and research

The checklist

- Established groups and charities may act like pressure groups if they want a particular policy to be changed.
- Government consultation means everyone can have their say and may lead to new protest groups being formed.
- Councils or government have to weigh up initial local anger over a proposal against wider concerns.

Further issues

- Should official bodies ever go against the wishes of large numbers of protesters?
- Should the needs or opinions of businesses count for more than voluntary bodies, religious groups or sports clubs?
- Do interests matter as much or more than opinions?

Taking it further

Find out about the 'progress' of government plans for wind farms, eco-towns and Crossrail.

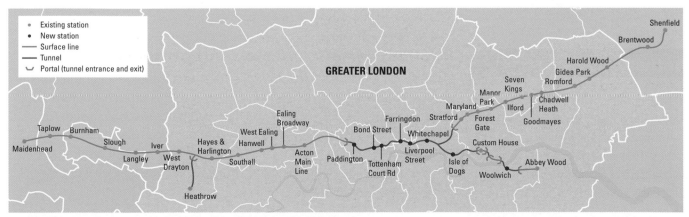

The proposed East-West railway line (Crossrail) to be built through London

Campaigning for or against change

You will learn about:

- ways citizens can try to mobilise opinion
- participation such as demonstrations and petitions
- local and national referendums.

What's the issue? Whatever did we do before the Internet?

- Individuals write blogs or e-mail TV-show presenters and broadcasters while their programme is on air.

- Within minutes an image can be captured on a mobile phone and flashed onto TV screens all over the world, providing us with immediate news.

- One person can express an opinion and moments later, millions of people can know about it.

- If we want to express a view and see how many people agree, we can start a petition on the 10 Downing St website. The proposal that gained the most support in 2008 was to 'scrap the planned vehicle tracking and road pricing policy'. It was proposed by Peter Roberts and gained 1,811,424 signatures.

- Nowadays fewer people join political parties but many people join groups and actively work to achieve their objectives (get what they want from the government). This helps explain why issues may 'take off' much more than previously; people can find out about and follow causes they support using the Internet. Almost ten times as many people are members of environmental groups than 30 years ago.

Thousands	1971	1981	1991	2002
National Trust	278	1,046	2,152	3,000
Royal Society for the Protection of Birds	98	441	852	1,020
Wildlife Trusts	64	142	233	413
World Wide Fund for Nature	12	60	227	320
National Trust for Scotland	37	105	234	260
Greenpeace	...	30	312	221
Ramblers' Association	22	37	87	137
Friends of the Earth	1	18	111	119

Membership of selected environmental organisations in the UK
Source: Social Trends 33, reproduced under the terms of the click-use lincense

- What are the advantages and disadvantages of today's 'immediate news'?

- Has the Internet really made individuals and groups more powerful?

- Why have pressure group memberships risen as the number of political party memberships has gone down?

Activity

In small groups look at any MP's website to get an idea of how they win support by campaigning on issues. Then all groups should come together and compare the information they have found.

Political parties, policies and progress

Increasingly councils switch from one party to another at local elections, and constituencies swing between parties too. This often happens when the 'out' party (the party that is not in power) picks up on an issue, for example, the building of a new bypass. The party campaigns to stop the bypass and local people who are also unhappy about it join in too. These people might then decide to vote for the party at a local or national election, or a **by-election**.

Do petitions and demonstrations work?

Local protests over school closures or other proposals can succeed if a community is determined and united. However, success does not often happen on a national scale. Three big protests were:

● In 1990 the **Anti-Poll Tax demonstrations** succeeded. The Conservative government gave up its unpopular policy to introduce a Community Charge (the 'poll tax'). This policy had been in its party **manifesto** and so, when the Conservatives won the 1987 general election, they claimed they had a **mandate** (the people's permission) to carry out the policy.

● In 2002 the Countryside Alliance brought its supporters to London to defend the 'liberty and livelihood' of country people who were against the anti-hunting bill. This bill was passed by Parliament anyway despite the strong feelings of opponents.

● In February 2003, hundreds of thousands of people protested in London against the Iraq war. However, Prime Minister Tony Blair and President George W Bush did not change their decision and went to war.

Demonstrating in favour of hunting

Local and national referendums

Referendums allow people to vote on issues which divide opinion in the political parties (when people within the same party cannot agree). Most referendums in which people vote 'yes' or 'no' to particular questions have been about how the country is governed, for example:

● whether we should stay in the European Union (previously known as the 'Common Market')

● whether the **Good Friday agreement** should go ahead in Northern Ireland

● whether Scotland should have a Parliament, and Wales an Assembly

● whether London should have a Mayor and Assembly.

All of these proposals were approved (allowed to go ahead) in referendums. However, a proposed elected regional government in north-east England was rejected in 2004 by 78% to 22%.

In 2008 a huge proportion of Greater Manchester residents rejected (79%–21%) a plan to introduce congestion charging. It was proposed that the money it brought in would be used to extend the Manchester Metrolink to places like Rochdale town centre and the airport, which are not served by the Metrolink at the moment.

Local and regional forms of government in the UK

84

You will learn about:

- councils, their duties and elected mayors
- devolution in Northern Ireland, Wales and Scotland
- minority, coalition and majority governments in the UK and constituent countries.

What's the issue? Local? How local?

Some local councils have combined to form bigger councils. Let's look at two councils.

Kirklees, West Yorkshire

- used to be made up of 11 councils
- now an area which used to have its own council may have only four or five councillors representing it on the new Kirklees council
- 69 councillors to represent 400,000 people
- 157 square miles.

Herefordshire, West Midlands

- used to be made up of 14 councils
- now an area which used to have its own council may have only four or five councillors representing it on the new Herefordshire council
- 58 councillors to represent 180,000 people
- 833 square miles.

The Kirklees area

Advantages and disadvantages of larger councils

Communication and efficiency have improved through local offices, computers, Internet access, better telephones, and combining services which all the areas need (e.g. catering and technology).

When a small area had its own council, all the councillors were focused on that area. In a larger council, the same area will only have a small number of members on the council. So it may be thought to be more difficult for individuals, groups and communities to make a difference or be heard.

The Herefordshire area

- Do local people have enough chance to *make a difference* with the new larger authorities?
- How does combining councils make services more efficient and cost-effective?
- Has the 'local' been taken out of 'local government'?

What is the ideal population size for delivering a service such as education, fire, police or social services?

What is local government?

In England and Wales two million people are employed by 410 local authorities to deliver key services (see the list opposite) that most of us use at some time in our lives. Decisions in these authorities are taken by

19,000 elected councillors who vote on most proposals. Local citizens can stand for council elections. However, in areas such as London, Bedford, Torbay and Watford there is an elected mayor (not to be confused with a ceremonial mayor or lord mayor) who acts as a 'chief policy maker'.

Sometimes councils join together to provide a particular service e.g. education, environmental health, fire services, highways, libraries, police, social services and waste management.

What is devolution?

Devolution means that political power becomes local. So if you live in Scotland or Wales, lots of decisions are made in Edinburgh or Cardiff now, when before devolution the decisions were mostly made in London.

In the past 15 years, the UK has become less centralised. The following have been established:

- Northern Ireland Assembly and power-sharing executive
- The Scottish Parliament
- The Welsh Assembly.

Although the UK government deals with nationwide matters such as defence, foreign policy and the economy, Scotland, Wales and Northern Ireland have control over matters such as their own country's arrangements for health, personal social care, rural affairs, tourism, transport and education. This gives people in these areas a greater chance to know about and influence what happens to them and their community.

Minority, coalition and majority governments

In January 2009:

- The UK had a one-party majority government led by Gordon Brown with Labour having a majority (350 seats out of 646) in the House of Commons. This means the party cannot be defeated as long as it remains united.

- In the Northern Ireland power sharing executive, all parties had ministers in proportion to their number of seats in the Northern Ireland Assembly at Stormont – this is a coalition government headed by Peter Robinson (Democratic Unionist).

- There was a coalition government in Wales, headed by Rhodri Morgan (Labour), with Labour and **Plaid Cymru** together commanding a majority in the Welsh Assembly (Labour 25 out of 60 and Plaid Cymru 15 out of 60).

- Scotland had a minority government (where a party does not have the overall majority of seats) headed by Alex Salmond of the **Scottish National Party (SNP)**, with under half the members of the Parliament belonging to the SNP (SNP 47 out of 129 and Green 2 out of 129). Therefore, the SNP looks for support on particular issues from Conservatives, Labour or Liberal Democrats.

Is there a reason why the devolved bodies (Northern Ireland, Wales and Scotland) all lack majority governments? What are the advantages or disadvantages of this?

Activity

Working in a small group or on your own, visit the websites of different councils with an elected mayor. Discuss the activities of councillors in places where there is an elected mayor and compare your information.

Review and research

The checklist

- The number of councils has gone down drastically over 50 years.
- The new authorities are much bigger and, some say, not close enough to many people and communities. Others say that local offices, telephone and the Internet make contact easier and faster than before.
- The devolved bodies and executives of Northern Ireland, Wales and Scotland mean the UK is now less centralised.

Further issues

- What are the strengths and weaknesses of having elected mayors?
- Does it matter if different policies apply in England, Wales and Scotland?
- What are the advantages and disadvantages of having majority, coalition or minority governments?

Taking it further

How much have councils in your area changed in recent years and how much easier (or harder) is it to contact departments and find out what is happening?

Government beyond the UK

You will learn about:

- presidential forms of government such as those in France or the USA
- democratic and non-democratic forms of government in other countries.

What's the issue? Head of state or head of government?

In the UK, the Queen is the neutral, impartial **head of state**. In 2007, Gordon Brown became the Prime Minister and **head of government** and, like Tony Blair and Margaret Thatcher before him, he is anything but neutral.

In the USA, President Barack Obama is both the head of state and the head of government, whereas in France President Nicolas Sarkozy is only the head of state. This is because there is also a Prime Minister, Francois Fillon, who is head of government. Although the relationships between the executive (the government) and the legislature (the law makers) differ between these three countries, they are all politically stable and are essentially democratic in that their populations can elect representatives.

President Obama

- Is it better for the head of state to be a neutral and non-controversial figure?

- Is it better for a head of government to be elected separately (as US and French presidents are) – from elections for **Congress (USA)** or the National Assembly (France)?

- Is the UK model better, in which the Prime Minister and Head of Government holds the office because his party has majority support in the House of Commons?

Democracy in the USA

US government works at both state and national (federal) level:

- There are 50 states and each of them has a governor who is head of government in the state, together with a state legislature which passes laws.

- At federal (national) level, Congress (parliament) has two chambers: the Senate and the House of Representatives. The members in both of them are elected democratically (voted for by the public). No one in either chamber is there by appointment or heredity as in the UK's House of Lords.

The two main parties in the USA are the Republicans and the Democrats.

The president is elected once every four years. There is a vote in all 50 states and the number of electoral votes held by that state (which is

Activity

In groups, look at the Amnesty International website. Read about the treatment of prisoners, the use of the death penalty and the fairness of government in different countries. Then compare the information you have found.

equal to its number of members of Congress) is then awarded to the winner in each state. In 2008, President Obama was the Democratic Party candidate who won by 365 electoral votes compared to 173 electoral votes gained by John McCain, the Republican Senator. Although President Obama won the popular vote by 66.8 million to 58.3 million, it is possible for one candidate to win the electoral votes but for another to be ahead in the popular vote.

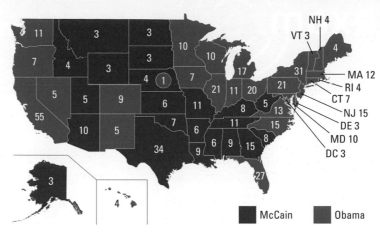

In most states the winner of the popular vote is awarded all that state's electoral votes. However, in 2000 Democrat Al Gore had more popular votes overall but Republican George W Bush became president because he had more electoral votes.

How much 'democracy' exists?

Many countries have elections, state ceremonies and parliaments but sometimes the images we see don't show the real picture. Sometimes the elections may be corrupt with candidates from just one party. Sometimes 'real' opposition candidates may be prevented from standing, victimised or not given any media coverage in newspapers or on TV.

In March 2008, Dmitri Medvedev was elected as President of Russia with 71% of the vote. However, this was only after the Central Election Commission had disqualified at least four candidates including Mikhail Kasyanov, a former Prime Minister and leader of the People's Democratic Union. Europe's Office for Democratic Institutions and Human Rights believed that the election was not fair and drew attention to the fact that the Russian government was not prepared to co-operate with it.

Also in March 2008, elections were held in Zimbabwe. President Robert Mugabe was in power and wanted to be re-elected. This was a good example of a country pretending to be democratic. During the elections there was murder, intimidation, brutality and starvation of the Zimbabwean people.

North Korea provides another example of a country where democracy does not really happen. According to the constitution, the country is a democratic **republic** and the government is elected with all voters being entitled to vote in secret. Voting rights are given to everyone aged 17 and over. This sounds fine until we learn that the elections only ever have one candidate for people to vote for, so there is no choice at all.

Activity

Use your knowledge gained from other subjects, newspapers and websites to identify five countries outside the EU where democracy is at least as strong as it is in the UK.

Review and research

The checklist
- The USA and EU member countries have fair and democratic elections, although the systems vary.
- Sometimes the responsibilities of Prime Minister and monarch or president differ.
- In many other countries, elections are often unfair and real democracy is not happening.

Further issues
- If a country treats its people badly, should other countries get involved? If so, what should they do?
- Which other countries have a good system of democracy and what ideas could we borrow from them to add to our own system of democracy?
- Where would you place Commonwealth countries on a democratic 'order of merit'?

Taking it further
Consider or debate whether a non-democratic government could still respect the dignity of its people, give them human rights and guarantee their well-being.

examzone

Know Zone

Source A: Changing behaviour in general elections

	Leeds North West constituency	
	2001 General Election	**2005 General Election**
Electorate (people with a right to vote if they wish)	72,941 (100%)	71,664 (100%)
Turnout (number of people who actually voted)	42,451 (58%)	44,711 (62%)
Labour	17,794 (42%)	14,735 (33%)
Conservative	12,558 (30%)	11,510 (26%)
Liberal Democrat	11,431 (27%)	16,612 (37%)
UKIP	668 (1%)	no candidate
Greens	no candidate	1,128 (2%)
Two others parties	no candidate	726 (2%)

Percentages given for each party show their share of the total vote, not of the total electorate.

ResultsPlus
Watch out!

Always aim to eliminate the 'impossible' options and then choose between the 'possible' ones. Always give an answer to multiple choice questions – marks will not be deducted if you give the wrong answer.

(a) In what way was the turnout of the election in Leeds North West in 2005 different from that in 2001? (1)

A About the same number of people voted

B About 1,300 fewer people voted

C About 2,300 fewer people voted

D About 2,300 more people voted

(b) How was the outcome of the election in Leeds North West in 2005 different from that in 2001? (1)

A Conservatives gained the seat from the Liberal Democrats

B Liberal Democrats gained the seat from Labour

C Labour gained the seat from the Conservatives

D Conservatives gained the seat from Labour

Results Plus
Maximise your marks

(a) Three statements have been made about the elections results in Leeds North West:

    (1) It is a great pity that the electorate declined from 72,941 to 71,664 in 2005.

    (2) When there are more than two or three candidates in a constituency, voters get confused.

    (3) There was a UKIP candidate in 2001 but not 2005.

(b) Give and briefly explain *two* reasons why it might be a good idea to replace the existing first-past-the-post voting system used in UK general elections (as in Leeds North West) with a system of proportional representation. Use information in the table and your own knowledge in your answer. (4)

    (i) State which statement contains fact only and explain why. (1)

    (ii) State which statement contains opinion only and explain why. (1)

    (iii) One of the statements contains both fact and opinion. Which statement is it? Identify the words which are factual and the words which are opinion. (2)

Student answer	Examiner's comments	Build a better answer
(a) (i) Statement 1 is obviously factual because the electorate did decline.	■ No, this isn't the correct choice. Statement 1 does refer to a fact (the electorate declined from 72,941 to 71,664 in 2005) but Statement 1 also includes an opinion (It's a great pity…) and the question asks for a statement containing fact only.	△ Statement 3 contains only fact. A factual statement such as this is objective because it can be tested or verified and proved to be correct.
(a) (ii) Statement 2 is an opinion because it is the person's own view.	■ Statement 2 is correctly identified as containing opinion only but the answer would gain no marks because it does not adequately explain why when it says 'it is the person's own view'.	△ Statement 2 contains only opinion. An opinion is a statement that not everyone would agree with. Some people may not agree that 'voters would get confused'. Opinions are often not supported by evidence and are simply value judgements.
(a) (iii) Statement 3 is fact and opinion because it's the only other choice offered.	■ This isn't the correct choice and the supporting reason offered is flippant and inadequate.	△ Statement 1 contains both fact and opinion. The opinion is 'It's a great pity..' and the fact part is 'the electorate declined from 72,941 to 71,664 in 2005'.
(b) In Leeds North West the winner in 2001 had 42% of the vote and in 2005 37%, so 58% voted against the 2001 MP and 63% against the 2005 MP. If the constituency was bigger and had more than one MP like in proportional representation, then lots of views could be represented. This is like the European elections system where constituencies are big, i.e. the whole North West.	● The answer makes reasonable points but they needed to be clearly separated. Answers should show an understanding that the first-past-the-post system offers no guarantee of any relationship at all between seats and votes – in 1951 and Feb 1974 the party winning most seats in Parliament did not have most votes. The advantages of having some if not all MPs elected via multi-member constituencies are briefly but effectively explained in the candidate's answer. This is important because it would take away the 'winner's bonus' discussed in Chapter 8.	△ My two reasons are: (1) that the first-past-the-post system gave the Labour Party in 2005 55% of the seats in the House of Commons when they only received 35% of the votes – this distortion happens partly because we choose MPs through first-past-the-post. (2) If we moved from first-past-the-post to a system of proportional representation, more people would elect an MP from a party of their own choice. If Leeds was a multi-member constituency all the voters would have at least one Labour, Con or LD MP to take their problems to; after all, in 2005 63% in Leeds NW did not want an LD MP!

Results Plus
Watch out!

If you are asked to 'state' something and also 'explain' you *must* give a clear explanation.

Practice Exam Question

'Sending more offenders to prison is an expensive mistake; there are better ways to reduce crime.'

Do you agree with this view? Give reasons for your opinion, showing you have considered another point of view. (12)

To answer the question above, you could consider the following points and other information of your own.

- Why has the prison population risen to over 80,000 in recent years?
- What are the advantages of sending offenders to prison?

- How many ex-prisoners re-offend and get sent back to prison?
- What other punishments could be given to offenders and why might they be 'better ways'?

Getting started

- Think about the material in Chapter 7 and the work you did in class on this topic.
- Focus on the key words in the question: *more* offenders, *expensive* mistake, *better* ways, *reduce* crime.
- If you answer the 'mini-questions', make sure your 'mini-answers' also clearly answer the main question.
- Even if you believe the statement is 100% right or 100% wrong you will lose marks if you do not include 'for' and 'against' points in your answer.
- Make sure your conclusion picks up the key words and explains why your final view is a clear 'yes' or 'no'. It isn't a good idea to sit on the fence without committing yourself.

Introduction

This is where you indicate the main points you are going to make and relate to the key words in the question. You can hint at what your conclusion will be but your *reasons* for coming to the conclusion should then be given in the final paragraph at the end.

Student answer

I think the best way to reduce crime is to send people to prison for long periods, make them do hard manual work and wear uncomfortable uniforms and have no television sets in their cells or sports kit or facilities or telephone calls. Many prisoners have a better life inside prison than they have when they are on the outside.

Examiner comment

This is a poor introduction – it wouldn't be possible to work out exactly what the question was asking because none of the key words are used or discussed: *more* offenders, *expensive* mistake, *better* ways, *reduce* crime. No definitions are offered and there is no sense of an answer plan. There is no suggestion of an alternative point of view being considered. The reader is unlikely to feel any confidence that this is going to be a strong answer.

Main body

Your answer has to establish a few clear points and the arguments you give must be supported with evidence. Most answers use the 'mini-questions' but remember this is one question not four mini-questions. Your whole answer needs to focus on answering the main question. The contrasting points you offer need to show in the conclusion why you believe one argument is stronger than the other.

Student answer

Why has the prison population risen to over 80,000 in recent years? Because crime has gone up. If everyone who committed crime was caught we would need prison places for two or three times as many people.

What are the advantages of sending offenders to prison? It keeps them away from the public and stabbing or murdering people. That is why we need more prisons.

How many ex-prisoners re-offend and get sent back to prison? About half the prisoners re-offend. Some learn their lesson. The others would learn to behave if they had a harder time doing manual work for at least 12 hours a day, no sport, television or phones.

What other punishments could be given to offenders and why might they be 'better ways'? In Singapore criminals get caned and in the USA they still have the electric chair. We should have the death penalty in Britain for second offenders. That would stop re-offending.

Examiner comment

The 'mini-questions' are used but none of the comments address the key words in the question, which the candidate seems to totally ignore. The arguments offered by the candidate are very simple and not really backed up by tangible evidence. They include opinions that are not backed up with facts. The candidate needed to make points involving the material from Chapter 7 to achieve a balance of 'for' and 'against' points in response to the main question.

Conclusion

Look again at the main question, which you should refer to in your conclusion. Don't introduce new information. Use the points you have already made to show which argument is stronger in your view and why it makes the best conclusion. The student who wrote the answer above didn't include a conclusion (and the final mark would probably have gained 2 or 3 marks). A student who had worked through Chapter 7 could have produced a suitable conclusion like this:

Student answer

Sending offenders to prison is essential where they present a danger to the public. Keeping society safe must be a main priority. But there are many people who offer little or no danger to society. It would be better and cost less to treat mentally ill people in the community or in hospitals than at £37,500 a year in prison. If offenders were helped to get qualifications and supported in getting a home and a job, it is very likely that crime would be reduced and that such people would settle down to happier and more productive lives.

Examiner comment

It would, of course, have been equally acceptable to argue that prison is an important deterrent and that if more effort and cash was spent on catching criminals and punishing them, the overall level of crime would possibly reduce in the long run.

Over to you

Chapters 5 and 6 will help you answer this question.

'There is no real difference between popular and quality newspapers.'

Do you agree with this view? Give reasons for your opinion, showing you have considered another point of view. (12)

To answer the question above, you could consider the following points and other information of your own.

- How do popular and quality newspapers look different?
- Do they have the same or different content?

- Are they equally biased or unbiased?
- Which types of paper have more readers and why?

Chapter 11: Saving our world
Global warming and sustainability

You will learn about:
- reasons for global warming and climate change
- the impact of renewable and non-renewable energy sources
- possible consequences of global warming and how they might be reduced.

What's the issue? Is global warming a threat to our future?

Global warming is perhaps the most important issue we face today. For the first time in our history the whole human race is under threat from the powerful forces of climate change. Will we be able to make the changes needed to save future generations from the impact of a changing climate?

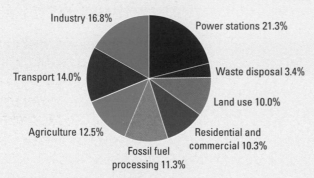

Annary greenhouse gas emissions by sector
Source: http://www.globalwarming.org.in

Industry 16.8%
Power stations 21.3%
Transport 14.0%
Waste disposal 3.4%
Land use 10.0%
Agriculture 12.5%
Residential and commercial 10.3%
Fossil fuel processing 11.3%

The possible effects of global warming

- Most scientists accept that global warming is taking place although some disagree. If global warming is really taking place, will it seriously affect our future?

- Should we be concerned about, or simply ignore, the possible effects of global warming?

Activity

Write a short questionnaire to find out what people think about the causes and consequences of global warming. Ask 20 people to answer the questions and make sure you ask people from different age groups. Analyse the results and summarise your findings.

What is global warming?

Earth's climate has always been subject to natural change. Since the 1950s the Earth's atmospheric temperature has risen as **greenhouse gases** have increased. The atmosphere consists mainly (99%) of safe but essential oxygen and nitrogen. Harmful gases include carbon dioxide (CO_2), methane and nitrous oxide.

Many scientists blame global warming on human activities which have raised the amount of these harmful gases in the atmosphere.

Renewable and non-renewable energy

We are rapidly using up the Earth's resources, which will bring huge problems for the future. A key to solving this is sustainability. To live sustainably we have to save resources, using them only at the rate at which they can be replaced. Where resources can't be replaced we must find alternatives or change the way we live. An important threat to sustainability, which is also part of the problem of global warming, is the way we use fuel to produce energy.

Non-renewable energy sources, including **nuclear power** and **fossil fuels**, cannot be replaced. Fossil fuels create greenhouses gases and nuclear power results in toxic waste. **Renewable energy** from wind, waves, water, and solar power, is expensive but has two advantages. It is cleaner and cannot be used up. However, critics say it is inefficient, unreliable and expensive and can result in environmental eyesores (e.g. wind farms in the countryside).

Which human activities are most likely to produce greenhouse gases?

Possible consequences of global warming

Increasing global temperature will:

- raise sea levels
- increase extreme weather
- expand desert areas.

This will lead to:

- extinction of animal species
- the retreat of glaciers and polar ice-caps
- flooding in low-lying areas.

Activity

In small groups discuss how these possible consequences might affect you and your families. Should we be so concerned with possible problems that may happen in 50 years time?

Can we reverse climate change?

The major cause of global warming is the increased amount of carbon that human activities, such as burning fossil fuels, release into the atmosphere. Scientists claim that if we all try to reduce global emissions of carbon we can overcome the worst effects of climate change. However, progress is slow. There is still debate about whether we can reduce or reverse global warming or adapt to its consequences. A real fear is that, even if we stabilise greenhouse gases, global warming will still continue.

Review and research

The checklist

- Scientists do not agree about whether climate change is really taking place as a result of global warming
- Some people fear that some forms of non-renewable energy will be used up before scientists have developed effective alternatives.
- Global warming could raise temperatures so much that we are forced to change our lifestyle.

Further issues

- How does the media present global warming?
- Are older people as concerned about global warming as younger people?
- How can you help to raise awareness and a willingness to take positive action?

Taking it further

Do you think there is enough evidence for global warming? Discuss in groups.

What can be done?

You will learn about:

- how individuals can make a difference through waste disposal, recycling and shared car schemes
- how new approaches to transport and commuting could help reduce greenhouse gases
- how changes in business practices and council initiatives could cut emissions of greenhouse gases.

What's the issue? It is easier to make waste than to dispose of it

A traditional method of getting rid of rubbish is to bury it in landfill sites. We produce so much rubbish now that these are getting filled up. Also, as the waste degrades, it gives off large quantities of methane, a powerful greenhouse gas. **Local authorities** are looking for alternatives. This extract outlines efforts made by Doncaster, a local authority in Yorkshire:

'A giant **waste incinerator** is to be built in the Doncaster area. The scheme aims to reduce pressure on local landfill sites. The Doncaster region is responsible for disposing of thousands of tonnes of waste every year, a third of which must be **recycled** or composted to achieve targets set by the **European Union**.

Incineration effectively replaces physical debris with toxic smoke and gases – but technology will 'clean' unpleasant gases before they are ejected. Chemical and biological waste will also be processed at the site. Unfortunately, incinerators are ugly and smelly, and unless incineration becomes completely 'clean', developers will face resistance from **NIMBY (Not In My Back Yard)** groups.'

Source: adapted from The Guides Network (2008) Recycling Guide, Fubra Ltd

What can be done to reduce traffic congestion and the pollution it causes?

Do as I say. Not as I do

- Is burning fossil fuels the major cause of the increasing amount of CO_2 in the atmosphere?
- How can road congestion, and the pollution it brings, be reduced?
- Why do NIMBY groups oppose efforts to improve the environment?

Making a difference

Most people agree that we must take action to help reverse global warming. It is easy to expect others to change their lifestyle while we continue to live as we wish. Individual actions may seem insignificant but we can't afford to leave everything to the world's **governments**. There are simple but effective actions that individuals can take:

- buying products that don't use a lot of packaging
- not throwing things away – re-using or recycling them

What recycling facilities exist where you live? Do people use them?

- using less energy, e.g. by switching off televisions and computers, and using energy-saving light bulbs
- walking or cycling more and using cars less.

Most people believe that actions like these can and will make a difference.

Better transport policies

Petrol-fuelled cars contribute a lot to global warming, so it is important to change attitudes to travel. Governments use taxes to encourage motorists to drive less and buy more energy-efficient vehicles. New **hybrid** or more fuel-efficient cars are available.

Councils could encourage car sharing on **commuter** journeys and extend **congestion charging**. **Public transport** must be improved in towns. Drivers can:

- stop using cars for short journeys
- share car journeys with others
- drive environmentally friendly cars
- improve their driving habits.

Has the government done anything to encourage congestion charging in cities? Has congestion charging reduced the number of car journeys in cities like London and Durham?

Will environmental taxes and restrictive **policies** succeed on their own or should we all change our attitudes?

Changes in business practice

Businesses must behave responsibly. They can:

- introduce energy saving measures and clean technology in the workplace
- avoid releasing harmful products into the atmosphere
- cut down packaging and travel.

Local councils can:

- recycle waste
- encourage use of public transport
- encourage energy efficiency and insulation in houses
- make car sharing easier.

Activity

Investigate the steps taken by your local authority to encourage the use of public transport. How effective has it been?

ResultsPlus
Exam Question Report

Give two reasons why environmentalists want petrol taxes raised, not lowered. (2)
May 2007, question 4

Answer: Driving cars burns petrol and adds to global warming. If petrol taxes were raised, people would not be able to afford to buy petrol as often and would drive less, so there would be less carbon dioxide emissions. They might choose to walk, cycle or use public transport.

How students answered

These candidates failed to recognise that raising taxes to discourage demand for petrol would reduce greenhouse gas emissions.

These candidates made a general point about cutting greenhouse gas emissions rather than giving two specific points.

These candidates often suggested that demand for petrol would be reduced if the price was increased through added taxation; this would mean fewer carbon emissions. If personal motoring costs rose, this could encourage more people to use public transport, which causes fewer greenhouse gas emissions.

Review and research

The checklist

- Individuals can make a difference with small 'lifestyle' changes.
- Modifying travel and transport can reduce harmful pollution.
- Better business practices, such as recycling at work, will reduce greenhouse gases.

Taking it further

Investigate what your school has done to improve energy efficiency and waste reduction. Are pupils encouraged to be aware of the benefits of recycling and energy efficiency?

Further issues

- How can we be more energy efficient in our homes?
- What can be done to make school more environmentally friendly?
- How well does your local council publicise energy saving initiatives?

Solutions to global problems

You will learn about:
- public attitudes and the nature, successes and impact of campaigns by environmental groups
- international efforts to combat global warming
- the role of councils, including Local Agenda 21.

What's the issue? How green are we really?

In May 2008 an online Opinion Research poll of 2,002 respondents showed that:

- 72% do not want to pay **green taxes**, even if the money is used for 'green' purposes

- 69% think that green taxes are just a way for the government to raise exta **revenue**

- 94% intend to behave more responsibly in environmental terms

- 36% of men and 22% of women oppose further 'green legislation'

- 34% believe that extreme weather is not related to global warming

- 43% of people aged over 55 believe extreme weather is not connected to global warming

- 10% believe climate change is entirely natural and 12% deny that extreme weather is becoming more common.

Good for holidays but bad for the environment
Source: www.dover.gov.uk/la21/

- Is a cartoon more effective than an opinion poll as a way of drawing attention to an issue like global warming?

- What does the opinion poll research tell you about attitudes to the environment?

- Why do you think men might oppose green legislation more than women? Do you think most people answer opinion poll questions honestly and accurately?

International efforts

Earth Summits are meetings arranged every five years by the **United Nations**. All members can take part in discussing issues relating to the environment and **sustainable development**. The Kyoto Summit (1997) reached an international agreement to reduce industrially produced gases in the atmosphere. However, the USA, one of the main polluters, refused to sign up to this agreement. Developing economies, like China and India, were let off from some Kyoto provisions so as not to stall their rate of development. The current round of climate change talks are scheduled to continue until at least 2012, so it will be some time before another agreement is made.

Agenda 21

In 1992, at the Rio de Janeiro Earth Summit, the United Nations developed an agenda for change in the 21st century. It recognised that to tackle global warming effectively, action is needed globally, regionally, nationally and locally. It claimed that environmental, social and economic issues are interlinked and must be tackled together.

Progress has been patchy. 179 countries signed the agreement but implementation is voluntary so it depends on how committed individual states are.

Have we heard so much about the dangers of global warming that we have started to lose interest?

Councils

Local authorities in the UK are required to work with the **community** to write a **Local Agenda 21** (LA21). The aim is to raise public awareness about what needs to be done and to outline positive actions that can be taken to improve quality of life now and for the future. The idea is to 'act local and think global'. Examples include encouraging local shops to stock (and therefore people to buy) **fair trade** goods, cleaning up local rivers and increasing recycling.

Environmental groups

Environmental groups operate at local, national and global levels. **Greenpeace International** and Friends of the Earth are dedicated to conserving and protecting the environment. Greenpeace is committed to non-violent action and Friends of the Earth emphasises grass-roots activities.

In the UK there are many other less well-known groups:

- *Keep Britain Tidy* focuses on litter
- *Carplus* encourages people to share cars when commuting
- *Flora locale* encourages the use of wild plants in planting schemes
- *Greendragon* sells second-hand books to raise money for woodlands and hedgerows
- *Resolve* encourages recycling in Cornwall.

Most rely on volunteers. Some work independently but others co-operate with authorities. They use various methods including awareness raising, leaflet distribution, advertising, lobbying, public **demonstrations** and obstruction.

Dramatic demonstrations grab the headlines but small-scale local activities can be more effective in the long term.

Activity

Find out the provisions of your Local Agenda 21. Can more be done to publicise them and encourage involvement?

Review and research

The checklist

- International action on global warming depends on the commitment of individual countries.
- Ordinary people have an important role in implementing Local Agenda 21.
- Environmental groups campaign at many levels to protect the environment.

Further issues

- How effective are international agreements on global warming?
- How does the media present the activities of environmental groups?
- Is it ever right for environmental campaigners to break the law?

Taking it further

Investigate the activities and successes of a local environmental group.

Activity

Investigate the Friends of the Earth campaign to raise awareness about the decline of the bee population (see www.birminghamfoe.org. uk). What other campaigns organised by Friends of the Earth have you heard about?

Chapter 12: The UK economy

A question of tax

You will learn about:

◉ different forms of national and local taxation, including income tax, VAT, council tax
◉ why poorer people often pay a higher proportion of their income in tax than rich people
◉ the decisions that the government has to make to provide services.

What's the issue? Are taxes fair?

Majority of Britons are opposed to increases in green taxation

72 per cent of people are not willing to pay more in green taxes like the congestion charge.

More than seven in ten voters insist that they would not be willing to pay higher taxes in order to fund projects to combat climate change, according to a new poll.

Most Britons believe 'green' taxes are imposed to raise cash rather than change behaviour.

Source: Adapted from The Independent, 2 May 2008

Council tax rises to exceed inflation

Council tax bills are likely to rise faster than inflation for the 12th year in a row, according to early estimates by the Local Government Association.

The LGA said average increases in 2009 would be between 3.5 percent and the cap of 5 percent.

The LGA prediction comes as councils experience a sharp fall in revenue from services.

There has also been a drop-off in fees from services related to the housing market.

Source: Adapted from www.ft.com, January 1 2009

◉ Why has the government introduced some green taxes and what will the money be spent on?
◉ What other reasons are there for creating green taxes? How might these taxes affect you?
◉ Why does the government have less money coming in from taxes and other sources than it expected?
◉ What does the government spend the money on that it receives from taxes?

Activity

Find out, for example by looking at your local council's website, how public money is being spent.

Should taxation be switched more from direct to indirect taxes? How important are green taxes?

Different types of tax

Direct taxes

◉ **Income tax** is tax on what you earn. You also pay income tax on savings.
◉ Local councils set Council tax, based on the value of homes. This tax helps pay for local services. You don't have to pay if you are under 18.
◉ Other **direct taxes** are: Capital Gains Tax (if you give money or property away), Stamp Duty (when you buy a house/flat or shares) and Inheritance Tax (tax on your house when you die and leave it to someone else) are other direct taxes.

Indirect taxes

- You pay **VAT (Value Added Tax)** when you buy **goods**. For many years it was fixed at 17.5%, but was reduced in 2008 to 15% to help boost the economy. A reduced rate of 5% is charged on domestic heating fuel and children's car seats. Zero rate applies to goods like books, children's clothes and food.
- Other **indirect taxes** are on: fuel, alcohol, tobacco and betting.
- Recently 'Green taxes' have been introduced to encourage a more responsible attitude to the environment.

You the taxpayer

You have probably heard of direct taxes like income tax and council tax which are paid directly to the government. But did you know that you are already a taxpayer? You pay indirect tax on things you buy like CDs. National taxes are fixed each year in the **Budget**.

Who pays the most tax?

Indirect taxes depend on what you buy, not on what you can afford. Compared to richer people, poorer people:

- pay a greater proportion of income in tax
- have similar basic needs but can't afford to buy in bulk
- have less money to use as they wish, after paying for essentials.

Is income tax fair?

Income tax is meant to be fair – you pay tax according to income and ability to pay. It 'works' by charging no tax on the first £6,475 of earned income (in 2009–10) and then 20% on the next £37,400 and 40% on the rest of earned income.

In 2008, the Chancellor of the Exchequer announced plans for a new 45% rate of tax. Some people think this is entirely fair; others feel that rich people will be penalised for their success.

What happens to the tax we pay?

Our taxes go to the government and become 'public money'. The government must decide how to spend money to help the most people. For example, public money is spent on the National Health Service to provide equipment and doctors and nurses in hospitals. It is also spent on schools, roads and defence.

Balancing spending and income

In the Budget, the government announces its tax and spending plans. If it wants to spend more money, it must raise more money. It does this by increasing taxes. This means people have less money to spend, as they have to pay more tax. The government must justify increased taxes by explaining the advantages of improved services. The government prioritises spending in areas that are important to a lot of people.

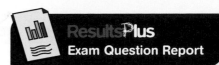

ResultsPlus
Exam Question Report

Which one of the following statements about income tax is correct?

A Income tax has to be paid by everyone who receives an income, no matter how large or small.

B The higher a person's income, the higher the proportion of their income which they must pay in income tax.

C Income tax is the tax we pay when we spend our wages – for example when we buy clothes or furniture. **(1)**

May 2007, question 8e

Answer: B

How students answered

Many students answered this incorrectly. Remember that income tax is paid on income (even if we don't spend it!), but only people earning over a certain amount will pay it.

Most students answered this correctly.

Review and research

The checklist
- Direct taxes take more money from the rich than the poor.
- People on low pay contribute a greater proportion of their income in tax than the higher paid, especially when tax allowances are included.
- Taxes are used to pay for public services.

Further issues
- Should people on high salaries be taxed at a higher rate than lower earners?
- Is income tax a good way to share out wealth?
- Are green taxes a way to change behaviour or are they just a way to raise extra revenue for the government?

Taking it further
Think about whether it is better to have high taxes and good services or low taxes and fewer services.

Benefits and spending

You will learn about:
- the 'means test' debate
- the boundary between public and private sectors
- choosing priorities between education, health, welfare and transport.

What's the issue? Is the Welfare State still effective?

Breadline Britain

About 700,000 pensioners live below the breadline because they don't claim the benefits they are due. Alarming figures reveal they are not applying for cash because of baffling forms. Now campaigners want the government to make asking for benefits much easier. Kate Jopling, of Help the Aged, said: 'Paying benefits automatically would solve this, ensure full take-up of benefits and help to reduce the number of pensioners struggling to get by'. The number of pensioners living on less than 60 per cent of average incomes – the official measure of **poverty** – soared by 300,000 last year.

Source: Adapted from www.ft.com

Pensioners protest at cuts to services for the elderly

A Worcestershire County Council spokesman said cutting back on council services, like no longer paying for hot meals for elderly people in sheltered housing, had saved the taxpayer £276,000 a year. 'The decision to withdraw the subsidies was a difficult one. It was necessary because savings of more than £6 million had to be made to achieve a **balanced budget.**'

Source: Adapted from www.independent.co.uk

- Who is at fault when people do not apply for the benefits they are entitled to?
- Should tax be increased to give more money to pensioners so that they do not live in poverty?
- Is it more important for local authorities to provide services for the elderly than for young people?

Should everyone be entitled to the same welfare cover or should state resources be targeted at those with the greatest needs? What is a 'minimum safety-net'?

Activity

Investigate which welfare benefits are means tested and which are available to all.

The 'means test' debate

UK governments use **taxation** to pay for welfare. The **Welfare State** provides a 'minimum safety-net' paid for by compulsory National Insurance contributions. Rising costs, particularly in the **NHS**, have led some people to ask whether everyone should be entitled to free health care.

Some benefits do depend on income and family circumstances. '**Means testing**' is used to decide what benefits a person really needs and some people think it should be used more widely. The problem is that many of the neediest people don't apply because they think it is unfair, that claiming is too complicated or that it is an invasion of their **privacy**. The only way to be sure everyone who needs help gets it, is by providing universal 'same for everyone' benefits. Others believe that if the majority of people paid for their own welfare it would free resources for those who need it most.

Public or private provision?

'Big' governments tax heavily and spend generously. 'Small' governments limit taxes and encourage private provision. UK governments provide basic welfare for all. Some people have private medical insurance, private or occupational **pension** schemes, and may pay for private education. In theory, anybody can do this but it is too expensive for most people – so the UK has a two-tier welfare system.

In the 1980s Margaret Thatcher's government sold off many **state-owned industries** – like airports, telephones, gas and electricity – because she believed the **private sector** organised things more efficiently than the **public sector**. Tony Blair's government introduced Public Private Partnerships (PPP) and Private Finance Initiatives (PFI), which involve co-operation between public and private bodies to build new facilities, e.g. prisons, roads, schools and hospitals. They are said to save taxpayers money but others criticise them for paying profits to **shareholders** rather than investing in more provision.

Choosing priorities

Government resources are limited. Politicians must decide how best to spend the money collected from taxes. Before a **general election**, **political parties** outline their policies and priorities for the **electorate** to make a choice. Recent governments have increased spending on education, health and welfare, but spending more in one area means there is less available to spend in others. Once spending decisions are made, governments must decide how to allocate resources within their chosen priorities. Inevitably some people feel government spending decisions are wrong.

Should we build more railways rather than more roads?

Will a new runway at Heathrow Airport be an expensive environmental disaster?

Are private toll motorways the best way to improve the road system?

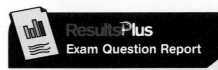

What are the advantages and disadvantages of PPP and PFI?

Review and research

The checklist
- Since government income is limited, benefits may be means tested but this often causes the most needy to miss out.
- Welfare services are provided by public and private organisations.
- Spending involves making choices about priorities.

Further issues
- Should the government ecourage people to use private health insurance so that more of the National Health budget can be used to help the really needy?
- Are state welfare costs too high and should they be reduced?
- How should governments decide welfare spending priorities?

Taking it further
Investigate how much it cost to build the Millennium Dome. Was it worth the money?

Managing the economy

You will learn about:
- how the government aims to reduce unemployment
- why the government has introduced a points-based immigration scheme for economic migrants with scarce skills
- the effect on the economy of the UK's ageing population and increased life expectancy.

What's the issue? Will more immigration create or solve our problems?

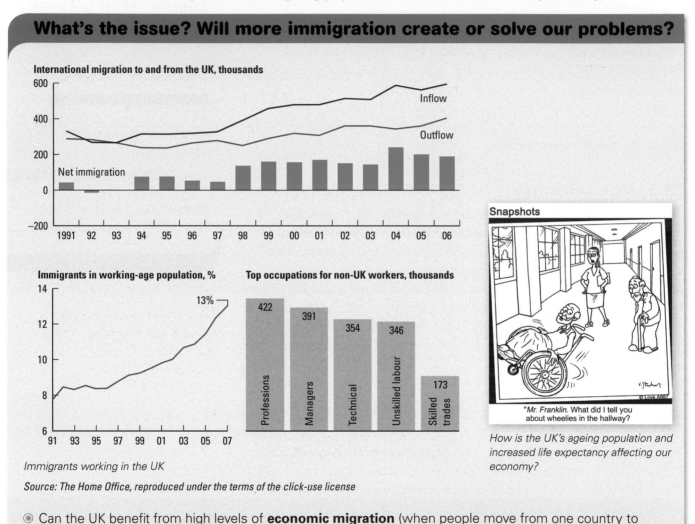

International migration to and from the UK, thousands

Inflow

Outflow

Net immigration

1991 92 93 94 95 96 97 98 99 00 01 02 03 04 05 06

Immigrants in working-age population, %

13%

91 93 95 97 99 01 03 05 07

Immigrants working in the UK

Top occupations for non-UK workers, thousands

422 Professions
391 Managers
354 Technical
346 Unskilled labour
173 Skilled trades

Snapshots

"Mr. Franklin. What did I tell you about wheelies in the hallway?"

How is the UK's ageing population and increased life expectancy affecting our economy?

Source: The Home Office, reproduced under the terms of the click-use license

- Can the UK benefit from high levels of **economic migration** (when people move from one country to another in search of employment or for other economic reasons)?
- What are the implications for the economy of rising numbers of healthy elderly people?
- Should we be more concerned by high levels of **migration** than by an increasingly elderly population?

Activity

Investigate what the government does to help the long-term unemployed prepare for work. How have they tried to reduce the numbers of those 'sick and unable to work'?

Employment and unemployment

The government's job is to manage the economy. If they are successful, living standards will rise and so will the amount of public money available to provide better services and welfare benefits. High employment levels will:

- cut the amount of money spent providing **unemployment benefits**
- improve living standards
- enable businesses to work at full capacity and make high profits
- increase national wealth.

Government departments help unemployed people find work, and provide support and training for those who can't. They also offer a range of services to help **employers** fill vacancies.

An ageing population

The UK's population is getting older. In 2006, 16% of the population were over 65. By 2031 this will rise to about 22% (out of 71 million). This is a serious economic problem because:

If pensions become inadequate, do you think some people might decide not to retire at all? Ask some adults whether they plan to retire.

- welfare, care, and health costs will increase
- the proportion of children in the population is getting smaller
- the working-age population is declining
- fewer working-age people must financially support increasing numbers of older people
- pension provision could become inadequate if people live longer.

The government plans to:

- raise the age for a pension to 68 by 2031
- protect the right to work beyond retirement age (the government has made it illegal to **discriminate** against people on grounds of age)
- encourage private retirement pension plans.

Points-based immigration

EU workers have the right to work in any EU country. Since about 2000 many have come to Britain to work. Britain also has large numbers of migrants who come from non-EU countries. There is concern that the UK can't cope with so many immigrants. The government has introduced strict new immigration controls.

Should the government try to reduce the need for skilled migrant workers? What could it do?

In 2008, a new points system limited immigration to workers with the skills needed by the UK's economy. The Home Office statement said that skilled foreign nationals can earn entry 'points' if they can show they will: do skilled work for which a British national can't be found, speak good English, earn over £24,000 a year, and have good qualifications. The government lists shortage skill areas where workers are needed.

Review and research

The checklist
- High levels of employment are necessary for the economy to grow.
- Increased life expectancy has economic implications.
- Britain's economy needs economic migrants with special skills.

Further issues
- Why is the age structure of the population changing?
- How can the government increase the proportion of the working-age population?
- Should people have greater responsibility to provide for their retirement?

Taking it further
Think about what contribution migrants make to Britain's culture and economy.

Chapter 13: Communities in the UK
Individuals making a difference

You will learn about:

- how individuals can make a difference to community life
- how individuals working together in groups can raise funds for causes they collectively support
- how individuals contribute to community cohesion.

What's the issue? All for one and one for all?

Communities in the UK may be geographical areas or they may involve groups of people who speak a particular language, share a religion or have interests in common – business leaders, ramblers, chess players or rugby enthusiasts, for example. Community cohesion exists when the members of a community work together and support each other.

Why volunteer?

Millions of people volunteer in the UK every year. They work to support their community for no payment.

What sort of things do they do? They may:

- raise money for a community service such as an air ambulance
- clean a local church or mosque
- coach children in football, rugby, tennis, swimming or other sports
- deliver meals to elderly or disabled people
- organise a **petition** to the local council or the local MP over a local issue
- run a charity shop in aid of a worthy cause such as animal welfare or a local hospice
- deliver leaflets or speak to voters on behalf of a local candidate or political party at election time.

Groups who put enormous effort into supporting good causes are often inspired by the work of individuals such as cancer sufferer Jane Tomlinson, who died in 2007 aged 43.

Athlete, Jane, was told in 2000 that she had terminal breast cancer and only six months to live. But she defied doctors, living for seven years and raising an amazing £1.7 million for charity. A very different source of inspiration for many was former Chief Executive of insurance firm Aviva, Richard Harvey, who gave up his £1 million-a-year job to do charity work in Malawi and Kenya. Now he wants UK companies – our business community – to help tackle more of Africa's problems.

Jane Tomlinson celebrates completing her attempt at the New York City Marathon.

- Why do so many people work hard for no pay or reward?
- How important is **voluntary work** to community cohesion?
- Is it better for social change to be brought about by voluntary work and charities or by government?

What would happen if people gave up doing voluntary work? What would happen if many more people did charity work?

Charities in the UK

UK charities may focus on a local hospice, children's nursery or disability organisation. Some, for example those that support research into disease, are national charities. Others, such as Oxfam or the Red Cross, operate nationwide or worldwide. All UK charities are regulated by the Charity Commission.

Examples of national charities include:

- National Trust
- Royal Society for the Prevention of Cruelty to Animals
- Cancer Research
- Royal National Lifeboat Institution
- Royal National Institute for the Blind.

Often charities are set up by – or in memory of – wealthy individuals. Examples of these include:

- Joseph Rowntree Reform Trust, which supports political reform, constitutional change and social justice.
- Esmée Fairbairn Foundation which makes grants to organisations that aim to improve the quality of life for people and communities in the UK, both now and in the future.
- The Bill and Melinda Gates Foundation, which believes science and technology have great potential to improve the lives of individuals and communities around the world.

Charities in the community

To support their air ambulance, Wiltshire people have to raise £320,000 a year doing everything from street collections to organising charity shops and garden fêtes. The service has airlifted some 1,500 seriously ill patients to hospitals in Bath, Swindon, Salisbury and Bristol in the past 12 years.

The Wiltshire air ambulance landing just 50 metres from the accident and emergency department at Swindon's Great Western Hospital.

Many local people raise money by getting their friends to sponsor them running a marathon. In the 2008 Wolverhampton Marathon £29,000 was shared by the four charities for whom the event was organised:

1 Mencap Wolverhampton & Mencap in the Midlands
2 The Mayor of Wolverhampton's Charity Fund
3 Children's Outpatients Department – New Cross Hospital
4 Brain Tumour UK.

Areas where a lot of people are involved in voluntary work for various causes tend to be strong communities, often meeting in the same church halls or community centres. If they are hit by a sudden problem, such as flooding, they pull together and help each other. Areas where such community networks do not exist or are much weaker are more likely to wait for others to come and help them out rather than rally round and help each other.

105

Activity

Find out from your local council, local newspaper or **Citizens Advice Bureau** about charities in the area where you live. What are their aims? What do they do? How much money have they raised in the last two or three years?

Review and research

The checklist

- Millions of people voluntarily spend hours every week doing things for others.
- Much voluntary work is poured into charities which support communities.
- Without this sort of support, important services such as an air ambulance might not exist at all.

Further issues

- Should hospitals depend on voluntary efforts to provide essential equipment such as an air ambulance?
- Why do strong voluntary and charitable networks seem to add to the self-confidence and cohesion of an area?
- Should all young people be expected to do national service in the community – locally, nationally or globally – for two years after leaving school, college or university?

Taking it further

Research on the Internet to find out the amount of funds held by UK charities, their annual income and what they spend their money on.

Working together

You will learn about:

◉ how and why communities change over time and the role of the voluntary sector in supporting them at local, national and global level

◉ the impact of business on employment opportunities and consumer spending

◉ the role of government in ensuring that business flourishes and citizens prosper in a free and fair economy.

What's the issue? UK communities – different and changing

Communities rarely stay the same for long: new people move in, new industries open up, or the community may go into decline. Over the last 30 to 40 years, rural communities have probably changed more than any others.

No more trains on Devon's Yelverton to Princetown line across Dartmoor

- Half a million people worked in the UK's rural areas in the 1960s. By 2005 that number had halved.
- Many rural areas now have no shop or post office.
- Train lines have been closed down, starting with cuts in the 1960s. Bus services have been reduced, so people without a car are increasingly isolated, though car-sharing schemes are sometimes organised in rural areas where people are keen to help each other.

Contrasts between urban and rural areas	Rural %	Urban %
Households comprising a married couple	44	35
Population aged 65 and over	65	15
Population born outside the UK	4	10
Population identifying as non-white	1	11
Population describing themselves as Christian	80	70
Self-employed	12	7
Employed in agriculture, hunting, forestry, mining, quarrying	5	1
People in employment aged 16–74 years working mainly at or from home	14	8
Proportion of workers travelling to work by car or van	69	59

Source: Office of National Statistics, reproduced under the terms of the click-use license

Urban areas may lack the beauty and clean air of the country but they have more services and better transport links, and people travel shorter distances to work – on average, 11 miles in rural areas and seven miles in urban areas.

◉ Why have rural communities declined in recent years?

◉ How do you account for the biggest differences between rural and urban communities?

◉ What steps could be taken to restore rural communities?

106

Countryside in decline?

- More and more houses in the countryside are second homes for wealthy people, who can afford to pay far more than locals. This means less **demand** for local services and employment levels fall. Shops and pubs close, and house prices go up, often beyond the reach of locals.

- Young people often leave the village where they grew up, moving to get a home they can afford – so their children will not be going to the village school they attended.

- There is a shortage of **social housing** in such areas – something government could change.

- Central and local governments have campaigned for high-speed broadband to be widely available in rural areas. This means that people can work from home; there is also much more self-employment in rural areas than before.

Reviving village life

People in the countryside don't all want the same things; 'original locals' may campaign to keep services going. Second-home owners may oppose new housing or developments such as wind farms, which may spoil their views. The villages where schools and businesses are threatened with closure might be where new housing could be built and the proposed closures could be reversed as new residents moved in.

Helping others, helping ourselves: the role of mutual organisations

The UK has always had a strong network of community organisations run by their own members, such as co-operatives for farming and groceries. Financially, **building societies** and **credit unions** helped many people when banks stopped lending to customers during the 2008/9 financial problems.

Promoting development and progress on a global scale: free and fair trade

For farmers in **less economically developed countries (LEDCs)**, **trade** is vital. That is why **free trade** is important – making sure that barriers to trade are removed and that subsidies which undercut prices for local farmers are avoided. **Fair trade** is also important. Fair trade products are those where fair prices are paid to producers in developing countries, rather than trying to buy everything as cheaply as possible. Fair trade products are often grown or made in some of the poorest parts of the world. Buying fair trade products (tea, coffee, chocolate, bananas, sugar, even footballs) means the local producers get a fair price. Fair trade supports the aim of Agenda 21 because it encourages sustainable development.

Would it be a good idea to re-open any rural railway stations that have been closed or would it just be a waste of money? What arguments could be put forward to support re-opening them? How might a new station support the local community?

Activity

Find out where your nearest building society and credit union are. Find out the difference between a bank, a building society and a credit union.

Review and research

The checklist

- Communities are constantly changing – as employment declines, demand for services falls.

- A problem in many rural areas is a shortage of social housing.

- Individuals and groups working together can make a big difference though government support is sometimes also needed.

Further issues

- How could incomes and business activity in rural areas be increased so that village shops, schools, pubs and post offices could be re-opened?

- When is it best to provide a service for the community through a partnership rather than through the government alone?

- Do goods imported as a result of free trade or fair trade help or hinder the prospects of UK producers and supermarkets?

Taking it further

Think about how government or business organisations can promote the growth of commerce locally and nationally within the UK.

Chapter 14: The UK's role in the world
An ethical foreign policy

You will learn about:
- how ethics can affect policy making and policy goals
- the nature and impact of UK global diplomacy
- key features of a morally-justifiable view of trade.

What's the issue? How much are ethical issues considered when deciding foreign policy?

British troops in Afganistan help reconstruct the country after the damage caused by war

'Our foreign policy must have an ethical dimension and must support the demands of other peoples for the democratic rights on which we insist for ourselves. The Labour Government will put **human rights** at the heart of our foreign policy and will publish an annual report on our work in promoting human rights abroad. The next twelve months provide the greatest opportunities in a generation for Britain to take a leading part on the world stage.'

Robin Cook (Foreign Secretary), May 1997

In a statement in December 2008, **Prime Minister** Gordon Brown said:

'Zimbabwe is now an international rather than a national emergency. International because disease crosses borders. International because the systems of government in Zimbabwe are now broken – there is no country capable or willing to protect its people. International because – not least in the week of the 60th anniversary of the **Universal Declaration of Human Rights** – we must stand together to defend human rights and **democracy**.'

- How has the government tried to support 'democratic rights' in other countries?
- Should Britain send troops or economic aid to places where people are suffering and starving as the result of corrupt government or civil war?
- Why should Britain's foreign policy be ethical?

An ethical policy

Foreign policy involves international relations. It includes trade and economics, international co-operation and political, social and military issues. The UK's foreign policy goals are decided by the government and carried out by the Foreign Secretary. Foreign policy is meant to protect and promote national interests. It requires international co-operation but can result in armed conflict if a country feels threatened.

In 1997 the Foreign Secretary promised an 'ethical' foreign policy, claiming it should be guided by moral values. Examples of an ethical approach are:

- helping famine victims in Africa
- combating climate change
- resisting discrimination
- opposing repressive regimes
- intervening militarily if necessary.

UK global diplomacy

Many international problems are solved by negotiation and persuasion. Britain, one of the world's wealthiest countries, is often involved in diplomatic activity. Recently this has included:

- negotiating climate change agreements, e.g. the EU Emissions Trading Scheme (ETS) 2008
- seeking solutions to the world economic crisis
- discussing trading agreements with other countries
- **peacekeeping** in trouble spots such as the Balkans, Sierra Leone and Afghanistan
- providing aid in cases of emergency and disaster such as famine in Ethiopia or after the 2001 tsunami.

Britain sometimes acts like the world's policeman to enforce international laws. Some people say recent activities have been guided by self-interest rather than genuine ethical principles. You should remember that foreign policy, like any other aspect of government, is influenced by many different factors.

Trade and moral values

The wealth of a country depends largely on **international trade**. Buying and selling goods or services helps maintain jobs and high living-standards. In order to help promote international trade, governments work to support businesses by:

- negotiating trade agreements, e.g. removing trade barriers which restrict the **import** of fair trade goods, like the EU Economic Partnership Agreements with African, Caribbean and Pacific (ACP) countries
- using government UKTI (UK Trade and Investment) to support the work of sales teams abroad, e.g. by providing information about business opportunities
- de-regulating trade to encourage the import and **export** of goods
- using export controls, e.g. to restrict the sale of military equipment to undemocratic regimes.

A wealthy country sells goods at the best possible price and buys as cheaply as possible. When we earn more than we spend, we have a positive **balance of trade**. Britain's government believes in free trade. This means that the price of goods from overseas is not increased to protect home producers. Surplus home production is not sent to less developed countries at reduced prices, since this may harm markets and ruin local farmers. The government also believes in fair trade which means producers in developing countries and paid fair prices for their goods.

Does the British government always follow an ethical foreign policy?

What different factors can influence foreign policy?

109

Activity

Investigate the difference between free trade and fair trade. What is the role of the **World Trade Organisation**? How does it encourage free trade and fair trade?

Review and research

The checklist

- Labour claims that the government follows an ethical foreign policy.
- Britain continues to play a major global role in international relations.
- The British government is committed to supporting free trade and fair trade.

Further issues

- Should foreign policy be based on ethical principles rather than UK self-interest?
- What are the benefits to the UK of a free trade policy?
- The government claims to believe in fair trade. What obstacles do they face when trying to encourage fair trade with developing countries?

Taking it further

Investigate the availability of fair trade goods in your local supermarket. How could shoppers be encouraged to buy fair trade goods, even if they are slightly more expensive?

Britain and the European Union

You will learn about:
- the aims, activities and membership of the EU
- the institutions of the EU
- debates about the effectiveness of UK membership of the EU.

What's the issue? How important are Britain and the EU to each other?

There has always been a lot of debate, both for and against British membership of the EU.

The UK Independence Party (UKIP) is one of the main political groups campaigning to get Britain out of the EU. This is what the UKIP leader said in October 2008:

'What the EU wants is increasing state control by **bureaucracy**, and that is what the Lisbon Treaty gives it the opportunity to achieve. … Government by centralised regulation will merely make problems worse and systems more rigid. Flexibility has to be the key – and that only comes with greater national independence.'

Nigel Farage, leader of UKIP (Blog 22 October 22 http://www.ukip.org/content/nigel-farages-blog/818-crisis-management-brusselsstyle)

The European Parliament is the only really democratic European institution. Members are elected by the citizens of EU countries.

- In what ways is the EU democratic and how is it bureaucratic?
- Is the EU too big and diverse to be effective internationally?
- Which major political party is the most enthusiastic supporter of EU membership and which is the least enthusiastic?

Activity

Investigate which European countries have currently applied to join the EU. Which European countries have chosen not to join? Why have they rejected membership?

The aims of the EU

The EU (European Union) is a political and economic organisation. In 2009 there were 27 member countries with several other eastern European countries hoping to join. Members agree to work together, obey community rules, and contribute to the central EU budget in return for benefits. Since 1992 the EU has operated as a single market. It aims to achieve free movement of trade and labour between member countries by removing barriers and subsidies.

Aims of the EU include:

- promoting economic and social progress
- being a united force internationally
- establishing a European citizenship
- developing Europe as an area of freedom, security and justice.

EU institutions

Parliament: Members of the European Parliament (MEPs) are elected every five years. They represent almost 500 million electors. Elections are based on proportional representation and universal suffrage (all eligible adults have the right to **vote**). The Parliament approves new laws proposed by the Commission. Its main duty is to approve the budget.

The Council of Ministers is the main decision-making body, made up of **ministers** from the governments of the 27 member countries. The minister who attends will depend on what is being discussed (e.g. if it is agriculture, it will be the agriculture ministers from each member country). It has more influence than Parliament but, like Parliament, is a legislative body and deals with the budget.

> **The main organisations that run the EU are**

The Commission represents European interests independently of national governments. It has **executive** powers, proposes new laws and is supported by a large **civil service**. It is responsible for the day-to-day working of the EU and makes sure EU laws are used properly.

The Presidency changes every six months. Each country takes a turn to run the EU for six months, deciding which issues will be considered or given priority. The President manages the work of the Council of Ministers.

How effective is UK membership?

Most UK political parties officially support membership of the EU but some are more committed than others. Some people think Britain has given up too much independence. Others see the economic benefits. Some want even stronger political ties. Some feel the EU will increase Britain's international influence.

UKIP is the only party that officially wants Britain to leave the EU. It wants to base relations with Europe only on trading agreements. Opponents of the EU are called **Eurosceptics**. This broad term covers a wide range of views about the future of Europe.

EU regulations have sometimes been laughed at or opposed – particularly those which try to control the size and shape of vegetables, like insisting that bananas should be straight, or that oddly shaped fruit and vegetables could not be sold. Many of these have now been relaxed. The use of EU funds to regenerate economically depressed areas like Cornwall or the North East have been more significant though.

What other institutions contribute to the work of the EU? Does it matter that the Parliament is the only democratically appointed EU institution?

Activity

The EU Council of Ministers, the European Council and the Council of Europe are different institutions. Find out more about the role and responsibilities of each one.

Review and research

The checklist

- The EU is a political and economic union of European countries.
- Power in the EU is shared by different institutions, each having different responsibilities.
- Britain has been a member of the EU since 1972 but there is still debate about the benefits and effectiveness of membership.

Further issues

- Is the EU too large? Should countries outside Europe be allowed to join the EU? What criteria should the EU expect new members to meet?
- What is the Eurozone? Why is Britain not a member?
- What benefits does Britain get in return for its contributions to the EU budget?
- Should the EU be involved in the climate change debate?

Taking it further

Find out and compare the official policy of each of the major UK political parties towards EU membership. Remember to include Nationalist parties and the Green Party.

Britain and the United Nations

You will learn about:
- membership of the United Nations
- the organisation and achievements of the United Nations
- UN Millennium Goals.

What's the issue? Can international co-operation solve global problems?

The United Nations is an international organisation set up after the Second World War to increase international co-operation. It is involved in many different activities including peacekeeping and works to improve education, health and humanitarian relief.

The Millennium Development Goals

In 2000 the UN set 'Millennium Development Goals' to be met by 2015 in response to the world's main development challenges. Progress has been uneven. In 2008, a practical programme agreed to:

- wipe out extreme poverty and hunger
- achieve primary education for all children
- promote gender **equality**
- reduce child mortality and improve maternal health
- combat HIV/AIDS, malaria and other diseases
- ensure environmental sustainability.

'Since 2000, the Millennium Declaration and the Millennium Development Goals (MDGs) have become a universal framework for development. We are now at the midpoint between the adoption of the MDGs and the 2015 target date. So far, our collective record is mixed. The results suggest that there have been some gains, and that success is still possible in most parts of the world. But they also point to how much remains to be done.

Adapted from the UN Secretary General's forward to 'The Millennium Development Goals report, 2007'

- Should the UN's main concern be humanitarian issues or peacekeeping?
- What humanitarian issues face the UN in Africa? How effectively are they dealt with?
- Is the UN truly representative of all member countries or is it too often influenced by the Great Powers like Britain, USA and China who are permanent members of the **Security Council**?

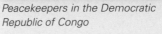

Peacekeepers in the Democratic Republic of Congo

UN relief agencies working in Africa

United Nations membership

The United Nations works to resolve international conflict before it escalates into war. It has 192 member countries, who all claim to accept the values and obligations of the **UN Charter** agreed in 1945.

UN organisation

The *Security Council* exists to maintain international peace. It investigates disputes, and can recommend solutions to disputes, apply economic **sanctions**, or take military action. It has five permanent members (Britain, France, Russia, China, USA) and ten non-permanent members who change every two years. Countries such as Germany, India, Brazil and Japan feel they should be permanent members. Only permanent members can **veto** (block) proposals.

The General Assembly meets in regular sessions. All member countries are represented and can speak and vote. Some critics have called for the establishment of a parliament elected by universal suffrage, to reflect the views of ordinary people.

The ***International Court of Justice*** examines disputes between countries.

UN agencies: many UN organisations and agencies exist to carry out its aims, e.g. UNESCO which helps countries work together on education, science and culture, and UNICEF which works to protect children, meet their basic needs and expand their opportunities.

Some UN members believe the Security Council prevents progress and must be reformed. A major concern is that the permanent members may use the veto to protect their own interests rather than world peace. This happened in 2008, when Russia and China vetoed sanctions against Zimbabwe. It was also criticised for being too slow in dealing with crises like Rwandan **genocide** (1994). Between 1984 and 2008, 63 resolutions were vetoed (including 43 by the USA and ten by the UK).

Achievements

Peacekeeping is an important UN role. The UN has no independent military force, so depends on those supplied by members. Much of the UN budget is spent on peacekeeping and it is claimed that two out of every three peacekeeping efforts are successful. Current peacekeeping operations (in 2009) include UNOCI (Ivory Coast), MINUSTAH (Haiti), UNMIT (East Timor) and UNIFIL (Lebanon).

Other work of the UN includes:
- encouraging **disarmament**
- supporting human rights
- supporting the political and economic rights of women
- providing humanitarian services to famine victims, war **refugees**, and victims of other disasters.

Activity

Find out how permanent members have used their ability to veto decisions agreed by other members. Does the veto give some countries too much power?

What arguments are there for and against the suggestion that the United Nations should have a democratically elected Parliamentary Assembly?

Activity

Investigate the role of UN agencies. How effectively have they acted to resolve (a) conflicts between states and (b) environmental issues?

ResultsPlus
Watch out!

Identify and explain one difference between the United Nations and the European Union. (2) June 2005, question 8b

Remember, strong answers will give examples of different things that the two organisations do e.g. that the EU ensures optimum trading conditions between members, but the UN doesn't involve itself in the market so obviously.

Review and research

The checklist
- UN membership is open to all countries.
- Some UN members believe it should be reformed to make it more democratic and reduce the domination of the major powers.
- The UN is successful in two out of three peace-keeping missions and in providing humanitarian aid.

Taking it further
Investigate the budget of the UN. Where do contributions come from and how is money spent?

Further issues
- Which of the Millennium Goals is the most important? Why do you think it is more important than the others?
- Is enough publicity given to UN humanitarian work?
- What is the purpose and moral justification for the International Court of Justice in The Hague?

Britain and the Commonwealth of Nations

You will learn about:
⊚ membership of the Commonwealth of Nations
⊚ the role and purpose of the Commonwealth of Nations
⊚ achievements of the Commonwealth of Nations.

What's the issue? Is the Commonwealth any more than a relic of Britian's colonial past?

The Commonwealth of Nations in 2008

The flag of the Commonwealth of Nations

The Commonwealth suspended Zimbabwe for 12 months over the conduct of its presidential election. The Commonwealth prides itself on being one of very few international organisations that is prepared to throw members out for violating democratic standards. Ironically, the Commonwealth's values are contained in the *Harare Declaration* (1991). This sets out democracy, fundamental human rights and the rule of **law** as the basis of membership.

The Commonwealth has little practical or financial leverage over Zimbabwe, so suspension is largely a symbolic move. It makes it more difficult for international institutions, such as the **World Bank** or the **International Monetary Fund (IMF)**, to deal with the country as normal.

⊚ What is the point of taking 'a symbolic move' which cannot be effectively enforced?

⊚ Do Commonwealth leaders have a moral right to condemn a **sovereign country**?

⊚ Does membership of the EU create conflict with membership of the Commonwealth?

⊚ What is ironic about the reference to the *Harare Declaration?*

Activity

Find out who is the current Secretary General of the Commonwealth and which country he or she is from.

Identify former British colonies which have resigned from or not joined the Commonwealth of Nations. Investigate why they made their decision.

What is the Commonwealth of Nations?

The Commonwealth of Nations, previously the British Commonwealth, is a voluntary organisation of 53 countries with a combined population of almost two billion people. Most members were part of the British **Empire** although some former British dependencies chose not to join. Members are countries which choose to maintain ties of friendship and co-operation with Britain. The Queen is appointed as Head of the Commonwealth. Commonwealth activities are managed by the Secretary General.

The role and purpose of the Commonwealth

The Commonwealth is different from other international organisations. It doesn't have power, a united policy, common principles, or shared institutions. Most member countries are parliamentary democracies. It might have become a preferential trade area if Britain hadn't joined the EU – that is, a group of countries which give better trading terms to each other.

The Commonwealth exists for informal discussion and co-operation between different nations. Commonwealth heads of government meet every two years. Decisions are not binding. Economic ties exist in trade, investment, and development programmes for new nations.

Commonwealth objectives include: world peace, representative democracy, individual liberty, the pursuit of equality, opposition to **racism**, the fight against poverty, ignorance and disease, free trade, joint action, opposition to gender-discrimination, and environmental sustainability.

Achievements of the Commonwealth of Nations

Members who do not uphold democratic government have been suspended. On a positive note, the Commonwealth provides:

- 'democracy experts' to promote democracy
- observers to see that election results are fair
- help to remove tension and conflict
- examples of best practice in human rights
- encouragement to achieve the Millennium Development Goals (MDGs) agreed in 2000
- support for socially sustainable 'green' economic activities such as the Iwokrama International Rain Forest Programme in Guyana.

Over 100 **non-government organisations (NGOs)** work in the areas of culture, education, charity and sport, to improve the lives of ordinary **citizens**. The Commonwealth (or 'Friendly') Games, the world's second largest festival of sport, take place every four years and are open to competitors from all member countries. The Commonwealth's main strengths are shared values and use of persuasion and moral authority.

How important are the Commonwealth Games? Why are they called 'the Friendly Games'?

Which one of the following countries is a member of the Commonwealth?

A Greenland   B Mexico   C Japan
D New Zealand (1)

May 2006, question 8c
Answer: New Zealand

How students answered

Many students answers failed to identify New Zealand as a member of the Commonwealth of Nations.

Most students answered this question correctly.

Activity

Investigate the Lake Victoria Commonwealth Climate Change Action Plan (2007). What steps have the Commonwealth of Nations taken to deal with problems of global warming and climate change?

Review and research

The checklist
- The Commonwealth of Nations is a voluntary global organisation.
- The Commonwealth supports and maintains democracy and human rights.
- Commonwealth agencies make significant cultural, social and educational contributions to the development of member countries.

Taking it further
Investigate how the Commonwealth supervises fair and free elections.

Further issues
- What features must be present for a place to be described as a sovereign country?
- In 1949 the British Commonwealth became the 'Commonwealth of Nations'. Why was the original name changed? How significant was it?
- Should the Commonwealth have a military peace-keeping force?

Chapter 15: Global citizenship

The strength of disagreements

You will learn about:

- International Humanitarian Law
- how international law can be enforced
- disagreements over human rights and equality.

What's the issue? Outlawing inhumanity

International Humanitarian Law (IHL) comes into force as soon as an armed conflict has started. It applies equally to all sides, regardless of who started the fighting. Its aim is to limit the suffering caused by war. The principles behind it were first developed in the **Geneva Convention** in 1864 and were extended by the Genocide convention 1948, when acts carried out with the intention of destroying a particular group of people were made unlawful. In the 1949 Geneva Convention the rights of wounded combatants, prisoners of war and civilians were clearly laid down.

According to IHL, those involved in armed conflict must:

- not use certain types of weapon, e.g. exploding bullets, biological or chemical weapons
- avoid injuring or killing civilians as far as possible
- not harm an opponent who surrenders or can no longer fight.

Exchange of Serbian and Bosnian prisoners of war in Sarajevo, 1993. This was done under the supervision of the International Committee of the Red Cross (ICRC), who help people innocently caught up in a conflict (e.g. children) and make sure prisoners of war are treated humanely. An important role of the ICRC is to encourage respect for International Humanitarian Law.

Activity

In groups, look at the ICRC website and work out how much difference their activities have made in the world in the past 20 years.

Former Leader on trial

After a conflict has ended, those who have broken the laws of war – especially those who have committed terrible acts – may be put on trial for war crimes. In 2008 trial proceedings began in the case of former Bosnian Serb leader, Radovan Karadzic who faces 11 counts of genocide (massacre of people, usually to try and wipe out a whole group or race), war crimes, crimes against humanity and other atrocities. Among other things, 12,000 people including 100 children were killed in the siege of Sarajevo. He faces a possible life sentence if convicted.

Former Serbian leader, Radovan Karadzic

Activity

Find out what progress the Karadzic trial has made.

- Why is International Humanitarian Law needed?
- How does the **International Committee of the Red Cross (ICRC)** make a difference?
- Why is IHL more difficult to enforce than other kinds of law?

Making international law work

- Making international law work depends on countries agreeing on the law and how it should be enforced.
- In 1998 a permanent war court to deal with war crimes, genocide and crimes against humanity was agreed – the **International Criminal Court (ICC)** in The Hague, The Netherlands. Its first trial started in January 2009, of Thomas Lubanga, accused of recruiting children as young as ten to fight for him.
- By December 2008, 148 states were in the process of signing up to be members of the Court. However, countries such as China, Russia, India and the USA have not joined.
- The ICC only applies international law where national courts are unable or unwilling to hear such cases.
- To date, the Court has started to investigate crimes in Uganda, the Democratic Republic of Congo, the Central African Republic and Darfur.

Human rights and equality

Although progress has been made in establishing human rights since 1945, the whole idea has yet to be fully accepted, particularly in Asia and Africa. In 2005, two Iranian teenagers received 228 lashes and were publicly hanged for admitting to a gay relationship. In the same year, **Amnesty International** reported a woman in Afghanistan was stoned to death for committing adultery. Over the years, **UN Human Rights Commissioners** have highlighted such cases and slowly the idea of human rights is being accepted in more countries – but still not in all.

Although the idea of every person being equal to every other person is generally accepted in theory, the reality is often different. This is true between different people in the UK too. We all have general rights (e.g. the right to vote), but some have more money and a better lifestyle than others. Across the world the difference is even greater.

Often, instead of aiming for equality, people talk about equality of opportunity. That is an easier goal to reach but it is not the same as equality. What is the difference between equality and equality of opportunity?

ResultsPlus
Watch out!

Do not confuse the ICC with the International Court of Justice. That is the UN organisation that settles disputes between member countries.

Activity

Look up cases raised by the UN Human Rights Commissioner with different countries over the past five years.

Review and research

The checklist

- International Humanitarian Law (IHL) aims to protect sick and wounded soldiers, prisoners of war, children and civilians in war-torn places.
- The International Committee of the Red Cross plays a key part in persuading countries to abide by IHL.
- Those who break IHL can be made to answer for war crimes, genocide and other crimes in court.

Taking it further

Check the ICRC and UN Human Rights websites for developments in IHL and human rights practices across the world.

Further issues

- Are wars caused mainly by economics, politics or geography?
- Are children, the elderly and the wounded adequately protected by IHL?
- Should it be just as much a criminal offence to injure someone in wartime as in peacetime?
- Why might countries such as China, Russia, India and the USA choose not to join the ICC?

A force for good

You will learn about:

- the effectiveness of UK action through the UN and other bodies in undertaking debt relief and peacekeeping
- the need for humanitarian aid and how it is provided.

What's the issue? Should we 'write off' third world debts?

Some of the world's poorest countries (sometimes called heavily indebted poor countries, or **HIPCs**) have borrowed enormous sums of money from wealthier countries. In 1999–2000 they were spending up to 50% or more of their export earnings on interest on such debts – and hardly reducing the debt at all. The UK led calls for these debts to be cancelled in full and the good news is that, in countries receiving this debt relief, initiatives to reduce poverty doubled between 1999 and 2005. Progress is very slow though.

Here you can see some of the ways countries have used the debt money they have saved:

- Tanzania used savings to eliminate school fees, hire more teachers, and build more schools.
- Burkina Faso drastically reduced the cost of life-saving drugs and increased access to clean water.
- Uganda more than doubled school enrolment.
- Zambia used savings to drastically increase its investment in health, education, and rural infrastructure.

Countries which currently qualify for HIPC relief

Countries which are eligible for HIPC relief but have not yet met the necessary conditions

Countries which debt campaigners wish to see added to HIPC list

Heavily indebted poor countries
Source: adapted from http://news.bbc.co.uk

Activity

Look at the DFID (Department for International Development) and UN websites to find out the current state of debt-reduction policies.

- Why can developing countries not solve their own problems?

- Why should rich countries give aid or cancel debts to developing countries?

- Why have debt reduction programmes made less progress than was generally hoped?

UN Peacekeeping

UK troops and diplomats are highly trained. As part of our commitment to world peace, UK troops have been sent to many conflicts in different parts of the world – such as former Yugoslavia, Afghanistan, Cyprus and Sierra Leone. They are not fighting for the UK but are part of an international force such as the North Atlantic Treaty Organisation (NATO) or the UN.

UK forces are part of NATO's UN mandated International Security Assistance Force (ISAF) in Afghanistan.

There are five different types of activity which can be part of peacekeeping:

- *Conflict prevention* involves working to keep disputes from turning into violent conflict.
- **Peacemaking** involves working to make the different sides in a conflict start to negotiate.
- **Peacekeeping** happens when the peacemakers have been successful and the fighting has stopped. It usually involves working with police and civilians.
- **Peace enforcement** involves the use, authorised by the UN Security Council, of force to restore international peace and security.
- **Peacebuilding** involves working to keep an agreement going and helping a country to become more stable by functioning as normally as possible.

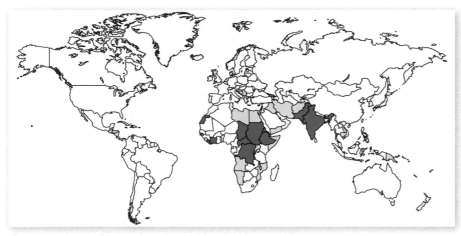

Current and past UN peacekeeping missions in March 2008
Dark Blue = Current UN peacekeeping missions
Light Blue = Former UN peacekeeping missions

Humanitarian aid

Humanitarian aid can suddenly be urgently needed. This may be because of:

- severe flooding (e.g. in Myanmar following the cyclone Nargis)
- serious earthquakes (e.g. in Pakistan in 2008)
- a tsunami (e.g. the one that hit Indonesia, Sri Lanka, India and Thailand in 2004)
- harvest failures (e.g. in Zimbabwe in 2007 and 2008).

The need may be to rescue people, to provide them with healthcare, clothing or housing, and to feed them. The UK government is the largest donor to the UN Central Emergency Response Fund (CERF), which provides humanitarian agencies with funds to respond immediately to sudden disasters. Aid is also provided by voluntary organisations such as the Red Cross, Christian Aid or Oxfam.

Where people flee in large numbers from their own homes, their need for humanitarian aid becomes the concern of the **United Nations High Commissioner for Refugees (UNHCR)** which in 2007 reported that over 21 million people were currently refugees. Of these, 8 million were in Asia, 4.7 million in Europe, 5 million in Africa, and 2.5 million in South America.

A call to conscience

You will learn about:
- the challenges facing the UN, EU and global community
- the relationship between More Economically Developed Countries (MEDCs) and Less Economically Developed Countries (LEDCs) in terms of trade and aid.

What's the issue? Life expectancy

Country	Life expectancy	Country	Life expectancy	Country	Life expectancy
Japan	82.67	Denmark	78.13	Vietnam	71.33
Australia	81.53	Ireland	78.07	Iraq	69.62
Canada	81.16	Portugal	78.04	India	69.25
France	80.87	European Union (average)	77.32	Ukraine	68.06
Israel	80.61	Cuba	77.27	World average	66.26
Sweden	80.74	Czech Republic	76.62	Pakistan	64.13
Iceland	80.55	Russia	65.94	Bangladesh	63.21
New Zealand	80.24	Mexico	75.84	Ghana	59.49
Italy	80.07	Poland	75.41	Kenya	56.64
Spain	79.92	Algeria	73.77	DR Congo	53.98
Germany	79.10	Jamaica	73.59	South Africa	48.89
UK	78.85	China	73.18	Zimbabwe	44.28
Finland	78.82	Estonia	72.56	Afghanistan	44.21
South Korea	78.64	North Korea	72.20	Sierra Leone	40.93
USA	78.14	Egypt	71.85	Swaziland	31.99

Estimated life expectancy for a child born on 18 December 2008 in selected countries. Green highlights G7 countries
Source adapted from https://www.cia.gov/library/publications/the-world-factbook/rankorder/2102rank.html

- On average, a newborn baby born anywhere in the world, would live 11 more years if born in an EU country. If born in Japan the baby would live to 82 (16 years more than the world average).

- In areas with low **life expectancy**, there can be great inequality and conflicts may occur over which group has most of the scarce resources.

- The figures for men and women are combined – in the UK women typically live longer than men.

- The averages also combine different groups – in South Africa, it is likely that white people live longer than black.

- There can be big variations within a country. In the UK, life expectancy in wealthy areas is 15 years higher than in some poorer areas such as Stoke-on-Trent or Glasgow. Life expectancy varies with health care, quality of public services, housing, wealth, and so on.

- Why is life expectancy higher in **G7** countries?

- Why is life expectancy in the EU different from the world average?

- What do many of the countries with life expectancy below the world average have in common?

Activity

Research the reasons why, in spite of the human right to life, life expectancy is six years higher in South Korea than North Korea.

Investigate why, although Cuba is much poorer than the USA, average life expectancy is quite similar.

MEDCs and LEDCs

In **MEDCs** workers tend to be more specialised – and so more productive. This is known as **division of labour**, where individual **employees** concentrate on what they do best. Employers can then afford to pay higher wages.

The greater a country's economic development, the higher up the life expectancy tables it is likely to be. Even if many of its population are ageing or have health problems such as HIV/AIDS, it will have the resources to provide good-quality care – in contrast to LEDCs, where HIV/AIDS continues to reduce life expectancy.

Trade or aid?

When a sudden disaster occurs, any country welcomes aid. Even the USA did when Hurricane Katrina devastated New Orleans in 2005. In the longer term, however, trade is more likely to help a country grow than aid. Giving a farmer food to eat every week would be a kindness but giving him or her skills, seeds, tools and a clean water supply will enable them to grow crops, join a fair-trade co-operative and – if he or she and their family work hard – to prosper without hand-outs. Because trade is so important in helping developing countries to achieve a higher level of average income, the **World Trade Organisation (WTO)** has been trying to increase trade. It does this by reducing the **tariffs** (taxes) which MEDCs impose on goods from LEDCs to protect their own industries from competition, and by reducing the subsidies which MEDCs give to their industries so that they can sell more to LEDCs at lower prices. Progress is very slow, though, and some countries resist.

Hurricane Katrina devastated New Orleans

World population

The top 20 countries in the world in 2009 in terms of population (in millions) are China (1338), India (1166), USA (307), Indonesia (240), Brazil (198), Pakistan (176), Bangladesh (156), Nigeria (149), Russia (140), Japan (127), Mexico (111), Philippines (97), Vietnam (86), Ethiopia (85), Egypt (83), Germany (82), Turkey (76), Democratic Republic of Congo (68), Iran (66), Thailand (65) – of which only three are G7 members (USA, Germany and Japan) and at least half are LEDCs.

Meeting the needs of a large population is a challenge for all countries but more so for a poor country where services are often very limited. Several of the countries in this list have, however, established an impressive rate of growth since 2000; particularly China, India, Russia and Brazil who are now part of the wealthier group of countries known as the **G20**. **Multinational companies** like BP, Shell, McDonald's, Coca Cola, Adidas, Nike and HSBC often want to invest in developing countries as a way of making more profits and maximising their 'global reach'. However, some multinationals have been accused of taking advantage of poor countries, using them for cheap labour and creating 'sweat shops'.

In the UK a house might be built by different groups of workers, each specialising in a trade, e.g. architects, foundation workers, bricklayers, plumbers, carpenters/joiners, electricians, painters/ decorators and landscapers. How might a house be built in an LEDC?

Review and research

The checklist
- Life expectancy varies greatly between developed and developing countries.
- MEDCs tend to be wealthier, partly because they can have a specialised workforce.
- Aid is best limited to short-term needs; trade is the best way for most economies to grow.

Further issues
- What steps could a country take to increase the life expectancy of its population?
- Why might a high level of life expectancy be seen as a disadvantage?
- Do multinational companies help developing countries in the long run?

Taking it further
Find out how life expectancy statistics have changed between any two countries over the past 20 years. What is the life expectancy in the area where you live? Has it risen or fallen in recent years?

Source A: Climate change is on the way...

- Fossil fuels cause greenhouse gases to warm the planet, leading to climate change which results in spreading deserts, rising temperatures, melting icecaps, violent hurricanes, serious flooding and rising sea levels. Climate change means wheat can now be grown in Iceland.

- As the planet warms up, areas of permafrost (long-frozen areas of land) thaw out, releasing methane which is twenty times more damaging than carbon dioxide, making things even worse.

- China is now building two new coal-fired power stations a week.

- World leaders haven't agreed new targets to cut gas emissions partly because developing countries such as India and China say it's not fair they should have to cut back when the problem was caused originally by developed countries such as the UK, France, Germany and the USA, who should do more.

- If all the world's ice melted, sea levels would rise and much of Britain and Ireland would be flooded, with odd-shaped islands replacing roads, railways, towns, homes and factories – the map would be totally changed.

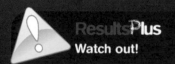

ResultsPlus
Watch out!

Sometimes multiple choice questions relate to a passage; sometimes they are set separately to test knowledge and understanding as these two questions are. Always give an answer to multiple choice questions – marks will not be deducted if you give the wrong answer.

(a) What is 'interest'?   (1)

A Money we borrow

B Money we lend

C The price we pay to a lender for borrowing money

D The price we pay to a borrower for lending money

(b) What is 'inflation'?   (1)

A Falling prices

B Falling production

C Rising prices

D Rising production

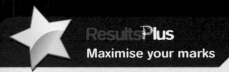

(c) Write an extract from Source A containing *one* fact and no opinion. (1)

(d) In what ways does a fact differ from an opinion? (2)

(e) Explain why large parts of Britain and Ireland could be lost to the sea by the year 2100. (2)

(f) Using the source and your own knowledge, explain why developing countries might say that demands that they should cut greenhouse gas emissions are an ethical issue. (3)

Student answer	Examiner comments	Build a better answer
(c) If all the world's ice melted, sea levels would rise and much of Britain and Ireland would be flooded, with odd-shaped islands replacing roads, railways, towns, homes and factories – the map would be totally changed.	■ The question asks for just one fact and no opinion. The extract quoted contains some opinions when it refers to 'odd-shaped islands' and 'the map would be totally changed'. Both statements are opinions because they are not generally agreed – some people might not consider the new islands 'odd-shaped' and the change to the map might not be agreed by everyone to be 'total'.	△ If all the world's ice melted, sea levels would rise.
(d) A fact is true while an opinion may be true.	● It is good to recognise that a fact is true but it would be better to say that it can be proved. An opinion is something that would not be generally agreed and in most cases cannot be proved or verified because it is a value judgment.	△ A fact is a statement that can be proved. This is not true of an opinion, which is a statement of values.
(e) Melting ice is likely to increase sea levels.	● This statement is true but the question requires explanation. This answer will only get one mark because an explanation of why sea levels will rise is needed for two marks.	△ Large parts of Britain and Ireland could be lost to the sea by 2100 if polar ice-caps melt, causing sea levels to rise and flood low lying land; the map of the UK would then look very different.
(f) Yes it is an ethical issue because ethical issues are about values – right and wrong.	■ This answer is a reasonable start which might gain one mark but it needs to go much further and add something like 'Greenhouse gases have been building up over hundreds of years as technology has developed power sources based on use of fossil fuels so developed countries are more responsible than today's developing countries; it would be unfair for developing countries to be asked to take the blame.'	△ An ethical question is one with a moral judgment of right or wrong. More of the damage was caused by developed countries over many years (before the dangers were understood) than developing countries more recently. But damage to the planet now is just as bad whoever causes it – we're all in this together.

examzone

Know Zone

Practice Exam Question

'Even in a small country such as the UK, living in a community can sometimes be a very different experience from one place to another.'

Do you agree with this view? Give reasons for your opinion, showing you have considered another point of view. (12)

To answer the question above, you could consider the following points and other information of your own.

- Do communities only exist in a specific geographical area?
- What do communities have in common? How do they communicate?
- What differences exist between geographical communities?

- How and why does life in a community change over time?
- Is it communities that change, or individuals, or both?

Getting started

- Think about the material in Chapter 13 and the work you did in class on this topic.
- Focus on the key issue in the question: *can* living in a community sometimes be a *very different* experience from one place to another? Think about your own community and different communities you belong to.
- A successful answer will need to focus on why, how and in what circumstances this might happen.
- If you answer the 'mini-questions', don't forget to tie all your points together before the end to make sure you do answer the main question.
- Even if you totally agree (or disagree) with the statement, you will lose a lot of marks if you do not look at the issue from different viewpoints in your answer, including both 'for' and 'against' points.
- Make sure your conclusion gives a clear 'yes' or 'no' to say whether you do or do not agree with the opening idea. It's important to commit yourself to a clear view at the end.

Introduction

From the start of your answer, focus on the key words in the question. Always show you are aware of more than one viewpoint. In the introduction, you can suggest what your conclusion will be, but state your *reasons* for reaching the conclusion nearer the end of the answer.

Student answer

A community is a group of people who are in close contact – they might all live in the same village or suburb or if they live at further distance from each other they may all speak the same language, e.g. Gaelic, Welsh or Chinese, and share the same interests or values. The link that unites them may be their religion, ethnicity, type of employment, beliefs or hobbies – and can be shared over the Internet if they do not live near to each other.

Examiner comment

Starting off with a definition is a good idea (and this one is comprehensive) but it doesn't give the answer a sense of direction – we can't see (yet) whether the student agrees or disagrees with the quotation in the question or whether the answer will contain a 'debate' between different points of view. You'll need to develop these points in your main answer.

Main body

Your answer has to establish a few clear points and the arguments you give must be supported with evidence. Your whole answer needs to focus on answering the main question, even if your strategy for this involves addressing the 'mini-questions'. You must include contrasting points in your answer and your conclusion needs to show clearly why you believe one argument is stronger than the other.

Student answer

Communities usually have shared loyalties, language and culture. If you were a miner in Wales, your community would not be very different from that of a mining community in Yorkshire. The same is true of a fishing community in Cornwall compared to a fishing community on the coast near Aberdeen. Living on a poor council or housing association estate in Dagenham will have a lot in common with a similar estate at Castle Vale in Birmingham. If you live in a small village in Suffolk, it may feel very much the same as living in a small village in Shropshire. If you live in a Bangladeshi community in Manchester, Leeds, Leicester or Hull, these communities will have a lot in common.

Communities change – as mines close, their communities change. Mining families sharing the same community centre, the same loyalties, the same lifestyles and the same dangers are not the same when people's interests and lives separate as the former miners get replacement jobs as lorry drivers, call centre workers, bus drivers or security guards or as some remain bitter and unemployed.

Individual friends will probably stay friends but when their interests are different and the things they had in common disappear, the community spirit becomes much weaker.

Examiner comment

The first two paragraphs make their points effectively. The third paragraph is vague and needs to be developed further. The answer never really explains how 'loyalties' work or the part communication plays in a community or how the Internet can bring a community together. There is some attempt to demonstrate differences – but is this a clear 'for' and 'against' the view expressed in the question?

Conclusion

In a conclusion the answer always needs to refer back clearly to the main question:

Student answer

So yes, even in a small country such as the UK, living in a community can sometimes be a very different experience from one place to another. Living in an inner city surrounded by graffiti has to be different from living in luxury in a big house in the country.

Examiner comment

It is good that the conclusion does refer back to the question but the rest of the comments seem to be more about housing or lifestyles without showing how these elements relate to communities. Overall this answer would gain about half marks. It is well expressed, makes some good points and does hint at differences but the second part is much weaker than the first, mostly because the points made are not specific enough and particularly how they help to answer the question.

Over to you

Chapter 15 will help you answer this question.

'In wartime military leaders and governments are more concerned with warring than with International Humanitarian Law.'

Do you agree with this view? Give reasons for your opinion, showing you have considered another point of view. (12)

To answer the question above, you could consider the following points and other information of your own.

- What is International Humanitarian Law and what actions and behaviour does it cover?

- In what ways does International Humanitarian Law change the basis of warfare?

- What might happen to someone found guilty of breaking International Humanitarian Law?

- What is the significance of the Geneva Conventions for participants in wars?

Participation in Society

Unit 2 gives you the opportunity to be active in your local community and to make a difference. Your local community could be your school, college, or local town or village. You'll be building on what you've learned in Unit 1, but whilst Unit 1 is about knowledge, and your exam, this unit is about *skills*.

What skills?

The skills that make up Unit 2 are:

Enquiry

This means finding out about an issue from different sources and involves questioning and evaluating different viewpoints.

Example

Chloe watched the news and saw a report on the effects of war on children in Uganda following a number of abductions. She decided to focus on this issue for Unit 2 and to complete an enquiry. First, after discussion with her teacher, she did a website search and found some articles on a national news website. This led her to a specific charity that supported the rights of children in Uganda and which quoted the children's views.

Her enquiries gave her greater understanding of the problems including realising that different governments in the region held different views on how and when children should be returned to their families.

Her enquiry led to her being able to produce evidence from the news website and the charity, and to be able to evaluate different viewpoints from the charity, the children, and different governments in the area.

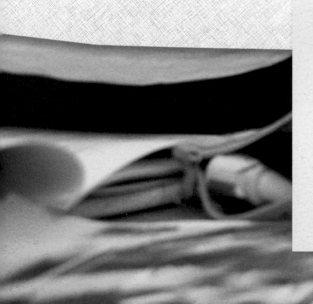

Advocacy and representation

This is about being able to explain viewpoints to others and present a view that might not be your own.

Example

Ahmed discovered that his local council did not recycle very much and decided to find out what his neighbours thought. After some discussions he discovered that roughly half of his neighbours were in favour of recycling, but half thought that it was a bad idea. Of those who disagreed, some thought it caused more pollution than throwing the rubbish away.

Ahmed did some web research with some other students he was working with on this Unit 2 project, to find out about the different arguments. Together they presented all the arguments to their class, including the views they didn't agree with.

Taking informed and responsible action

This is researching, planning and initiating action to address a citizenship issue and involves negotiating and deciding on the action, assessing the action and reflecting critically on the action when complete.

Example

David wanted to do something for his local community centre to promote diversity within his local community for his Unit 2 controlled assessment. He spoke to the community centre organiser and they agreed that it would be good if David could make a display to promote diversity.

David worked with his school who helped him to set up a meeting inviting representatives from the different communities. Following David's suggestion and some discussion, each community agreed to contribute to the display. (Negotiation)

After the display had been put up, David and his group created and conducted a brief survey to find out what people thought about the display and whether people had a better understanding of different cultures. (Reflecting critically)

No exam?

There's no exam for Unit 2. Instead you'll take a *controlled assessment* which will be 60% of your Short Course, or 30% of your Full Course GCSE. This means that you'll need to make sure you collect the right evidence of what you've done, and submit this evidence, with some writing, on a response form.

It's called controlled assessment because you'll gather your evidence and do your writing in class, not at home.

How do I choose what to do?

There are *five stages* to preparing for your controlled assessment.

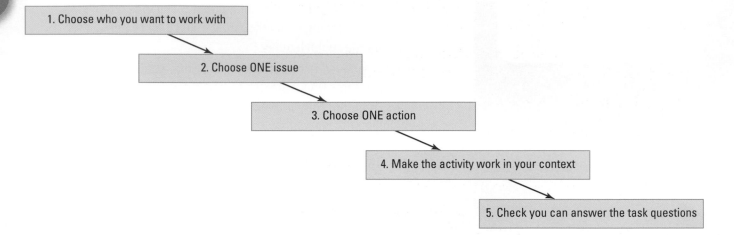

A: Choose who you want to work with

You can complete Unit 2 by yourself or you can work in a group. Remember though that you have to pull together your evidence and write your controlled assessment by yourself.

There are advantages to working alone if you have an issue that really interests you but not others.

There are advantages to working with other people if you have different points of view, which can make discussion interesting! You can also share the work, as long as you have enough of your own evidence to answer the controlled assessment questions.

B: Choose ONE issue

You need to choose *one* issue that relates to one of the nine *range and content areas* from the specification.

If you've studied Unit 1 you'll recognise these areas because they relate to the content of Unit 1. You don't have to learn new content in Unit 2!

It's important to choose a citizenship issue that's important to you.

The nine range and content areas from the specification are listed opposite. As you read them, think about what you've learned in Unit 1. Are these areas important locally and nationally?

Examiner speak

What is a citizenship issue?

A citizenship issue is any issue relating to the nine range and content areas, and therefore to the three themes in Unit 1. It could be a well-known problem or question, or a statement of fact.

1 Political, legal and human rights and freedoms in a range of contexts from local to global (see pages 10–41).

2 Civil and criminal law and the justice system – police, youth offending teams, courts, lawyers, prisons and probation (see pages 56–67).

3 Democratic and electoral processes and the operation of parliamentary democracy (see pages 68–87).

4 The development, and struggle for, different types of freedoms both in the UK and abroad (see pages 10–41, 104–107 and 116–121).

5 The media (see pages 48–55).

6 Policies and practices for sustainable development (see pages 92–97).

7 The economy in relation to citizenship and the relationship between employers and employees (see pages 26–29 and 98–103).

8 Origins and implications of diversity and the changing nature of society in the UK (see pages 10–25 and 104–107).

9 The European Union, the Commonwealth and the UN (see pages 30–35 and 108–121).

Look at the nine areas again. This time, you'll see some ideas of how these range and content areas might relate to a citizenship issue that you could study for your controlled assessment task in Unit 2.

Range and content	Issue
1 Political, legal and human rights and freedoms in a range of contexts from local to global.	How does war overseas affect children's rights?
2 Civil and criminal law and the justice system – police, youth offending teams, courts, lawyers, prisons and probation.	Should young offenders be given a prison sentence or a community punishment?
3 Democratic and electoral processes and the operation of parliamentary democracy.	Elections to a school council.
4 The development, and struggle for, different types of freedoms both in the UK and abroad.	The diversity of a local community in the UK.
5 The media.	Does your local newspaper represent the views of old people?
6 Policies and practices for sustainable development.	Is recycling worthwhile?
7 The economy in relation to citizenship and the relationship between employers and employees.	Is it right for people to go on strike?
8 Origins and implications of diversity and the changing nature of society in the UK.	How can we make sure that people understand each other's religious beliefs?
9 The European Union, the Commonwealth and the UN.	Should the UK still be a member of the EU?

Try to think of some other issues for the nine areas. You may have talked in class about some of the issues raised in Unit 1. It's important that the issue you choose is relevant and interesting to you (and your group).

130

C: Choose ONE action

You might now have an idea of what issue you'd like to focus on, or maybe you're still making up your mind.

Choosing an action will help you to make your decision. This will be the main focus of Unit 2 and has to be an action that is relevant to your issue. You only need to choose one action.

Here are the actions to choose from:

1 Presenting a case to others about a concern.
2 Conducting a consultation, vote or election.
3 Organising a meeting, event or forum to raise awareness and debate issues.
4 Representing the views of others at a meeting or event.
5 Creating, reviewing or revisiting an organisational policy.
6 Contributing to local community policies.
7 Lobbying and communicating views publicly via a website or display.
8 Setting up an action group or network.
9 Training others in democratic skills such as advocacy, campaigning or leadership.

Let's take an issue from the list on page 129.

Is it right for people to go on strike?

Which action would help you to address this issue?

You could:

* conduct a consultation, vote or election
* organise a meeting, event or forum to raise awareness and debate issues
* represent the views of others at a meeting or event.

Think about how these actions might be used to address the issue.

If you've chosen an issue, think about which of the actions might be appropriate. This next table has some possible actions for each of the issues. Remember that these are just suggestions – there are many different actions that can address an issue.

Range and content	Issue	Action
1 Political, legal and human rights and freedoms in a range of contexts from local to global.	How does war overseas affect children's rights?	Organising a meeting, event or forum to raise awareness and debate issues.
2 Civil and criminal law and the justice system – police, youth offending teams, courts, lawyers, prisons and probation.	Should young offenders be given a prison sentence or a community punishment?	Presenting a case to others about a concern.
3 Democratic and electoral processes and the operation of parliamentary democracy.	Elections to a school council.	Conducting a consultation, vote or election.
4 The development, and struggle for, different types of freedoms both in the UK and abroad.	The diversity of a local community in the UK.	Lobbying and communicating views publicly via a website or display.
5 The media	Does your local newspaper represent the views of old people?	Training others in democratic skills such as advocacy, campaigning or leadership.
6 Policies and practices for sustainable development.	Is recycling worthwhile?	Contributing to local community policies.
7 The economy in relation to citizenship and the relationship between employers and employees.	Is it right for people to go on strike?	Representing the views of others at a meeting or event.
8 Origins and implications of diversity and the changing nature of society in the UK.	How can we make sure that people understand each other's religious beliefs?	Creating, reviewing or revisiting an organisational policy.
9 The European Union, the Commonwealth and the UN.	Should the UK still be a member of the EU?	Setting up an action group or network.

D: Make the action work in your context

Every school and college is different, just as every area of the UK is different. This means that you have to make your Unit 2 activity work where you are. The table below shows how you might put your issue into an appropriate context for your school or college.

If you've chosen your issue and action, your context might be different – there are many different ways of being active in citizenship.

Range and content	Issue	Action	Context
1 Political, legal and human rights and freedoms in a range of contexts from local to global.	How does war overseas affect children's rights?	Organising a meeting, event or forum to raise awareness and debate issues.	You could organise a fundraising event, inviting a charity representative to introduce the event, and follow it up with a debate of the issues.
2 Civil and criminal law and the justice system – police, youth offending teams, courts, lawyers, prisons and probation.	Should young offenders be given a prison sentence or a community punishment?	Presenting a case to others about a concern.	In school, as part of a group, you might set up a meeting in which you present a case and take questions.
3 Democratic and electoral processes and the operation of parliamentary democracy.	Elections to a school council.	Conducting a consultation, vote or election.	You might stage an election in your college, organising hustings and a vote.
4 The development, and struggle for, different types of freedoms both in the UK and abroad.	The diversity of a local community in the UK.	Lobbying and communicating views publicly via a website or display.	You and your group could create a display in a local community centre representing the diversity of the local population.

Range and content	Issue	Action	Context
5 The media	Does your local newspaper represent the views of old people?	Training others in democratic skills such as advocacy, campaigning or leadership.	You and your group could canvass older people in a local community centre and help them to be better heard by establishing a petition, or enabling them to make contact with the newspaper.
6 Policies and practices for sustainable development.	Is recycling worthwhile?	Contributing to local community policies.	You could attend a local council meeting and make your views heard, and respond to a consultation process.
7 The economy in relation to citizenship and the relationship between employers and employees.	Is it right for people to go on strike?	Representing the views of others at a meeting or event.	In school you might set up a meeting to explain why people go on strike. If you have some views from strikers, you'd be representing the views of others.
8 Origins and implications of diversity and the changing nature of society in the UK.	How can we make sure that people understand each other's religious beliefs?	Creating, reviewing or revisiting an organisational policy.	You could review and update your school/ college policy on religious tolerance.
9 The European Union, the Commonwealth and the UN.	Should the UK still be a member of the EU?	Setting up an action group or network.	You could set up an online network or forum to debate the issue of EU membership.

E: Check you can answer the task questions

The task questions are the questions that appear on the exam paper. There are four of them.

1: Enquire into the citizenship issue (10 marks)

This section allows you to find out about the issue you have chosen, collect information and viewpoints and express your own opinion. You need to make sure that you select relevant parts of the issues and communicate them clearly, saying why they are important locally and nationally. You should clearly state the links between the issue and the citizenship themes you learned in Unit 1.

You need to produce evidence of your issue. This could be in the form of:

- leaflets
- newspaper articles
- websites
- video or audio recordings of people involved.

Your evidence should show that you understand why the issue is important and the different views about it, both locally and nationally.

Examiner hints

- You will get marks for your knowledge of the citizenship issue that you choose.

- To reach the top level you need to show understanding of values, ideas and viewpoints, both locally and nationally, related to your issue.

- You need to make the links to the citizenship themes you studied in Unit 1.

- There's no need to attach a lot of evidence – one or two more detailed pieces are better than lots of evidence that's only partly related to your issue.

2: Application of skills of advocacy and representation (15 marks)

You need to communicate with *two* different people in positions of authority on the issue and find out why they have these opinions. Try to present more than one viewpoint, and make sure you provide evidence of why these people have these views.

It is important to provide evidence that you can communicate clearly with these people. It's not enough to describe your meeting – you will need

Examiner speak

What is 'advocacy'?

Advocacy is the act of speaking to present an idea or cause that may or may not be your own.

independent evidence such as a video or audio recording, or a signed witness testimony or observation record. You must include evidence of your own contribution (e.g. the questions you asked), not just what the other person says.

Appendix B: Witness testimony/statements

Candidate name:	Candidate number:

Unit title:

Activity context:

Assessment evidence:

Observation notes:

Witness: _____	Signature: _____
Job role: _____	Date: _____

Assessor comments:

Assessor: _____	Signature: _____
	Date: _____

Appendix E – Observation records

Candidate name: Ian Barnes

Unit title: Unit 2: Marketing in Leisure and Tourism

Activity context: The above named student was asked to work in pairs and give a presentation on the marketing mix of their selected organisation. The organisation selected was Alton Towers.

Assessment criteria: Describe the 4Ps in relation to the selected organisation and show how they work together to meet the organisation's objectives.

Activity: Ian outlined three of the organisation's objectives. Ian described in detail the products of Alton Towers.

Ian also described the price element of Alton Towers. He gave details of the price of rooms and the restaurant at the hotel. He described entrance prices to the theme park for different types of client. he also described the prices of food and merchandise.

His colleague in the presentation described promotion and place. To confirm that Ian also had understanding of these elements of the marketing mix, I asked Ian questions relating to both promotion and place. I asked Ian to explain different ways I could get to the theme park and also how I could book tickets over the Internet. I also asked him to describe how the new ride 'Air' had been promoted. Although these had been mentioned in the presentation I asked Ian to give more details. He referred to the website and gave a detailed account of its content relating to the promotion of 'Air'.

In the presentation Ian explained how product and price enabled the organisation to meet their objectives. I asked him questions relating to 'how they work together to meet the objectives'. He gave me two examples of product and price working together to meet objectives but was unable to give a satisfactory response related to all four elements of the marking mix.

Supporting evidence: Copies of visual aids are attached.

Assessment summary: Ian gave a detailed description of the 4Ps of Alton Towers. He was able to give some explanation of how elemetns of the marketing mix worked together to meet the organisation's objectives but this was limited.

Assessor: _A N Assessor_____

Signature: _A N Assessor_____

Date: _____

Then present your own viewpoint clearly and persuasively, referring to the evidence to show that your opinion is valid. There's no need to write about your communication if it's in your evidence.

3: Participate in action to address the citizenship issue (15 marks)

You include evidence of your action in this section. You need to show how you can have an impact on the issue.

Your evidence should focus on negotiation, decision making and action taking. You should also consider:

- how the group worked together
- how decisions were made
- how effectively different skills were used
- what sort of 'negotiation' took place (within a group)
- how you negotiated with school staff or local people in your action (if you worked alone).

You also need to produce evidence of your action and of the fact that you were involved in the action – it's not enough to just write about it. You should provide good quality evidence that you gathered during your participation in the action. There are different ways of doing this, such as drawing up a questionnaire, distributing it and analysing the results (which will often provide some important data) or getting an observation record or witness statement from a responsible adult such as your teacher. Or the evidence could be a video recording, a recorded observation from your teacher or evidence of the outcome of your action. You could also include notes from a meeting with your group to decide what action to take.

You will be trying to work out the *consequences* or results of the various actions that you took. These will depend on the range and quality of evidence gathered during your participation in the action.

Examiner hints

- You are assessed on how your action addresses your citizenship issue. Make sure that you fully describe how your action links to your issue.

- Your evidence should clearly show how you negotiated, decided on and took action. The evidence could include notes from a meeting with your group to decide what action to take and a witness testimony or video that details the action taken.

- Top level marks are reserved for those who produce valid evidence and clearly present the case for action.

4: Assess the impact of your own action (10 marks)

This section requires you to think about what went well and what went badly in the action taken, in the context what impact the action has had locally and beyond.

Think back to the different stages:

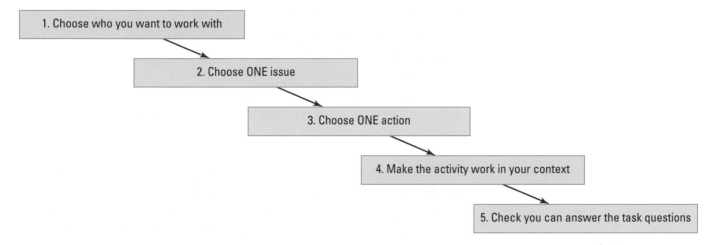

1. Choose who you want to work with
2. Choose ONE issue
3. Choose ONE action
4. Make the activity work in your context
5. Check you can answer the task questions

Then consider:

- What did you (and your group) contribute to the issue?
- Did your action support an argument? The way arguments are put forward is important and so is the ability to separate fact from opinion and to recognise the presence of bias. A number of different views might be expressed and these should be discussed and evaluated.
- What difficulties were met and, perhaps, overcome?
- Did your action make a positive impact?
- Overall, how successful was the action, at least in the short term?
- What were your views when you started, and what are your views now? How has your view changed?

You should make a considered conclusion, considering each stage in the task, and how it relates to the citizenship issues. You should think about whether your view has changed, and if so, how and why. It's important that you write clearly, accurately and use the correct citizenship terms.

Examiner speak

What does 'bias' mean?

When people give their own one-sided opinions, without taking a balanced view.

Examiner hints

- Top level responses will include a detailed and well-structured assessment of the action, and analysis of the impact of the action on your own view.

- Your response should show how your action impacted locally and nationally. For example, a national impact might be where you contributed to a national campaign at a local level.

Example actions

Now look at some examples of actions other students have chosen.

Example 1: Chloe (p126)

Issue

Chloe's Unit 2 focus is the effects of war on children in Uganda.

Chloe's action

Setting up a network.

How this will work in my context

- Digital television has meant that viewers have lots more channels to choose from. As part of a study of global citizenship, we are advised to watch selections from 24 hour news. I was very moved by pictures of children caught up in war in Uganda.
- There were two things in particular that interested me.
  (a) What rights children in Uganda had and the dangers of them being taken as child soldiers.
  (b) How vulnerable some children were, often because they lacked food and many were orphans.
- I Googled the topic using children in Uganda. This helped me to come up with research sites on the Internet.
- I then made enquiries and conducted research on my chosen topic and collected research evidence. I was also able to use newspapers online to find out more. All the time I was working to build up some evidence to include in my final work.
- In searching for evidence I was able to build up different views on the situation – my own, people in Uganda, politicians and aid organisations like the Red Cross.
- I interviewed a representative from the Red Cross and a local journalist about the perspectives in preparation for my website.
- Having built up my knowledge I felt that I wanted to share it with others in my class. This would also enable me to get a wider range of viewpoints and to have a wider discussion as part of a citizenship lesson. This helped me with advocacy and representation.
- With the help of some other students I decided to set up my own website designed especially for 16-year-olds who were interested in the rights of children in Uganda.

Example 2: Ahmed (p127)

Issue

Ahmed's Unit 2 focus is his local council's recycling policy.

Ahmed's action

Contributing to local community policies.

How this will work in my context

- My uncle is a councillor for the Rushington district of the city where my family live. We have talked about council policies. One of my interests is recycling.
- Three other people in my Citizenship class were also interested in recycling so we decided to work as a group. We discussed what we would do and agreed our roles.
- After talking to my Citizenship teacher I decided to do a study of recycling in the Rushington district.
- Besides the Internet, I was able to base my research on materials from the council and the local newspaper library.
- My enquiries led me to believe that the city council worked hard to encourage local residents to recycle, organising skips, collecting large items and providing bins for different recycling materials. I found a lot of evidence but I realise that I will have to sort this out and select the most important pieces.
- I contacted a city councillor from The Green Party. He explained the party's policies and the importance of sustainable development both now and in the future.
- Through my uncle, I had an interview with a senior member of the council's Environment and Energy Department. She explained why the council had to increase its rate of recycling instead of using landfill, why not all residents co-operated with the council's scheme and the fall in demand for some recycled materials.
- Our teacher allowed us to do a Powerpoint presentation to the class. Those who thought recycling was a waste of time put their points of view and later we had a vote.
- We worked out ways of evaluating our work and devised a questionnaire so that we could see if we had made a difference in helping to encourage recycling.

Example 3: David (p127)

Issue

David's focus is on the promotion of diversity within his local community centre using a display to promote diversity.

David's action

Lobbying and communicating views publicly via a website or display.

How this will work in my context

- In my leisure time, I attend a community centre which tries to attract people of all ages and races.
- Attendance is not very high and, after talking to the community centre organiser, I am worried that, because of the credit crunch, the council will have to close less popular centres to save money.
- I wanted to find ways of encouraging more local people to attend the community centre and to do this in a way that would help to promote diversity in our community.
- Two other members of my Citizenship class, who also attend the community centre, were also interested and we decided to form a group.
- I decided to find out as much as I could about local community centres in the area. I was able to use the council's website and the local library to find out information and gather evidence.
- First I arranged to meet the organiser from a community centre that seemed to be very successful. This provided me with more evidence to support my ideas.
- Through my Citizenship teacher and Head of Year, a meeting was arranged with representatives from different groups in the community.
- It was decided as a result of our discussions to set up displays both in my school, arranged by our group, and the community centre. These displays were publicised in the school newsletter and by community representatives. The displays ran for a week. I negotiated this arrangement with the Assistant Head.

- We needed to evaluate the impact of our display, although we realised that our actions would need to be judged over a longer period when, hopefully, more people would come to the community centre and would represent more diversity.
- We also wanted to find out how much people had a better understanding of different cultures as a result of the displays. To help us do this, we did a survey using a questionnaire to which we all contributed.

Final checklist

Now copy this checklist, fill it in and decide your action for Unit 2.
Good Luck!

1 Choose who you want to work with	
2 Choose ONE issue	
3 Choose ONE action	
4 Make the activity work in your context	
5 Check you can answer the task questions	

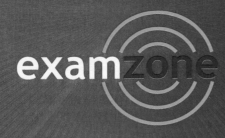

Welcome to ExamZone! Revising for your exams can sometimes be a scary prospect. In this section of the book we'll take you through the best way of revising for your exams, step-by-step, to ensure you get the best results that you can achieve.

142

"I used to think I was no good at revision. I got distracted and worried about the actual exam and panicked. I thought I was going to forget everything as soon as I arrived in the exam room. But for the mock exams I got myself sorted, planned it out, knew what I was doing and it worked OK." Alfie, GCSE student

Have you ever had that same feeling in any activity in your life when a challenging task feels easy, and you feel totally absorbed in the task, without worrying about all the other issues in your life? This is a feeling familiar to many athletes and performers, and is one that they strive hard to recreate in order to perform at their very best. It's a feeling of being 'in the zone'.

On the other hand, we all know what it feels like when our brains start running away when we are under pressure. We end up saying lots of negative things like 'I've always been bad at exams', or 'I know I am going to forget everything I thought I knew when I look at the exam paper' — as Alfie did until he worked out that making a plan and sticking to it can make all the difference.

The good news is that 'being in the zone' can be achieved by taking some steps in advance of the exam. Here are our top tips on getting 'into the zone':

- First — start early. The biggest problem facing many students is that they don't give themselves enough time to get everything done. Alfie started earlier than his friends and was pleased he did so when they started to run out of time.

- Be familiar with how the exam will be run, how many questions you will need to answer, what sort of questions they will be and whether you need to answer in two or three lines or at greater length — then you can work out what revision you need to do. This will give you confidence and also help you to organise your time. These pages will help you to do well in the exam.

- Think about the issues in your life that may interfere with revision. Write them all down. Then think about how you can deal with each so they don't affect your revision. Share your revision plan with your friends and family so they know when you want to revise. Don't let them distract you from revising — then you can have more quality time with them when you have done the work planned for that day or week and you won't be worrying about what you should be doing.

- You might not be able to deal with everything. For example, you may be worried about a friend or relative who is ill. Try to focus on your exam goals and understand that you can't do everything at once! Focussing on your goals and what you want to achieve will help you to concentrate on the tasks at hand.

- Use your revision time not just to read and revise content but make brief notes, then reduce these notes to even shorter notes which you can learn. Be systematic about it.

- Look at past questions, answer them in note form and check your answer against a mark scheme or ask your teacher.

- Make sure you eat well and exercise! If your body is not in the right state, how can your mind be?

Planning Zone

The key to success in exams and revision often lies in the right planning. Knowing what you need to do and when you need to do it is your best path to a stress-free

JUNE

SUNDAY

✓ Find out your exam dates. Check with your teacher.

✓ Draw up a calendar or list of all the dates from when you will start your revision through to your exams.

• First of all, know your strengths and weaknesses. Go through each topic making a list of how well you think you know the topic. Look at your notes and use your mock examination results and/or any further tests that are available to you as a check on your self-assessment. This will help you to plan your personal revision effectively by putting more time into your weaker areas.

✓ Give yourself regular breaks or different activities to give your life some variety. Revision need not be a prison sentence!

✓ Chunk your revision in each subject down into smaller sections. This will make it more manageable and less daunting. In Citizenship Studies you could follow the order of Themes (1.Rights & Responsibilities, 2.Power, politics and the media, 3.The Global Community) and sub-divisions within topics in the specification, which is clearly divided up already. Revise one chunk at a time, but make sure you give more time to topics that you have identified weaknesses in.

✓ Be realistic in how much time you can devote to your revision, but also make sure you put in enough time. That's why you need to start early and build up a good set of notes to work from. Use the glossary in this book to help you learn key terms on which there may be questions.

✓ Also make time for considering how topics fit together. In Citizenship Studies, ideas such as democracy and justice, identities and diversity and rights and responsibilities cut across everything in all three themes. You will be tested in the exam on how well you can link related ideas together and can gain valuable marks by showing you can do this.

Try the Keyword Quiz again

✓ Make sure you know what types of questions will be on the exam paper. Practice answering past exam questions and time yourself doing them (unless, like Alfie, you just write practice exam answers in note form so you can cover more ground). It is important to learn how to tackle the exam as well as learning about the subject.

EXAM DAY!

• Finally (and this is the fun part, I promise!) follow the plan! You can use the Know Zone revision section in the following pages to kick-start your revision and for some great ideas for helping you to revise and remember key points. Good Luck!

28

29

30

31

In the Unit 1 Citizenship Studies exam you will have one hour in which to answer 4 questions and you should spend about a quarter of your time on each. You must answer all parts of Questions 1, 2 and 3:

- Question 1 will be based on Rights and Responsibilities,
- Question 2 will be based on Power, Politics and Media and
- Question 3 will be based on The Global Community.

In each of these questions there will be one or two pieces of stimulus material (a paragraph of information, picture, diagram, table, etc) and seven sub-questions relating to them, all of which you must answer. The space beneath the question will indicate roughly how long your answer should be – but if you have small handwriting it is ok to write less. You do not have to fill up all the space. The more marks a sub-question carries, the longer the answer is expected to be.

Some of these sub-questions will call for short written answers, often asking you to explain a particular term or to give reasons for a particular event or development. Sometimes they may take the form of multiple choice questions in which you have to choose between four options – if you are not totally sure of the correct answer, work backwards by eliminating the choices that couldn't possibly be correct!

The fourth question asks you to write a long answer from a choice of three, one on each of the themes listed for questions 1, 2 and 3. Typically a statement is made and you are asked whether you agree. There will be four or five mini-questions which you could take into account in answering the main question. Don't get so involved in the mini-questions that you forget about the main question – and you are expected to add ideas, arguments and evidence of your own. You need to argue for and against the idea expressed in the statement and to reach a clear conclusion at the end, which refers back to the question asked; it isn't a good idea to 'sit on the fence'.

As you have worked through the book and perhaps received handouts from your teacher, you will probably have made notes of your own. As you get near to starting your own revision, you need to start making notes on your notes. Alfie had 20 pages of notes on Justice (police, probation, courts, criminal and civil law, etc) which he summarised down to 6 pages and then cut down to 2 pages, so a paragraph of 10 lines in his original notes on criminal courts may have become a few phrases in the shorter notes.

Sometimes a diagram or picture might help you remember something – at other times it may be better to produce bullet points. Sometimes people remember key points by recalling a doodle on the page! As you start to learn the key points, it's good to get friends to test you or for you to test others who are also taking the Citizenship Studies exam. If you are using the glossary in the book to learn key terms, maybe your mum or dad or brothers or sisters would test you from that (or be like Alfie and get your girlfriend or boyfriend to test you). When you start preparing to answer exam questions – especially the longer ones - try bouncing ideas off friends on the same course. Try to think about what works best for you by trialling a few of these different methods for the first topic.

Remember that each part of the specification will be tested so you should revise it all.

To be successful in the Citizenship Studies exam you need to see the subject as a jig-saw and work out how to fit together all the different pieces and topics. You can use the summaries on the next few pages as revision points to remind you of what you've covered.

Citizenship starts with individuals and we met four characters in the All about you section of the book. This was important for three reasons:

- Firstly it helped to explain the important ideas of identities & diversity, rights & responsibilities and democracy & justice.

- Second it reminded us that individuals see things differently, have different loyalties, characteristics and beliefs which make up their identity and that we all have many different identities – son, daughter, student, member of a choir or football or netball team, religion, the school we attend, ethnicity, etc.

- Third it helped us understand that communities (whether a particular town or village or as a grouping of individuals with things in common) are made up of many different individuals – if we expect to enjoy our rights, we have a responsibility that we recognise that others have similar rights.

You can use these chapter summaries as revision points to remind you of what you've covered.

Chapter 1 – A changing and diverse society emphasises how society doesn't stand still.

1. We learned that human rights mean little unless they are built into the laws of a country to also become legal rights. It's important that we treat others with respect and don't let people down, so moral rights are important.

2. Rights or freedoms mean little if the five giant evils (ignorance, ill-health, squalid housing, poverty or unemployment) have not been largely conquered – we learned to distinguish between freedom to… and freedom from… Sometimes individuals want to do things for which a minimum age currently applies in the UK.

3. To appreciate how a community can change, we looked at London's East End where many new arrivals to the UK have settled over the years. It is a strongly multicultural area – yet there are the clear signs of poverty and deprivation alongside evidence of wealth in the riverside apartments and iconic buildings such as Canary Wharf.

4. Different communities and lifestyles were highlighted, showing how political, social and economic factors are all linked, with one measure – life expectancy at birth – highlighting the effect of such factors when taken together. Well off people who lead healthy lifestyles are expected to live much longer than poorer people with less satisfactory diets who may do dangerous work or live in more crowded housing.

Chapter 2 – Consumption and Employment focuses on our rights and responsibilities as buyers and/or sellers of goods and services and also as employers and/or employees.

5. To ensure consumers are treated fairly, we now all have many rights set out in laws to prevent people being swindled either by shopkeepers or financial organisations wanting to lend us money at very high rates of interest; sellers also have rights and we need to understand these when we buy goods from them.

6. Terms such as contract of employment, dismissal, redundancy and trade unions are important and there are seven laws affecting employment: (i) Sex Discrimination Act 1975, (ii) Race Relations Act 1976, (iii) Equal Pay Act 1970, (iv) Disability Discrimination Act 1995, (v) Health and Safety at Work Act 1974, (vi) Employment Rights Act 1996 and (vii) National Minimum Wage Act 1998.

Chapter 3 – Where did our rights and freedoms come from? examines the rights we have been given by the UN Universal Declaration of Human Rights, various European bodies and also by the 1998 Human Rights Act in the UK.

7. In addition to the rights listed from the Universal Declaration of Human Rights, you could look up the full list on the UN website. There is also the UN Convention on the Rights of the Child. Generally UN Human Rights Commissioners have effectively pressured governments over human rights. A body intended to do this is the UN Council on Human Rights, though this has been criticised because neighbouring countries seem to turn a blind eye to abuses committed by their friends.

8. European and Western countries are often keener on human rights than some Asian or African countries. In Europe, citizens are covered by the European Convention on Human Rights and disputes can by settled by the European Court of Human Rights in Strasbourg. This has no connection with the European Union which also guarantees some rights and freedoms for citizens in member countries such as the UK. Any EU disputes are settled by the European Court of Justice in Luxembourg.

9. In 1998, the provisions of the European Convention were largely built into UK law by the Human Rights Act, so now 'human rights' cases can be heard by UK judges in UK courts, saving expense, cost and time for UK citizens. If the UK courts do not give the ruling citizens hope for, they can still take their case to the European Court of Human Rights, as the McLibel Two did in 2005. For those who find it difficult to access human rights, the UN has established the International Criminal Court to deal with crimes such as genocide but in 2008 countries such as the USA, China, Russia and India had yet to join.

Chapter 4 Can our rights be overruled? aims to separate theory from practice and to focus on practical realities of rights.

10. If people expect health care how much should be expected of them? Should smokers or people who eat or drink too much (and become obese) be refused treatment on the NHS? Rights may conflict, as the case of Natallie Evans and Howard Johnson demonstrated. Natallie wanted to have a child but Howard withdrew consent for embryos he had fertilised to be used.

11. The Labour government believes identity cards are essential to protect against identity fraud, illegal working and terrorism but Conservatives and Liberal Democrats disagree saying identity cards would not have stopped the London bombers in 2005 or the Madrid train bombers. The fear is that UK citizens' civil liberties are being sacrificed by government policy in an attempt to thwart terrorists.

12. Does the freedom to practice ones own religion in the UK effectively divide or unite society? The bitter disputes between Protestants and Catholics in Northern Ireland were largely overcome, thanks to the Good Friday Agreement – but there are still disputes in which different faiths sometimes object to the presentation of plays or publication of books, perhaps showing an unwelcome lack of tolerance in a multicultural society; also, practices such as female circumcision or honour killings or inciting racial or religious hatred clearly break UK laws.

13. Nowhere is the problem of freedoms clashing clearer than when we look at freedom of expression and the right of privacy. Newspapers may want to print accounts of individuals' private lives but privacy rights say they must not do so. A similar clash comes with the right to work enjoyed by UK citizens and the freedom of movement enjoyed by EU citizens from other countries.

Chapter 5 – Media representations looks at where people in the UK get news and opinions from.

14. Key features of popular and quality newspapers should be understood and you should recognise that the press is generally more biased than terrestrial broadcasters such as BBC and ITV. Often our opinions depend on empathy – putting ourselves in the position of someone else and this often occurs when we relate to a particular character in a soap such as *Eastenders* or *Coronation Street*.

15. The press can, however, be influential when they campaign for or against an issue such as the 'mosquito' device which was initially supported and then opposed because it denied young people dignity and respect. When people object to things said about them in the media they can appeal to the Press Complaints Commission or, in the case of broadcasting and/or the Internet to the regulator, Ofcom.

Chapter 6 – Public debate and policy formation investigates the idea that 'information is power' and considers ways in which public opinion is formed.

16. Being open about government proposals means that those who are for or against a proposal have a chance to put their point of view forward, something they could not do if the idea was kept secret. This is why government increasingly issues consultations, though some people question whether they take much notice of the feedback received. Often politicians try to use the media to publicise their views, though some people believe the press excessively influence the results of UK general elections.

17. There is a big debate over which types of press have the biggest impact on public opinion – the readership of many quality papers is relatively low but the readers themselves often include the most influential people in the country; but many more people read popular papers so in elections such people form an overwhelming majority. It is also debated whether opinion polls reflect or influence public opinion.

Chapter 7 – Law and Society looks at courts and those who work in them, criminal and civil law, different types of crimes and the punishments awarded to those who commit them as well as the work of the police, probation service and youth offending teams.

18. Crime statistics are hotly debated because the numbers of crimes reported to the police are only about half the number estimated by the British Crime Survey (BCS). Though the elderly are said to fear crime most, it is the young who are often the victims. There are continuing debates over laws on moral issues, such as abortion (allowed) and assisted suicide (not allowed), and whether changes are desirable.

19. It seems that for only 27% of crimes reported to the police, offenders are detected and punished; if the BCS figures are correct, the figure may be barely half that. So are more police needed? With so few offenders being caught, the possibility of being punished is hardly an effective deterrent. Could the Youth Offending Teams and the National Probation Service play a bigger or more effective role?

20. The main courts delivering justice in criminal cases need to be understood and so do the roles of judges (or magistrates), prosecution and defence teams (of solicitors or barristers) and the role and usefulness of juries is particularly important.

Sometimes a jury may feel sympathetic to an accused person and find them 'not guilty' because they do not want to see the person receive punishment in the circumstances.

21. Prisoners are more likely to have no qualifications, be unemployed, to have run away from home as a child or to suffer mental illness than the rest of the population. They are also more likely to have fewer reading, writing and number skills than an 11-year-old, so perhaps society should focus more on their social problems to get them out of the crime 'habit'. For those who do need to go to prison, make sure you understand how Grendon Prison differs from other prisons. Also look at the pros and cons of ASBOs, community punishments and the idea of restorative justice.

22. It's important to know that criminal law is about punishing those who commit crime while civil law is about family matters (e.g., divorce and adoption) or settling disputes over contracts or employment. Those who 'win' such cases get compensation or a specific decision (e.g., over a disputed land boundary) will be ordered. Look at the courts that deal with civil cases.

23. The civil disputes which you have learnt about are those concerning employment, consumer matters (contracts), divorce, custody of children, adoption and how inheritance (wills) work.

Chapter 8 – Democracy at work looks at voting, elections, political parties, MPs, parliament, law-making and government.

24. The rules for general elections are much tighter than those for *X Factor* or *Strictly Come Dancing*. You can only vote once. You have to be 18. You cannot vote by telephone. And the results decide which party will run the government and put its (perhaps very different) policies into action. In the 1950s 80% voted and almost everyone supported Labour or Conservative; in 2005 barely 60% voted and many people voted for other parties such as Liberal Democrats, Greens, UKIP and Scottish Nationalists.

25. In the 2005 geneal election Labour got 35% of the votes but received 55% of the seats – a big 'winner's bonus' caused by the first-past-the-post voting system. Try to understand how and why this happens and what steps could be taken so that a party got the same share of seats as the votes it receives as happens in elections for the European and Scottish Parliaments and the Welsh and Northern Ireland Assemblies.

26. Eleven different parties had MPs in the House of Commons in 2009 but there were 320 political parties registered with the Electoral Commission – some are serious parties aiming for representation on local councils, others stand as a joke. Some people vote for parties according to their policies for the future or their record in the past, while others are influenced most by party leaders.

27. Each MP represents an area of about 70,000 people aged 18 or over. MPs are there to speak for their party, to voice the needs and concerns of their constituency (taking up voters' complaints or grievances) and to keep an eye on government actions (asking questions and working on committees). They vote on finance matters, decide the content of new laws or whether old laws need to be replaced and some MPs also become government ministers.

28. Most government ministers are MPs from the party with most seats in the House of Commons, though a few are peers in the House of Lords. Although ministers are almost always political appointees, their departments are effectively run

by full-time civil servants, headed by a permanent secretary. The Prime Minister and about 20 senior ministers form the Cabinet which meets regularly to take policy decisions and review progress. The effectiveness of government depends on the success of the opposition in making them justify and explain their policies and decisions.

29. There are four types of laws – public bills proposed by (i) the government, or (ii) backbench MPs (sometimes called private members' bills), and (iii) private bills proposed by companies or organisations such as railways, harbours or universities (not MPs) – all of these become law when approved by the House of Commons and House of Lords and granted the Royal Assent. The fourth type is delegated legislation in which a minister writes a regulation, based on powers given previously.

Chapter 9 – Active participation influencing decisions reviews the work of pressure groups and the voluntary sector and considers the impact of demonstrations, petitions and referendums.

30. Some pressure groups have expert knowledge, so the government is pleased to receive information from them – they are called 'insider groups' and include bodies such as the National Farmers Union, Age Concern and Help the Aged and the National Society for the Prevention of Cruelty to Children. Other groups, which have strong feelings but lack expertise will have less influence over government, so they are known as 'outsider groups' including bodies such as Plane Stupid and Fathers4Justice or local groups protesting against eco-towns. When consultations and referendums are held, pressure groups work hard to sway public opinion towards their point of view

31. Much pressure group and political party campaigning activity now occurs over the Internet. Anyone who wants to start a petition to the Prime Minister can do so on the 10 Downing St website, though generally petitions and demonstrations are over-rated in terms of their real impact – probably the most successful demonstrations being those against the Community Charge ('poll tax') in the early 1990s.

Chapter 10 – Decision-making in the UK and beyond looks at local government, devolved bodies and the impact of minority and coalition governments.

32. Many councils providing services such as education, social services, fire services, police and waste management, have merged to create larger units which are said to be more efficient, but some critics say they are less democratic. Devolution, locating power in Cardiff and Edinburgh instead of London, has given Wales and Scotland a bigger say over their own affairs. These new bodies use proportional representation, so no one party has won control of the Scottish Parliament or the Welsh Assembly but coalition or minority governments appear to have operated effectively.

33. Other western countries such as France and the USA have systems that are just as democratic as ours though different in various ways. Russia has elections but prevents some candidates from standing. Elsewhere some countries have elaborate rituals, putting on a show of democracy (one party elections in North Korea, brutality and corruption in Robert Mugabe's Zimbabwe) which fools few people.

Chapter 11 – Saving our world examines the causes and consequences of global warming and actions that can be taken to reduce the extent of climate change.

34. Should the world accept that global warming is happening? Or else try to limit or reverse the trend, recognising that harmful gases include carbon dioxide, methane and nitrous oxide. Possible consequences could see raised sea levels, more extreme weather and expansion of deserts leading to extinction of animal species, melting of glaciers and polar ice caps and flooding in low-lying areas.

35. Individuals and communities can make a difference through recycling, cutting down on packaging, insulating their homes, not wasting energy and switching to public transport or car-sharing where possible. There is a big debate over whether green taxes should be used to discourage people from wasting energy.

36. International efforts have been slow to take effect, partly because many people are still in denial over the causes of global warming. You learnt about Earth Summits such as those held in Rio de Janiero (1992), Kyoto (1997) and planned for Copenhagen (2009); also the Local Agenda 21 plans in which each local area works out its own way to help arrest global warming and to support the environment.

Chapter 12 – The UK economy discusses different types of taxation, how and why benefits are paid, the activities of public and private sectors and the challenges facing economic managers in the 21st century.

37. You looked at the difference between direct taxes (e.g., income tax or council tax) and indirect taxes (e.g., VAT). Many people reduce their tax by paying money into pensions or investing in new businesses – these sound like good ideas but such rules mean that high-paid people may pay less income tax than many low-paid people, a situation strongly criticised by people such as Lib Dem leader, Nick Clegg.

38. As the share of elderly people in the population rises, the financial burden of supporting their needs falls on a shrinking number of people at work – leading to cuts in services and protests by pensioners and their families. One way of overcoming such problems is to get the private sector involved in providing care for the elderly, or running prisons or providing healthcare though some suggest that letting private companies make profits out of providing such services is wasteful and wrong.

39. The 2008/9 credit crunch showed that when economic problems occur, massive solutions are required on a global scale. The UK is raising the retirement age and is encouraging elderly people to continue working beyond the retirement age. Also, new rules have been made to allow economic migrants to come to the UK only if they have skills for which there is a shortage in the UK labour market.

Chapter 13 – Communities in the UK examines how far individuals can make a difference through personal effort, voluntary work and community activities.

40. Volunteers sometimes work for purely local projects but some do things locally to support national or international concerns such as Childline, Christian Aid, Oxfam or the Red Cross. Jane Tomlinson and Richard Harvey both made a big difference personally – look at why and how. Charities to support local projects such as a hospice or an air ambulance not only help the good causes themselves but also strengthen the local community feeling as well.

41. In the UK urban dwellers live in tower block, estates or leafy suburbs, or new or regenerated homes while in rural areas locals often find that young people cannot afford a home in their own village (because so many second home owners have moved in) and as they move away, the community's demand for the local school, shop, post office or pub diminishes, causing them to close. UK communities can also be important in supporting producers in less economically developed countries get a better return for their produce through fair trade initiatives.

Chapter 14 – The UK's role in the world discusses the UK's changing role in world affairs.

42. The UK has long been a trading nation, originally buying raw materials from overseas and manufacturing them into finished products; that pattern has changed as more multinational companies find it cheaper get their manufacturing done in low-wage countries such as India or China. The UK is still at the forefront of peacekeeping and provision of humanitarian aid and (in pursuing an ethical foreign policy) have opposed repressive regimes, though the war against Saddam Hussein's Iraq was unpopular among many people in the UK.

43. In 1972 the UK joined the EU – there are now 27 member countries and business is conducted in 23 different languages. The credit crunch in 2008/9 demonstrated the importance of countries working together. Look at the main duties of the European Commission, the European Council of Ministers and the European Parliament and both sides of the debate over the UK's membership.

44. The UN was formed in 1945. Its declaration of human rights has had a major impact on the whole world and in 2000 it set down a new set of Millennium Goals. The UK (like France, Russia, China and the USA) has a veto on the Security Council which is criticised because it only takes one country to prevent action if a country abuses its own population (e.g., Myanmar or Zimbabwe) or attacks another country (e.g., Israel attacking Gaza Strip), even when the rest of the Security Council wishes to intervene.

45. The Commonwealth of Nations comprises 53 member countries with a combined population of 2 billion. Most members were formerly colonies of the British Empire. The organisation promotes democracy and co-operation between member countries.

Chapter 15 – Global citizenship examines the development of international humanitarian law, debt relief and the need to raise living standards in less economically developed countries throughout the world.

46. Since the first Geneva convention of 1864 the international community has adopted rules to ban particularly cruel weapons, to avoid injuring or killing civilians and to not harm opponents who surrender or who can no longer fight. Legal processes are now in place to try and punish those who break the laws of war at the International Criminal Court. There is, however, still much work to be done to promote human rights in some countries (e.g., where women guilty of adultery are stoned to death).

47. Many LEDCs pay a big proportion of their earnings to richer countries as interest on past debts – and this prevents them improving their own countries. That is why Western nations favour writing off such debts so the money saved can go to genuine development projects. This programme started in 2000 but has yet to make significant progress. Apart from debt relief and humanitarian aid, the five stages of peace keeping are important.

48. There is no better test of living standards in the world than to look at life expectancy figures. A baby born somewhere in the world in 2008 could expect to live to 66 (world average) but if she was born in one of the G7 countries the average would be 77 or if born in Zimbabwe or Afghanistan, her life would be expected to last for just 44 years. When people ask why we should bother about other countries, these figures tell us why it would be wrong to do nothing in terms of trade or aid or combating AIDS or international co-operation.

Don't Panic Zone

Once you have completed your revision in your plan, you'll be coming closer and closer to The Big Day. Many students find this the most stressful time and tend to go into panic-mode, either working long hours without really giving their brain a chance to absorb information, or giving up and staring blankly at the wall. Some top tips are:

The week before the exam:

- Do a practice exam and check your answers with a mark scheme.
- Write notes on how you could improve.
- Check through your notes and consolidate them — this means write a shorter version. This will get you thinking about what is really important to remember.

- Make sure you know the day and time of the exam, how long it will last, and the building or room in which it is located. Get there with plenty of time to spare. Make sure you have a good pen to write with, use black ink or black biro, and have a spare one with you, just in case.

The night before the exam:

- Relax! You've done all the hard work. Cramming will just make you more anxious. Have a relaxing evening with family and get an early night. Wake up early so you have enough time to get ready and get to the exam without rushing.

Exam Zone

Finally, exam day itself will dawn. In the exam, spend your first five minutes reading the paper and planning your time. Be sure you know exactly how many questions you need to answer.

Finally, think of this as your cup final. Visualise that you are ready and better prepared for this examination than any examination you have ever taken before, and you will truly be 'in the zone'.

Good luck!, be confident, you can do it!

Zone Out

So you made it through the exam — well done! But what happens next? Well, you'll be able to have some well deserved rest time and wait for your results.

You'll probably want to start thinking about what you want to do next. If you have enjoyed your Citizenship Studies course there is always the option of carrying on studying and going on to do AS or A level in Government and Politics or General Studies.

If you are unsure about when you will get your marks, or have any questions about what your results slips will look like, or what to do if your results weren't what you wanted or expected, you can find some useful information on Edexcel's ExamZone website at: www.edexcel.com/quals

Glossary

accountability: requires ministers to take responsibility for their department, their own actions and the civil servants who support them

Act of Parliament: law passed by Parliament

adjournment debate: debate in Parliament when an MP raises matters of concern to his/her constituents

allegiance: loyalty to the country or the Crown or another body

alternative dispute resolution (ADR): use of activities such as mediation and counselling to avoid formal judicial process

additional member electoral system (AMS): proportional representation voting system used for Scottish Parliament and Welsh Assembly

Agenda 21: global plan following 1992 Earth Summit; organised by government and councils to encourage people to help improve their local environment

Amnesty International: pressure group campaigning for the welfare of prisoners around the world

anti-social behaviour order (ASBO): civil orders which aim to protect the public from anti-social behaviour, established by the Crime & Disorder Act 1998

anti-poll tax demonstration 1990: successful campaign against the community charge or 'poll tax' initiated by the Conservatives in the late 1980s

appeal: attempt by a person found guilty of a crime or who loses a civil court case, to get the verdict, sentence or civil judgement reviewed

Assembly – Welsh: devolved assembly for Wales established in 1999 following a referendum in 1997, located in Cardiff

Assembly – Northern Ireland: devolved assembly for Northern Ireland established following the Good Friday Agreement in 1998, located at Stormont

asylum seekers: people who flee from their home country and seek asylum in another because they fear persecution based on their ethnicity, religion or political beliefs

balanced budget: when government spending is matched by taxation or other sources of income

balance of trade: compares the value of imports and exports over a particular period to establish whether a surplus (more exports than imports) or a deficit (more imports than exports) is being made

barrister: specialist lawyer entitled to practise in senior courts; many barristers go on to become judges

BBC Charter: rights and duties of the BBC, including impartiality requirement

belief: an idea, fact or opinion which is believed by at least one person

benefits: financial support provided by government, e.g. child benefit (weekly payment to parents for each child) or jobseekers' allowance (paid to unemployed seeking work)

bias: promotes a one-sided view; newspapers are not required to avoid bias as terrestrial broadcasters are

bill: proposed law being considered by Parliament

blog: or 'weblog' is a website maintained by an individual with regular entries, descriptions of events – may include graphics or video; blogs run by experts, celebrities or opinion leaders may influence public opinion.

British Crime Survey: measures the amount of crime in England and Wales by asking people about crimes they have experienced – including crimes not reported to the police – so it is an important alternative to police records and contains information about both criminals and their victims

Budget: annual statement by Chancellor of the Exchequer on taxation, spending and borrowing levels for future years

building society: mutual organisation owned by its members (not shareholders) engaged in savings, investments and mortgage business

bureaucracy: form of administration often used in large organisations which may be slow to respond and is regarded as oppressive and inflexible

by-election: election to fill a vacancy if an elected person such as an MP or councillor dies or retires

Cabinet: (i) in national government, this is a committee chaired by the Prime Minister including about 20 of the most senior ministers in the government; (ii) in local government, committee

chaired by leader of the council comprising 6–10 councillors each with lead responsibility for provision of key services

capitalism: form of economic organisation involving investment and risk-taking with a view to making profits

caution: formal warning given to those guilty of minor offences

censorship: not allowing publication of certain information in the media

chair or chairperson: person who presides over a meeting; every council has a chair who is sometimes called the mayor

child benefit: weekly payment to parents for each child

Children's Commissioners: aim to promote and protect the rights and welfare of children and young people. In 2006 Sir Al Aynsley-Green was appointed as Children's Commissioner for England

citizen: an individual who exercises his or her rights and recognises there are also responsibilities to be fulfilled; to become a UK citizen a person from overseas needs to be able to speak English and successfully pass a **Citizenship test**; if accepted, the person will be invited to attend a **Citizenship ceremony** to celebrate their status as a UK citizen

Citizens Advice Bureau: national organisation with local branches run mainly by trained volunteers who offer free and confidential information about rights and the law

civil partnership: situation in which two people of the same gender have registered their partnership

civil servants/service: employees of government implementing decisions taken by Parliament and government

claimant: someone who claims benefit, e.g. for housing allowance

coalition government: local or national government comprising members of different parties

co-habitation/co-habiting: unmarried couple living together in emotional relationship

collective cabinet responsibility: principle that once a decision is made, all members of the cabinet will support it, even if they did not originally support it

colonialism: process in which one country rules another, often gaining great wealth from them – sometimes regarded as a form of exploitation

Commission for Equality and Human Rights (CEHR): established in 2007, it enforces equality legislation on age, disability, gender, gender reassignment, race, religion or belief, and sexual orientation and encourages compliance with the Human Rights Act

Commonwealth of Nations: organisation of 53 countries – mainly former members of the British Empire

community/communities: network of individuals living in a particular community or of people working together or with a shared interest, e.g. athletics or fashion

community integration: aims to ensure people with disabilities are not socially excluded from community activity and involvement

community sentence/punishment: may involve the offender doing unpaid work for up to 300 hours on local community projects under close supervision; community sentences help the charities, community organisations and local authorities that benefit from the offender's work – re-offending rates are lower following this type of punishment than after prison sentences

commuter: regularly travels between home and place of work

compensation: a cash sum may be ordered by a court as a result of a civil claim in cases of damage to a person, their feelings or their property

congestion-charging: form of road pricing, e.g. in London, where drivers pay a fee on any day when they enter the charging zone – intended to encourage use of public transport to reduce congestion caused by individual vehicles

conscience: an individual's moral sense of 'right' and 'wrong'

Conservative Party: party with right wing beliefs established in 19th century – in government for 35 years between 1945 and 2009

constituency: geographical area represented by an MP

constituent: a resident in an MP's constituency

consultation: process to test public views on ideas under consideration

consumer: individual purchaser of goods and services

Consumer Credit Acts, 1974–2006: says that if you use a credit card to buy faulty goods or a service which provides less than it promises, you may be able to claim from the credit card company

Consumer Protection Act, 1987: says it is always illegal to sell unsafe goods; you can claim damages from the manufacturer if you are injured using faulty goods – also when a 'sale' is held the product must have been offered for sale at the higher price in the same shop for at least 28 days in the previous 6 months

contract: legally binding agreement, e.g. between buyers and sellers

contract of employment: legally binding agreement covering all terms and conditions between employer and employee

cost of living: costs of buying goods and services for a typical family – often measured by retail prices index

costs of production: costs arising from production of goods or service – wages, raw materials, electricity, etc

council/local authority: district, borough, city, county or unitary council delivering local government services

Council of Europe: works for European integration – developed the European Convention on Human Rights in 1951; now has 47 member countries and aims to promote legal standards, human rights, democratic development, the rule of law and cultural co-operation

councillor: person elected to serve on a council

council tax: tax paid by householders to partly finance local government – based on theoretical value of property

county court: courts which deal with civil disputes

Court of Appeal: has two Divisions, the Civil Division and the Criminal Division to hear appeals from the High Court and, in criminal matters, the Crown Court

credit card: can be used to pay for goods and services – the purchaser will be charged interest on the money which has effectively been borrowed until repayment is made in full

credit union: a co-operative which is owned and controlled by its members, encourages saving and provides credit to members at reasonable rates

criminal law: includes offences such as theft, violence, dangerous driving and other breaches of law where the government, through the Crown Prosecution Service, prosecutes offenders

criminal responsibility: holding a person responsible if they commit crime/break the criminal law

Crown Courts: deal mainly with more serious criminal cases referred to them by magistrates – a jury decides innocence or guilt and the judge decides the sentence

CPS: Crown Prosecution Service decides whether or not a suspected wrongdoer should be prosecuted

culture: attitudes, values, norms and beliefs of a society or community

custody: imprisonment

custody of child: having guardianship of a child

DA Notice: (called a **D-Notice** until 1993) is a formal request to news editors not to publish or broadcast stories on certain subjects, to safeguard national security

Daily Mail: popular newspaper usually supports the Conservatives

Daily Mirror: popular newspaper usually supports Labour

debit card: can be used to pay for goods and services purchased – withdraws money directly from purchaser's bank account

debt cancellation: richer countries cancel debts of poorer countries so the money they would otherwise have spent on interest and debt repayment can be spent on education, health, housing and infrastructure improvement schemes

defamation: wrongfully and unfairly damaging someone's reputation in spoken (slander) or written (libel) form

defendant: person accused of an offence in a criminal court or being sued in a civil court

degrading treatment: humiliating an individual – such treatment is contrary to human rights provisions, though a difficulty is that treatment which is thought degrading or humiliating may differ over time

delegate: someone at a conference or other meeting with clear instructions from those sending them as to how they should speak and/or vote

delegated legislation: specific regulations produced by a minister based on a general permission granted in an Act of Parliament

demand/supply: while **demand** is the amount of a good or service purchased in a given period at a given price, **supply** is the amount that would be supplied – generally as the price goes up, more would be supplied and less demanded

democracy: one person, one vote and majority rule

demonstration: form of protest

dependency: situation in which people look to others to meet their needs – as welfare state provision has grown, there is a fear that a dependency culture has developed, i.e. those who receive benefits see them as a right without recognising a responsibility to do things for themselves

deterrence: belief that the prospect of receiving a heavy punishment may put someone off the idea of committing a crime – and discourage others too

devolution: system of establishing parliaments or assemblies to undertake limited government functions in parts of the UK, giving greater power to local communities

dictator: a ruler who hasn't been elected

direct/indirect tax: while a **direct** tax is a tax we know we are paying such as income tax or council tax, **indirect** taxes are added to other spending so we may be less aware of them, e.g. VAT or airport tax

division of labour: belief that splitting a task into several smaller activities leads to greater efficiency, e.g. production line in a factory

Disability Discrimination Act 1995: aims to end discrimination against disabled people, particularly in employment

disarmament: giving up weapons – sometimes happens as a **bilateral** bargain between two countries or on a **multilateral** basis by more countries while others favour **unilateral** disarmament, for example of nuclear weapons

disciplinary code: most firms adopt a code which involves a **verbal warning** for an employee who 'breaks the rules'. This would typically be followed by a **written warning** if the poor performance continued; if the person's conduct does not improve, the next stage could be **dismissal**. If a person is found guilty of **gross misconduct** such as racial or sexual harassment or dishonesty, they may be instantly dismissed

discrimination: treating an individual or group in a prejudiced way

dismissal: the ending of a person's contract of employment – commonly referred to as 'getting the sack'; this is different from **redundancy** where the job itself is ending, e.g. if a business is closing down

district judge: trained and experienced lawyer who decides cases on his/her own in some Magistrates' Courts

diversity: celebration of diverse social, cultural and religious backgrounds in a multicultural society

divorce: ending a marriage – the number of divorces increased after a 1969 Act which made it easier to divorce, but more recently, numbers have been affected by fewer marriages taking place and the increase in people living together

e-petition: signing a petition, using the Internet – for example signing a petition to the Prime Minister on the 10 Downing St website

Earth summit: such as conferences at Rio de Janeiro, 1992, which introduced the idea of sustainable development or Kyoto in 1997 which aimed to reduce carbon emissions to combat global warming

economic growth: amount of annual increase in national income, usually as measured by GDP (gross domestic product)

economic migrant: a person who migrates to a country to improve their economic circumstances, adding to the GDP of the country in doing so

eco-town: new town to combine sustainable living and affordable housing – the government wants to build twelve eco-towns by 2020

editor: person in charge of deciding content of newspaper or TV/radio programmes

election: opportunity to vote for candidates to be members of a council (**local election** – usually held on dates fixed in advance) or to be MPs in a **general election** on a date usually chosen by the Prime Minister – must be within five years of the previous election

Electoral Commission: organisation established in 2000 to monitor UK elections, referendums and political parties

electorate: everyone listed in the electoral register for an area

emigration: act of moving from one country to another – many UK pensioners emigrate on retirement to live in warmer countries

empathy: ability to recognise or understand how another person feels – often characterised as the ability to 'put oneself into someone else's shoes'

Empire: group of countries conquered or colonised by another country, e.g. British Empire

employee: person working for money or other payment

employer: person or body providing **employment** (work) for others for which they are paid

employment laws: relate to employment terms, contracts and conditions including working hours, minimum pay rates, health and safety arrangements and rights to holidays

employment tribunals: independent judicial bodies that determine disputes between employers and employees over employment rights

Employment Rights Act 1996: deals with rights that most employees can get when they work, including protection against unfair dismissal, reasonable notice before dismissal, time off rights for parenting, redundancy and more – amendments since 1997 have included the right to request flexible working time

euthanasia: terminating the life of someone by merciful or painless means, to prevent further suffering

equality: social state in which all people have the same status and equal rights before the law including voting, freedom of speech and access to education, health care and social security. For reasons such as poverty, inadequate education or lack of confidence, some people may not have the capacity to benefit fully from such rights

Equal Pay Act 1970: says women and men doing the same or similar work should get equal pay and benefits

ethnicity/ethnicities: cultural values and norms, including language or national origin, which distinguish the members of a given group from other groups

European Commission: body which proposes new laws for the EU and implements laws once agreed

European Convention on Human Rights: statement of human rights published by the Council of Europe to which the UK committed itself in 1951 – most of its provisions were incorporated into UK law in the Human Rights Act 1998

European Council of Ministers: principal law-making body of the European Union

European Court of Justice: judicial branch of the EU, based in Luxembourg

European Court of Human Rights: hears human rights cases based on the European Convention on Human Rights, based in Strasbourg

European law: EU law has direct effect within the legal systems of member countries, and overrides national law in many areas, especially those covered by the Single Market

European Parliament: includes members elected from every EU country; deals with legislative work not undertaken by the Council or Ministers and is the body which decides the EU budget – it also has the power to amend the decisions of the Commission

European Union: 27 (in Feb 2009) European countries aiming to gain the benefits of free trade and some social, political and economic integration

Eurosceptic: widely-used term for opposition to the process of further European integration, with some seeking the withdrawal of their own country from the EU while others favour the complete dissolution of the EU

exchange rate: rate at which one currency can be exchanged for another; such rates vary over time

executive: function of government to implement laws and policies

exports: goods or services sold by an individual or business in one country to an individual or business in another country

fair trade: system of trading in which growers receive a fair share of the value of the final product

FSA: Financial Services Authority – body set up to regulate those providing financial services

first-past-the-post electoral system: system used in UK general elections in which the candidate with most votes in a constituency is declared elected even if the person has secured less than 50% of the voting electorate; Scotland and Northern Ireland use a form of proportional representation

first reading: first formal stage of a bill in the legislative process

Food Safety Act 1990: says it is illegal to sell food or drink that does not comply with food safety rules

foreign aid: gifts by richer countries to poorer countries; may be to eliminate short term humanitarian needs or to meet longer term development needs – sometimes such aid unfairly requires the recipient to spend the 'gift' on products or services from the donor country

fossil fuel: decomposed animal and plant life which over long periods of time turns into fuels such as coal or natural gas

free trade: a system in which the trade of goods and services between or within countries is free from government-imposed taxes, tariffs and subsidies, non-tariff barriers or regulatory legislation and quotas

Freedom of Information Act 2000: a UK Act of Parliament that introduces a public 'right to know' in relation to public bodies; often the right is used by media and opposition political parties to highlight weaknesses in the government's implementation of its policies

G7: a group of finance ministers from seven developed, industrialised nations, (Canada, France, Germany, Italy, Japan, United Kingdom, and United States of America), who meet several times a year to discuss economic policies – not to be confused with the **G8** – the annual meeting of the heads of government of the same nations, plus Russia.

G20: group of finance ministers and central bank governors from 20 economies: 19 of the world's largest national economies, plus the European Union, together comprising 90% of global gross national product, 80% of world trade and two-thirds of the world population; there has also been one meeting at heads of government level, in November 2008

general election: election for all seats in the House of Commons – must be held once every five years; most Prime Ministers choose a date about four years after previous election

Geneva Conventions: consist of four treaties agreed in Geneva, which set the standards for international humanitarian law concerning the treatment of non-combatants and prisoners of war

genocide: deliberate and systematic attempt to destroy an ethnic, racial, religious, or national group

'giant evils': five 'evils' which the Welfare State was designed to combat – ignorance (education), idleness (full employment), poverty (social security), disease (NHS) and squalor (housing)

globalisation: production and consumption of goods and services organised across international boundaries, often by multinational companies, making it more likely that what happens in one country will affect other countries

global warming: gradual rise in the Earth's average surface temperature often linked to climate change

GNP: Gross National Product – the total value of all goods and services made by UK companies in a year

goods: tangible items which are bought or sold, e.g. cars, cabbages, packets of cornflakes

Good Friday agreement: (also known as the **Belfast Agreement**) this was a key stage in the Northern Ireland peace process, signed in Belfast on 10 April 1998 (Good Friday) by the British and Irish governments and endorsed by most Northern Ireland political parties, except the DUP

government: (i) practice of governing, (ii) ministers led by the Prime Minister who together govern the country

Government, Head of: role heading the decision-making machine; this is the Prime Minister in the UK and France but the President in the USA

green belt: area of largely undeveloped, wild, or agricultural land next to towns or cities – further building is generally not permitted within the green belt

greenhouse effect/gases: effect of burning fossil fuels leading to more CO_2 in the atmosphere; thought to result in global warming

Green Party: UK political party which campaigns on ecological policies

Greenpeace: international pressure group campaigning on environmental issues

green taxes: attempt to shift the tax burden to the things we want to discourage such as use of fossil fuels in motoring and air travel, and away from things we want to encourage such as recycling or home insulation

gross misconduct: misconduct so serious that the employer is entitled to dismiss for a first offence, e.g. fighting, stealing, arson and deliberate falsification of time-sheets

Health & Safety at Work Acts: intended to ensure that the workplace is a safe working environment

HM The Queen: monarch in the UK, Head of the Commonwealth

HIPC: heavily indebted poor country

High Court: split into three main divisions: the Queen's Bench Division, the Chancery Division and the Family Division; most proceedings in the High Court are held before a single judge

hire purchase: where a buyer theoretically hires goods for a monthly rent and becomes the owner when a sum equal to the original full price plus interest and any final charge has been paid

Holocaust: systematic, state-sponsored persecution and murder of approximately six million Jews by Germany's Nazi regime during the Second World War

Home Secretary: senior member of the UK government responsible for the Home Office which deals with immigration, passports, drugs policy, counter-terrorism, police, and science and research

homophobia: fear or hatred of homosexuals

House of Commons: elected chamber of UK Parliament with 646 MPs in January 2009 (650 after next election)

House of Lords: second chamber of UK Parliament with about 750 members, of whom 92 are hereditary peers

household: person living alone or group of people who share a housing unit including living/sitting room

human rights: stated in documents such as the Universal Declaration of Human

Rights and supposedly apply to every citizen in the world – but they usually do not apply in a country until they are written into its laws and then become legal or social rights; this is different from **moral rights** based on values or conscience or a person's sense of 'right' and 'wrong'.

Human Rights Act 1998: incorporates most of the provisions of the European Convention on Human Rights into UK law

humanitarian aid: food, clothing, shelter and healthcare provided to people in a country after a serious emergency such as flooding, earthquake, act of terrorism, failed harvest or civil war

hybrid (car): car which can run partly on electricity or hydrogen, reducing carbon emissions

ICRC: International Committee of the Red Cross

identity: an individual's self-image, the way the person views her or himself

identity card: card to confirm who a person is

identities – multiple: recognition that an individual may have many different identities, e.g. father, husband, son, employee, angler, Christian, being Welsh

IMF: International Monetary Fund

immigration/emigration: when an individual moves from one country to another, he **emigrates** from his former country and is regarded as an **immigrant** in his new country

impartial: a view which isn't biased

imports: goods or services bought by an individual or business in one country from an individual or business in another country

income tax: is levied on earnings – generally the greater your income, the more tax you pay; however income tax can be offset by **tax allowances** which mean that a person who can afford to invest £10,000 in a pension or £20,000 in start-up businesses through a venture capital trust would pay little or no tax on such sums; this is how some people are able to pay a smaller proportion of their income in tax than those who earn less than they do

inflation/deflation: when prices of goods and services are rising, this is **inflation**, if they fall it is **deflation**

Inland Revenue: familiar term for tax authorities – now officially Her Majesty's Revenue & Customs (HMRC)

International Criminal Court: established in 2002 to prosecute individuals for genocide, crimes against humanity and war crimes

International Court of Justice: the principal judicial arm of the United Nations (UN), established in 1945 by the Charter of the UN, situated in The Hague (Netherlands). Its role is to settle legal disputes submitted to it by States and to give advisory opinions on legal questions referred to it by UN bodies and specialised agencies

international humanitarian law: defines the conduct and responsibilities of nations at war, neutral nations and individuals engaged in warfare, in relation to each other and to protected persons, i.e. children and civilians.

interest rate: the amount a bank pays for invested money and the return a lender receives for lending it to the borrower. Interest rates are normally expressed as a percentage rate over the period of one year

international trade: exchange of capital, goods, and services across international borders or territories.

ITV: public service network of commercial television stations and programme providers

job description: list of tasks to be undertaken by post-holder, usually provided to applicants prior to job interview

judge: legally trained and qualified person who decides questions of law in a court and passes sentence on a guilty person

judgement: court ruling

judicial review: review by judges of the actions of government or others to determine legality

jury: a group of (usually 12) citizens aged 18–70 selected from the register of electors to hear evidence and decide if an accused person is guilty or not guilty

Justice: a law reform and human rights pressure group working to improve the legal system and the quality of justice in the UK

Kyoto Protocol: plan agreed in Kyoto, Japan to cut carbon emissions to below 1990 levels by 2012

Labour Party: left wing party supported by trade unions; in government for 29 years between 1945 and 2009

landfill: an area of land filled with rubbish/ waste material

law: rules laid down in an Act passed by Parliament

lawyer: qualified barrister or solicitor; gives legal advice and may appear in court for defence or prosecution

LEDC: Less Economically Developed Country such as Sudan or Vietnam

legal aid: public funds to provide legal advice and representation for defendants in criminal cases and a minority of civil cases

legislate/legislature: law-making

libel: written form of defamation, unfairly lowering someone's reputation in the eyes of society

Liberal Democrat Party: formed in 1987 when the Liberals merged with the Social Democratic Party (SDP)

life expectancy: the average number of years of life remaining at a given age; life expectancy results at birth may be low because of a high level of infant mortality in some developing countries

life peer: person appointed to be a baron or baroness for their lifetime with the right to be a member of the House of Lords; the title does not pass to a son or daughter on the death of the life peer

lifestyle: how a person lives in terms of cost of living, or because of choice

Local Agenda 21: local plans to help achieve sustainable development throughout the world, established following the 1992 Earth Summit in Rio de Janeiro

local authority: county, district, unitary or city council

magistrates: local people who receive limited training to decide innocence or guilt and punishments (for the guilty) in a **magistrates court** – such courts deal with 95% of all cases and are usually decided by three magistrates or, in some larger cities, a professionally qualified district judge, sitting alone

majority rule: democratic idea that rule should be based on more than 50% support as opposed to **plurality rule** – simply having more support than another candidate or party

mandate: permission or duty to govern given to Government as a result of winning an election

manifesto: policies put forward by a candidate or party before an election

mayor: (i) ceremonial chairman of council or (ii) elected person to head decision-making by council, e.g. Boris Johnson as Mayor of London, elected 2008

MacPherson report: following the racist killing of Stephen Lawrence, an A-level student, the 1999 report labelled London's police force 'institutionally racist' and condemned officers for 'fundamental errors' in the way they conducted their investigation

means test: some benefits are means tested, meaning that those with higher incomes or more savings can't claim the benefit; the problem is that many elderly people who would be entitled to more benefits don't apply, either because they do not wish to provide personal information or because they find the whole process too complicated

MEDC: More Economically Developed Country such as UK, France or Canada

MEP: Member of the European Parliament – the UK has 78 MEPs

Mr Speaker: i.e. effectively 'chairman' of the House of Commons

MP: Member of Parliament

middle class: traditionally viewed as professional and managerial workers and their families, the middle class is increasingly seen as those who choose to identify themselves in this way

migration: historically those deciding to come and settle in the UK have done so either for **pull factors** – advantages they saw in the UK or **push factors** such as poor harvests or economic turmoil which they saw as disadvantages in their home country

minister: political head of a government department

minority government: government which controls less than half the seats in a parliament

monarch/monarchy: UK head of state

money bill: A bill certified as a money bill by the Speaker of the House of Commons can become law without being approved by the House of Lords

moral considerations: the need to consider issues of right and wrong, fairness and honesty when making a decision

multicultural: community or society made up of people from many different cultural and ethnic groups

multinational company: companies like Microsoft and Coca Cola which operate in many countries and base their activities where they can make most profit

National Minimum Wage Act 1998: established minimum wage in the UK

National Probation Service: aims to rehabilitate offenders given community sentences and those released from prison and to take whatever steps in their power to protect the public

newspapers: sometimes described s either **popular** or **quality**; more people buy popular papers perhaps as much for entertainment as news – but quality papers offer more analysis of events and tend not to introduce their own opinions into a news story

NGO: Non-government Organisation such as Oxfam or the Red Cross

NHS: National Health Service founded as a result of the Beveridge Report 1942

non-renewable energy: energy sources such as coal, petroleum, natural gas, and propane are all fossil fuels – like uranium ore, these energy sources are considered non-renewable because they cannot be replenished in a short period of time.

'Not in my backyard' (NIMBY): attitude of some who oppose new developments near their homes such as wind farms, offender hostels or new housing

nuclear power: seen as an alternative to burning fossil fuels, though how to dispose of spent fuel remains a concern

numeracy: capacity to use numbers and do calculations

obligation: sense of moral commitment or responsibility

OFCOM: the Office of Communications is the independent regulator and competition authority for the UK communications industries

Ombudsman: official who examines files of government or council to check whether 'maladministration' has occurred and, if so, suggests remedies

opinion: a non-factual statement which expresses a value judgement which may or may not be supported by evidence

opinion leaders: well-known individual or celebrity whose ideas and behavior influence the attitudes and behavior of those who know, like and trust them

opinion poll: prediction of public opinion based on small sample of interviews; often used to indicate popularity of political parties, leaders or opinions on policy proposals

opposition: parties opposed to the government in Parliament

Parliament – UK: comprises two houses; House of Commons and House of Lords

party political broadcasts: short programmes made for radio and/or television by political parties as part of a campaign to gain support, particularly at election times

peacebuilding: involves measures intended to reduce the risk of an agreement falling apart and to lay the foundation for sustainable peace and development by helping a state to carry out its core functions

peace enforcement: involves the use, with the authorisation of the UN Security Council, of coercive measures, including the use of military force, to restore international peace and security

peacekeeping: occurs where fighting has been halted to help implement agreements achieved by the peacemakers – usually involving military, police and civilian personnel working together.

peacemaking: involves measures to tackle a conflict and bring hostile parties to a negotiated agreement

peers: holders of hereditary or life title such as baron, baroness, duke, etc

pension: regular payment made to retired person

permanent secretary: the most senior civil servant in a government department who is responsible for recruitment and gives advice to the ministerial team

petition: request for change

perjury: telling lies under oath in a court

persecution: the mistreatment of an individual or group by another individual or group on account of e.g. their religion, politics or ethnicity

person specification: qualifications, experience and any other requirements for an individual to be able to carry out a particular post, usually given to enquirers before they submit an application

Plaid Cymru: Welsh Nationalist Party – describes itself as 'the party of Wales'

plurality: more support for one party or candidate than for other parties or candidates but not a 50% majority

political party: seeks to form government or control council by presenting policies and nominating candidates at elections, e.g. Labour, Conservative, Liberal Democrat; other parties with little chance of immediate success also contest elections as a means of gaining publicity and winning new supporters

policies: proposals put forward by political parties and/or pressure groups

poverty: lack of basic necessities such as food, clothing, shelter and safe drinking water

power-sharing executive: system of government in Northern Ireland

presidential rule: system as in USA where the President has final say over whether laws are passed. In the UK, Parliament has the authority

Press Code: code of conduct for journalists

Press Complaints Commission: enforces a code of practice agreed with the newspaper and periodicals industry which focuses on such matters as accuracy, privacy, opportunity to reply and the national interest

pressure groups: voluntary and campaigning groups which may be categorised into **insider groups** on which the government relies for specialist knowledge and technical advice, e.g. Age Concern, British Medical Association or National Farmers Union and **outsider groups** such as Fathers4Justice or Plane Stupid which try to get publicity any way they can because they feel the causes for which they campaign are ignored by government

Prime Minister: head of government in UK

Prince's Trust: charity formed by HRH Prince of Wales to support and empower young people

privacy: right given in Human Rights Act 1998 to be allowed to keep one's lifestyle private and not to be intruded upon against one's wishes

Private Bill: bill which applies only to a specific business or geographical area such as a railway or harbour or area of natural beauty

Private Member's Bill: public bill sponsored by a backbench MP

probation: involves the suspension of all or part of a jail sentence; so a convicted offender will be returned to the community for a certain period during which they must abide by conditions set by the Court under the supervision of a probation officer

profit: where a business's income exceeds its outgoings

progressive/regressive taxation: the idea that the more income a person has, the larger the proportion of income they should pay as tax is **progressive taxation**; this is the reverse of **regressive taxation** where poorer people pay a larger share of their income than richer people

proportional representation: voting systems in which the number of people elected for each party is proportional to the votes gained – forms used in the UK are (i) single transferable vote (ii) regional list and (iii) additional member system

public bill: bill that applies throughout the country, regardless of whether it was originally introduced by a backbench MP or by the government

public/private sector: services provided by government are part of the public sector (e.g. state schools, police and NHS) while goods and services provided by business (e.g. supermarkets, telephones) are part of the private sector

public transport: travel by train, tram or bus rather than car

punishment – capital: death penalty (hanging, electric chair, etc) as punishment

question time: set times for MPs to ask ministers questions about their department in the House of Commons – the Prime Minister answers questions on Wednesdays

Race Relations Act 1976: forbids employers from treating a person such as an applicant for appointment or promotion less favourably because of their race, colour, nationality or ethnicity

Racial and Religious Hatred Act 2006: made it an offence to stir up hatred against persons on racial or religious grounds

racism: acting in a prejudiced way through the belief that some people of different origins are not as good as others

recidivism: when a prisoner is released from prison but commits another crime

recycling: processing products – bottles, cans, wood, paper – so they can be used again

redundancy: loss of a job by an employee because it is no longer needed or the firm has closed down

referendum: form of direct democracy – ballot in which public are asked to decide a policy issue

refugee: someone who flees from their home or country from fear, often seeking asylum in another country

regional list electoral system: used in England, Scotland and Wales for elections to the European Parliament

rehabilitation: aim to teach offenders in prison or youth offender institutions reading, writing and skills for work so they do not commit crime in future

religion: everyone has the right to practise their faith but also the responsibility not to promote hatred of other faiths

renewable energy/resource: a source that can be replaced or reused such as wind, wave or tidal power or solar energy

report stage: comes between the committee stage and third reading in legislative process

republic: country where the head of state (and sometimes government as well) is a president

respect: recognition of or esteem for the worth or excellence of a person, their personal qualities or ability, and their endeavours

responsibilities: every right comes with duties or responsibilities, e.g. to expect to be protected by the law, we need to be law-abiding ourselves

restorative justice: theory of justice which emphasises the importance of repairing the harm caused by criminal behaviour; and suggests this is best accomplished through co-operation between all stakeholders, with the offender apologising face-to-face to the victim

retribution: the idea that an offender must be punished because that is what he/she deserves

revenue: income

right to life: right claimed for unborn babies by those who oppose abortion

Rights – Universal Declaration of Human: statement of rights organised by the United Nations in 1945

Royal Assent: formal approval of bills passed by Parliament given by HM Queen as constitutional monarch or by a commission appointed by her

Sale of Goods Act 1979: says that new or second hand goods bought from a trade or mail order firm must be (i) of satisfactory quality, (ii) do what the seller or manufacturer says they will do (iii) as described in an advert, on the packaging or by a sales assistant

sanctions: agreements among states to cease trade with a state they believe has violated international law

Scottish National Party (SNP): seeks independence for Scotland – formed a minority government in the Scottish Parliament in 2007

scrutiny: function of Parliament achieved mainly through question time and select committees

second reading: first serious consideration for the principles of a bill in the UK legislative process

secretary of state: senior minister in government heading a major department

select committee: investigatory committees of House of Commons which each mainly monitor the work of a particular government department

service: non-tangible purchase such as travelling on a train or a dental examination by a dentist or going to watch a film at the cinema

Sex Discrimination Act 1975: this established guidelines for fair employment practices and gave those treated unfairly on grounds of gender or sexual orientation the support of the Commission for Equality and Human Rights

shadow cabinet: groups of policy spokespeople of opposition parties

shareholder: part owner of a business holding shares and receiving part of the profits

single transferable vote electoral system (STV): used in Northern Ireland for all elections and in Scotland for local government elections

slander: saying lies about someone in public; unfairly lowering the reputation of the person slandered

Small Claims Court: simplified and informal procedure in which a county court judge will decide claims up to £5,000 in value (£1,000 for personal injury claims)

social exclusion: a situation where people are unable to achieve a quality of life regarded as acceptable by most people or where an underclass of individuals have little or no stake in society (qualifications, jobs, homes, income) or who feel they are not part of society, opposite of social inclusion

social housing: affordable housing for rent offered by councils and housing associations

socialist: person who supports economic theories of social organisation, advocates state ownership and control and a society with equal opportunities for all and a fair distribution of wealth

society: an economic, social and industrial network, of which a varied group of people are a part; members may be from different ethnic groups or a particular nation state, or broader cultural group, such as a Western society

solicitor: legally qualified person who gives advice to clients

sovereign country: each country has sovereignty over its own affairs and does not expect other countries to intervene, no matter how badly its regime treats its people

State, Head of: a country's monarch (king or queen) or president

state-owned industries: previously known as 'nationalised industries' including airports, gas, electricity, steel, telephones – now mostly sold off to the private sector

state benefits: regular payments such as child benefit, state pension or jobseeker's allowance

state/private pension: benefits such as state pension are funded by a person's national insurance contributions during their working lifetime, while a private pension will be funded partly by the employer and partly by the employee and paid on retirement by a private provider such as Aviva, Prudential or Standard Life

statutory instrument: form of delegated legislation in which detailed regulations are made or updated by a minister based on authority given by an earlier Act

stealth taxes: term used for a tax levied in such a way that it is largely unnoticed, or not recognised as a tax, e.g. government decision to impose tax on pension funds

store card: can be used to pay for goods and services; the card is offered by the store from which purchases are made and generally charges interest on the outstanding balance at a significantly higher rate than a credit card

strike: withdrawal of labour by workers seeking to overcome a grievance over pay or working conditions or allegedly unfair treatment to a worker or workers

subculture: variations from the culture of the country, e.g. teenage culture, referring to the values of teenagers which differ from those of older citizens

subsidy: selling goods at a price below costs – can cause problems for a developing country if a richer country offers cheap food or raw materials, thereby undercutting producers in the developing country

supplementary vote: preferential voting system used for Mayoral elections in which second preferences of less successful candidates are counted to ensure winning candidate has 50% support

Supply of Goods & Services Act 1994: says goods sold must be fit for purpose, safe, durable, of acceptable appearance/finish and free from minor defects; people providing a service must do so with reasonable skill and care, within a reasonable time and at a reasonable price.

Supreme Court: will assume the jurisdiction of the current Appellate Committee of the House of Lords and the devolution jurisdiction of the Judicial Committee of the Privy Council when it starts work in September 2009

surveillance: monitoring individuals and their activities – UK is said by the Information Commissioner to be a 'surveillance society'

sustainable development: aiming to meet the needs of people today without threatening similar needs of future generations

tariffs: taxes imposed on imports to protect a domestic market from foreign competition

taxation: money collected by government or local councils from individuals or businesses

tax credits: method of providing additional financial support to low income pensioners and working families

terrestrial (broadcaster): programmes (e.g. BBC and ITV) transmitted via land-based transmitters as opposed to satellite transmissions

terrorism: systematic use of terror to create fear with no apparent regard for the safety of innocent bystanders

The Guardian: quality newspaper with socially progressive opinions

The Guardian: quality newspaper with socially progressive opinions

The Independent: quality newspaper with strong social conscience

The Sun: largest circulation popular newspaper in the UK

tolerance/toleration: a fair, objective, and accepting attitude toward those whose opinions, practices, race, religion, nationality, etc., differ from one's own

Trade Descriptions Act 1968: makes misleading claims about items for sale a criminal offence

Trading Standards: departments in larger local authorities which enforce consumer laws

trade: sale and purchase of goods and services

trade union: an employee organisation which exists to protect and improve pay and working conditions of members

TUC: Trade Union Congress is a 'union for unions' whose affliated unions have six and a half million members

turnout: proportion of those entitled to vote in an election who actually do so – 61% voted in 2005 general election but turnouts for local and European elections are usually much less than this

unemployment: not in paid employment

unemployment benefits: weekly allowance paid to active job-seekers

Unison: trade union for public sector workers

unitary council: council carrying out all local government functions, e.g. Medway, Isle of Wight and Herefordshire

universal benefits: benefits paid to individuals regardless of their income, e.g. child benefit

universal suffrage: right to vote applying to all citizens over 18

Unite: combined trade union for workers who previously belonged to either Amicus or TGWU trade unions

United Nations: organisation which acts as a world forum and seeks to achieve humanitarian, peacekeeping, development and other goals agreed by the 192 member countries

UN Charter: statement of principles and provisions agreed in 1945 which brought the UN into existence; in 2000 these were updated by the **UN Millennium Goals**

UN Convention on the Rights of the Child: basic human rights of children declared by the UN in 1989

UN Declaration of Human Rights: statement of human rights agreed by the UN in 1948

UN General Assembly: meeting of representatives of all 192 member countries

UN Human Rights Commissioner: monitors human rights issues in all countries, seeking wide publicity for breaches of the UN declaration and to specifically draw such matters to the attention of governments on a case by case basis

UN Security Council: made up of five permanent members, including the UK, who hold a veto power and ten members who are elected to serve for a limited period

UN relief agencies: provide support for those in need of humanitarian aid; include the Office for Co-ordination of Humanitarian Affairs (OCHA) and UN

Relief and Works Agency for Palestine Refugees (UNRWA)

UN resolutions: declarations of policy agreed by the General Assembly or Security Council

UNHCR: UN High Commissioner for Refugees who protects and supports refugees and assists in their return or resettlement

US Congress: the 'parliament' of the USA comprising two chambers – the House of Representatives and the Senate

values: accepted forms of behaviour, sometimes absolute values will apply which all law-abiding citizens agree on, e.g. it is always wrong to murder or act dishonestly

VAT: Value Added Tax is an indirect tax which we do not pay directly as a tax but indirectly – it is included in the price when we purchase goods or services

voluntary work: charitable activities voluntarily undertaken in the UK or overseas by people of all ages for little or no reward, sometimes with only their expenses met

veto: the effect of a veto is to forbid something – if one country vetoes a proposal in the UN Security Council, the proposal will make no more progress even if every other member of the Security Council supports it.

vote/voting: UK citizens over 18 have the right to vote in elections as long as they make sure they are listed on the electoral register for the area where they live

warning – verbal/written/final: normally a **verbal** warning is the first stage in an employer's disciplinary process; the second stage is usually a **written** warning and the third stage a **final** warning after which an employee whose conduct continues to be unsatisfactory may well be dismissed

waste incinerator: burning waste is an alternative to burying it in landfill sites. Waste incinerators can be used to generate electricity or to divert the heat to domestic uses in **heat and power** schemes. But incinerators emit varying levels of carbon dioxide and also heavy metals such as lead and cadmium, which can be toxic at very minute levels.

Weights and Measures Act 1985: makes it a crime to sell short measures or underweight goods

Welfare State: state provision of welfare services such as education, health, housing, pensions and social security

'winner's bonus': the gap between the percentage share of votes a winning party receives and its percentage share of seats – in 2001 and 2005 Labour's bonus was about 20%

witness: person who gives evidence in court

working age: the earliest age for full time employment is 16; older workers are encouraged to retire later in life – by the year 2046 the state retirement age for both men and women will be 68, though workers can continue working beyond this age if they wish to

working class: official classifications indicate this refers to unskilled manual workers and their families; however, when asked to which class they felt they belonged 57% said 'working class' in 2006, referring to their family's roots rather than the job they do now

World Bank: provides financial and technical assistance to developing countries usually via the International Bank for Reconstruction and Development (IBRD) and the International Development Association (IDA)

WTO: World Trade Organisation

youth offending team: YOTs bring together professionals from education, social services, careers and police to address offending behaviour by 10–17 year olds

Youth Parliament: debating and campaigning organisation for young people to promote social change

Index